access to history

Britain and the American Colonies 1740–89

access to history

Britain and the American Colonies 1740–89

Alan Farmer

HODDER
EDUCATION
AN HACHETTE UK COMPANY

Study guides written in 2008, by Sally Waller (AQA) and Angela Leonard (Edexcel).

The Publishers would like to thank the following for permission to reproduce copyright material:

Photo credits
p.7 Library of Congress LC-USZC4-12540; **p.17** © Classic Image/Alamy; **p.19** © Jonathan Edwards Center at Yale University; **p.23** © Alan King engraving/Alamy; **p.28** © Mary Evans Picture Library; **p.35** © Mary Evans Picture Library; **p.51** © North Wind Picture Archives/Alamy; **p.55** Library of Congress LC-USZ62-45554; **p.60** Library of Congress LC-USZ62-9487; **p.67** © Classic Image/Alamy; **p.73** © Classic Image/Alamy; **p.80** © Mary Evans Picture Library; **p.90** © North Wind Picture Archives/Alamy; **p.99** © 2007 Getty Images; **p.100** © Mary Evans Picture Library; **p.102** Courtesy of the Mount Vernon Ladies' Association; **p.104** © Mary Evans Picture Library; **p.114** © 2007 Getty Images; **p.120** © 2007 Getty Images; **p.147** © Mary Evans Picture Library; **p.155** © Lebrecht Music and Arts Photo Library/Alamy; **p.166** © Visual Arts Library (London)/Alamy; **p.172** Library of Congress LC-USZC4-4097; **p.178** © Mary Evans Picture Library; **p.186** Library of Congress LC-USZ62-45589

Acknowledgements
p.147 the US Census Bureau for the 1790 Census

Every effort has been made to trace all copyright holders, but if any have been inadvertently overlooked the Publishers will be pleased to make the necessary arrangements at the first opportunity.

Although every effort has been made to ensure that website addresses are correct at time of going to press, Hodder Education cannot be held responsible for the content of any website mentioned in this book. It is sometimes possible to find a relocated web page by typing in the address of the home page for a website in the URL window of your browser.

Hachette Livre UK's policy is to use papers that are natural, renewable and recyclable products and made from wood grown in sustainable forests. The logging and manufacturing processes are expected to conform to the environmental regulations of the country of origin.

Orders: please contact Bookpoint Ltd, 130 Milton Park, Abingdon, Oxon OX14 4SB. Telephone: (44) 01235 827720. Fax: (44) 01235 400454. Lines are open 9.00–5.00, Monday to Saturday, with a 24-hour message answering service. Visit our website at www.hoddereducation.co.uk

© Alan Farmer 2008
First published in 2008 by
Hodder Education,
An Hachette UK Company
338 Euston Road
London NW1 3BH

| Impression number | 5 4 3 2 |
| Year | 2012 2011 2010 2009 |

Cover photo shows 'Washington crossing the Delaware' by Emanuel Gottlieb Leutze, © Bettmann/Corbis
Illustrations by Barking Dog Art and GreenGate Publishing
Typeset in New Baskerville 10/12pt by GreenGate Publishing Services, Tonbridge, Kent
Printed in Malta

A catalogue record for this title is available from the British Library.

ISBN: 978 0340 965 962

Contents

Dedication

Keith Randell (1943–2002)

The *Access to History* series was conceived and developed by Keith, who created a series to 'cater for students as they are, not as we might wish them to be'. He leaves a living legacy of a series that for over twenty years has provided a trusted, stimulating and well-loved accompaniment to the post-sixteen study. Our aim with these new editions is to continue to offer students the best possible support for their studies.

Note on maps

CT	Connecticut
DE	Delaware
GA	Georgia
IL	Illinois
IN	Indiana
KY	Kentucky
MA	Massachusetts
MD	Maryland
ME	Maine
MI	Michigan
NC	North Carolina
NH	New Hampshire
NJ	New Jersey
NY	New York
OH	Ohio
PA	Pennsylvania
RI	Rhode Island
SC	South Carolina
TN	Tennessee
VA	Virginia
VT	Vermont
WI	Wisconsin

1

The American Colonies by 1763

POINTS TO CONSIDER

The establishment of the British colonies in North America seemed, by the mid-eighteenth century, to have been a huge success. In 1763 British North America ran from Hudson Bay in the North to Florida in the South. Few Americans or Britons expected that within twelve years they would be at war – a war which the Americans were to win. The American War of Independence was perhaps the most important event of the eighteenth century. It resulted in the creation of a nation state of enormous potential wealth and power, governed in a significantly different way from Britain. But were there any signs pre-1763 that Americans wanted independence from Britain? This chapter will examine the relationship between Britain and her American colonies by focusing on the following themes:

- The development of the thirteen colonies
- Colonial government
- Colonial economy, society and culture
- The struggle with France
- Britain by 1763

Key dates

1607	Virginia established
1688–89	The Glorious Revolution
1756–63	The French–Indian (or Seven Years') War
1759	Britain captured Québec
1760	Accession of George III
1763	Peace of Paris

1 | The Development of the Thirteen Colonies

In 1607 a group of settlers established the first English **colony** in Virginia. The second major colony followed the sailing of the **Mayflower** to Massachusetts in 1620. By 1650, four further colonies – Connecticut, New Hampshire, Rhode Island and Maryland – had been added. New York was captured from the Dutch in 1664, New Jersey and North and South Carolina founded during the 1660s and Pennsylvania and Delaware during the 1680s. The establishment of Georgia in 1732 completed the thirteen British colonies on the American mainland. They stretched about 2400 km (1500 miles) along the Atlantic seaboard from Canada in the North to Florida in the South. Although settlers were starting to move west in search of new lands, in 1763 the vast majority of Americans lived to the east of the Appalachian mountains (see Figure 1.1).

Colonial division

The colonies are usually divided into three main groups:

- the New England Colonies – New Hampshire, Massachusetts, Rhode Island and Connecticut
- the Middle Colonies – New York, New Jersey, Pennsylvania and Delaware
- the Southern Colonies – Maryland, Virginia, North Carolina, South Carolina and Georgia.

Key question
How divided were the thirteen colonies in 1763?

Virginia established: 1607

Colony
Territory, usually overseas, occupied by settlers from a 'mother country' that continues to have power over the settlers.

Mayflower
The name of the ship on which the Pilgrim Fathers – a small group of English Puritans – sailed to America in 1620.

Key date · Key terms

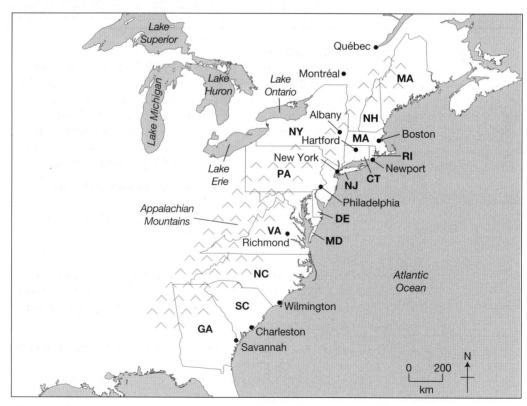

Figure 1.1: The thirteen colonies in 1763.

Figure 1.2: Colonial settlement: 1660–1760.

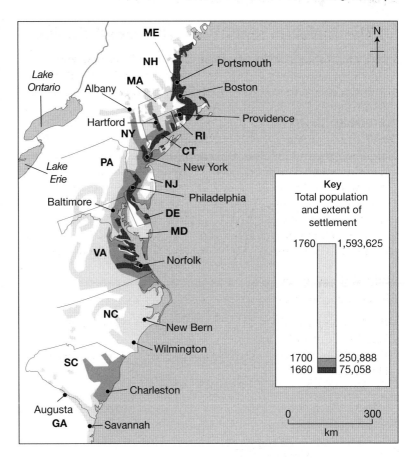

Population growth

Key question
Why did the American population grow so quickly in the eighteenth century?

Between 1700 and 1763 the population of the thirteen colonies increased eightfold from 250,000 to reach 2 million. Between 1750 and 1770 the population of England and Wales rose from 6.5 million to 7.5 million – a fifteen per cent increase. In the same period, the population of the thirteen colonies expanded from 1.25 million to over 2.3 million – almost a one hundred per cent increase. There were three reasons for the population growth:

- a high birth rate. The average American woman had a family of seven children
- a low death rate. Americans, well fed and generally prosperous, lived longer than most Europeans
- large-scale immigration (see below).

Nevertheless, America was far from densely populated. The vast majority of colonists lived on farms. Almost half the people lived in the South, a quarter in the Middle Colonies and a quarter in New England. By 1770:

- Virginia was the largest colony in population and land area, with some 500,000 inhabitants.
- Pennsylvania and Massachusetts each had about 275,000 inhabitants.
- Maryland and North Carolina each had 200,000.

- New York, South Carolina and New Jersey each had more than 100,000.
- New Hampshire and Rhode Island each had just over 50,000.
- Delaware had 40,000.
- Georgia (the newest colony) had only 30,000.

American towns

There were only five towns of any size – all seaports: Boston, Newport, New York, Philadelphia and Charleston. By 1760 their combined population was 73,000 – only 3.5 per cent of the total population. In 1760:

- Philadelphia had 23,750 inhabitants.
- New York had 18,000 inhabitants.
- Boston had 15,600 inhabitants.
- Charleston and Newport each had about 10,000 inhabitants.

The towns were the hub of the local economy as well as being major trading centres.

The colonial melting pot

Some 400,000 people from Europe and Africa migrated to the thirteen colonies between 1700 and 1763. While most of the seventeenth-century settlers were of English stock, less than twenty per cent of the eighteenth-century migrants were English.

Key question
What impact did immigration have on the thirteen colonies?

European settlement

The largest group of immigrants (some 150,000) were Scots-Irish, descendents of Scottish **Presbyterians** who had settled in Ulster in the early seventeenth century. Discontented with the land system, recurrent bad harvests and the decline of the linen trade, most left Ulster for economic reasons. Religious and political discrimination provided an additional impetus. Many of the Scots-Irish settled along the Western frontier.

About 65,000 Germans, mainly peasants from the Rhineland, hoping to improve their economic lot and attracted by the religious tolerance in the colonies, crossed the Atlantic. Many settled in Pennsylvania, making up almost a third of the colony's population by the 1760s and maintaining an important degree of religious and cultural **autonomy**. Smaller immigrant groups included Dutch, Swedes and Jews.

Presbyterians
Protestants with a system of church government by elders or presbyters, rather than bishops and archbishops.

Autonomy
Independence or self-government.

Key terms

Indentured servitude

Few European immigrants crossed the Atlantic under their own resources. They tended to travel in groups, either as part of colonisation schemes or, more frequently, under a system of temporary servitude designed to meet the chronic labour shortage in the colonies. The system enabled the less well off to obtain free passage by entering into a contract (or indenture) pledging their labour for a specified number of years – usually four. Between a half and two-thirds of all white immigrants during the colonial period were indentured servants.

Jacobites
Supporters of James (*Jacobus* in Latin) Stuart, the eldest son of James II, who was driven from the throne in 1688. Strong in the Highlands of Scotland, the Jacobites led rebellions in 1715 and 1745.

Undesirables

The British authorities used the colonies as a dumping ground for undesirables. Despite colonial protests, Britain transported at least 30,000 felons, vagrants, paupers and political prisoners (mainly **Jacobites**) to America during the eighteenth century.

African settlement

The first black slaves arrived in Virginia in 1619. Their numbers at first grew slowly. In the eighteenth century, however, the importation of slaves soared. By 1763 there were 350,000 slaves – one in six of the overall population. Most came from West Africa. The demand for slaves was so high that the black population in America grew faster than the white population. While there were African Americans in all the colonies, 90 per cent lived in the South. They made up less than five per cent of the total population in New England but forty per cent in Virginia, Maryland and Georgia, and sixty-seven per cent in South Carolina.

Indians (Native Americans)

The British and European settlers did not assimilate with the Native Americans. Divided, less advanced technologically and hit hard by European diseases, the Indians had been unable to resist the newcomers advancing down the Atlantic seaboard and then further inland. Nevertheless, the Indians remained a powerful force to the west of the Appalachian mountains (see Figure 1.1).

The results of immigration

By 1760 only about half the American population was of English stock. Another fifteen per cent were Welsh, Scottish or Scots-Irish. Africans comprised over twenty per cent and Germans eight per cent of the population. European newcomers quickly blended into the colonial culture and society, although Germans tended to resist complete amalgamation.

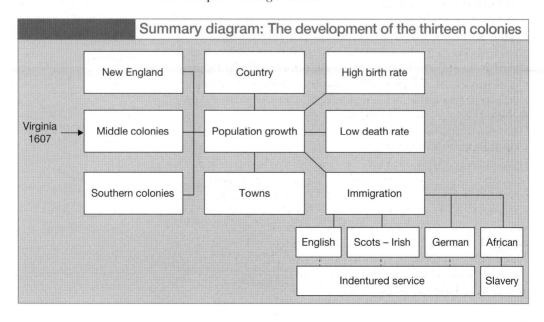

Summary diagram: The development of the thirteen colonies

2 | Colonial Government

Key question
To what extent did the colonists govern themselves?

Most of the colonies were royal colonies. Legal authority flowed from the Crown, in Massachusetts through its **charter** (granted by the king), and in others technically through the authority granted to its governor by virtue of his royal commission. The only exceptions were the **proprietary colonies** of Maryland, Pennsylvania and Delaware and the **corporate colonies** of Connecticut and Rhode Island. All the colonies, whether royal, propriety or corporate, had, by 1760, a very similar governmental structure. This consisted of a governor and a legislative assembly.

Governors

Key question
How powerful were the colonial governors?

In most colonies the governor was appointed and could be removed only by the British king, to whom he was responsible. The exceptions were the proprietary colonies, where the proprietor who ran the colony appointed the executive, and the corporate colonies, where governors were popularly elected and responsible to the legislatures. The governors were responsible for internal administration, enforcement of laws and granting lands. As well as being legal heads of the established church in their colonies, they also acted as military commander-in-chief. They could:

- veto acts adopted by the assemblies
- summon and dissolve assemblies
- appoint and dismiss judges
- nominate members of the upper house
- appoint and remove officials
- pardon criminals.

Although, in theory, they had greater powers than the Crown exercised at that time in Britain, in reality the governors' authority was limited.

- As royal officials, they could be dismissed at will by the British government.
- Their average term of office was only five years.
- They were dependent for political support, revenue and even their own salaries on the lower houses of the colonial assemblies. Governors were obliged to co-operate with their assemblies (see below) if they wished to achieve anything.

Colonial legislatures

Most colonial legislatures (usually called assemblies) consisted of two houses:

- The upper house (or colonial council) was usually appointed by the governor. Chosen from the colonial elite, its members served as an advisory board to the governor and as the highest court of appeal within the colony.
- The lower house was elected by a wide **franchise**. In theory, its powers were restricted. Most could be summoned, **prorogued** and dissolved at the will of their governors. Moreover, the

Key terms

Charter
A formal document, granting or confirming titles, rights or privileges.

Proprietary colonies
These were colonies in which the Crown had vested political authority in the hands of certain families: the Calvert family (in Maryland) and the Penn family (in Pennsylvania and Delaware).

Corporate colonies
The corporate colonies Connecticut and Rhode Island possessed charters granted by the king which gave them extensive autonomy.

Franchise
The right to vote.

Prorogued
Dismissed or postponed.

legislation of the lower house could be vetoed by the governor or disallowed by the **Privy Council** in London.

In practice, however, the power of the assemblies was considerable:

- They were responsible for initiating money bills and controlling expenditures – not least the governors' salaries.
- The core of the lower houses' political influence lay in the fact that they represented their provincial communities in a way that neither the governors nor the upper houses did.

The assemblies usually met in the spring or autumn for a session of four to six weeks. While the main item on their agendas was to vote on taxes to pay the expenses of the colonial government, the assemblies also made local laws and acted as protectors of local interests. They offered lively arenas of debate. Though political parties did not exist, factionalism was endemic in most colonies and political controversy intense. The most persistent disputes were between Easterners and Westerners over political representation. Westerners felt they did not have enough seats in the assemblies.

Key term

Privy Council
The private council of the British king, advising on the administration of government.

The Massachusetts assembly met in the State House in Boston. What does the nature of the building suggest about the power of the colony's legislature?

Colonial democracy

Representative government had a greater democratic base in the colonies than in Britain. Most American adult white males owned enough property (usually land) to be able to vote. At least fifty (and sometimes as much as eighty) per cent could do so, compared with only fifteen per cent in Britain.

Nevertheless, the colonies were far from democratic:

- Not all men owned enough property to be able to vote. (The amount of property varied from colony to colony and from time to time.)
- Women and slaves could not vote.
- Higher property qualifications for office as well as custom and deference towards men of high social standing ensured that great landowners, rich merchants or lawyers were usually elected.

Key question
How democratic were the colonial governments?

Local government

In New England, where settlements were relatively compact, authority over local affairs was vested in town meetings in which all **freeholders** had voting rights. Elected annually, the town meetings fixed local taxes and chose men to administer the town's business. In the Middle and Southern Colonies a wider variety of practices prevailed. Some communities had New England-style town governments: in others local government was organised by county or parish. In the counties there was no democracy. The county court, an administrative as well as a judicial body, consisted of justices of the peace (JPs) appointed by the governor. County sheriffs, responsible for keeping the peace, supervising elections and collecting taxes, were also governor-appointed.

Freeholders
People who own, rather than rent, their land.

The Glorious Revolution
In 1688 King James II fled from Britain. William III and Mary became joint monarchs. Parliament assumed greater control.

Key terms

British rule in the colonies

The charters were the umbilical cords attaching the colonies to Britain – the mother country (see pages 26–28 for the political situation in Britain at the time). Granted in the seventeenth century, the charters tied the colonies to the Crown rather than to Parliament. The governors continued to be appointed by – and represented – the Crown as if nothing had changed in England with the advent of parliamentary supremacy in **The Glorious Revolution**. The crown's authority was somewhat ambiguous in the proprietary colonies and even more tenuous in the corporate colonies. After 1696 the British sovereign and the Privy Council had joint authority, conferred by Parliament, to review colonial laws. (Only five per cent of the 8500 colonial measures submitted between 1691 and 1775 were disallowed by Britain.)

For most of the eighteenth century, responsibility for the supervision of the colonies fell to the lords commissioners for trade and plantations – commonly known as the Board of Trade. The sixteen-man board advised on colonial appointments, drew up government instructions and reviewed colonial legislation.

Key question
How did British rule in the colonies operate?

The Glorious Revolution: 1688–89

Key date

The board answered to the Parliamentary Committee on Plantation Affairs which then made recommendations to the Privy Council. However, the secretary of state for the Southern Department also had responsibility for colonial affairs. Both the Board of Trade and the secretary communicated with governors on policy and routine administration. Governors submitted regular reports to the secretary on colonial affairs generally and to the Board of Trade on commercial matters.

Besides the Privy Council, Board of Trade and secretary of state, other agencies had some role in imperial administration. These included the Treasury, the War Office and the Admiralty. Given that British administration affecting the colonies lacked central control, confusion and duplication often characterised the bureaucracy.

In order to follow developments concerning colonial affairs, as well as to lobby Parliament and the Board of Trade on behalf of their interests, most colonies employed agents in Britain. These agents warned the colonies of pending measures by the Crown or Parliament and informed British officials of colonial thinking.

Salutary neglect

In the early eighteenth century, British governments realised it was best not to stir up trouble in the colonies. When coupled with the difficulty of communications – the colonies were 4800 km (3000 miles) away from Britain – it is not surprising that the colonies were left largely to their own devices. This detached policy is often referred to as 'salutary neglect'.

Despite salutary neglect, the common presumption in Britain was that the colonies were subject to parliamentary legislation. The colonists did not necessarily accept this view. However, this was not a major issue pre-1763 because Parliament gave so little attention to colonial affairs. Trade regulation apart, there was hardly a single parliamentary act that touched on the internal affairs of the colonies. Few colonists, therefore, gave much thought to their relationship with Britain. Most viewed their rights and political practices as fitting in with the principles of the British constitution, though adapted to their own specific situation.

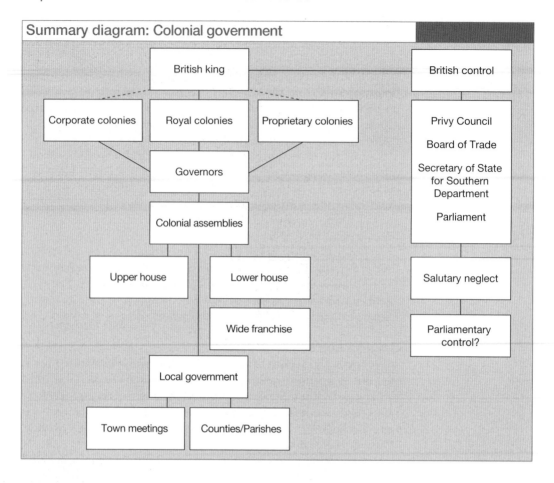

Summary diagram: Colonial government

3 | Colonial Economy, Society and Culture

The colonial economy

Between 1650 and 1770 the colonial gross product grew by an annual average of 3.2 per cent. Colonial economic growth was the result of several factors:

Key question
Why were the American colonies so prosperous?

- expanding intercolonial trade
- urban growth
- trade with Britain and its empire
- the availability of credit and capital from Britain
- the rapid increase in population
- the availability of new land
- increasing overseas demand for colonial products such as tobacco and grain
- increasing diversification; for example, the development of iron production, textiles and shipbuilding.

The importance of agriculture (and fishing)

There was no large-scale industrial development. Farming remained the dominant economic activity, employing nine-tenths of the working population. There was great diversity from region to region:

Figure 1.3: The colonial economy.

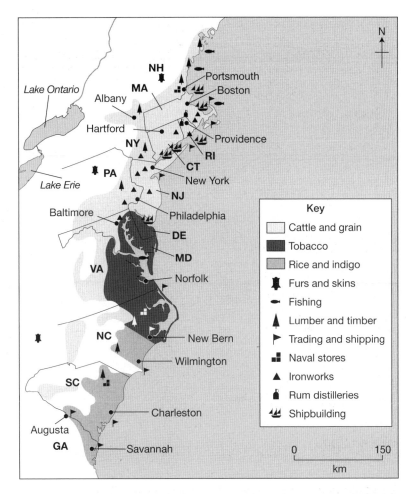

Key

☐ Cattle and grain
■ Tobacco
▨ Rice and indigo
♜ Furs and skins
◠ Fishing
▲ Lumber and timber
► Trading and shipping
▪▪ Naval stores
▲ Ironworks
🍾 Rum distilleries
⛵ Shipbuilding

0   150
km

- Lacking extensive rich soils, New England remained a land of small subsistence farms. The sea, however, provided it with a profitable alternative. From the Newfoundland Banks and the shores of Nova Scotia, New England fishermen brought back great quantities of cod, to be dried and exported, along with livestock and lumber. More than half of New England's thriving export trade was with the West Indies, which supplied her in return with sugar, molasses and other tropical products. New England distillers turned molasses into rum.
- Pennsylvania and the Middle Colonies were a major source of wheat and flour products for export to other colonies, the West Indies and southern Europe.
- The South was even more rural and agricultural than the other regions. Tobacco remained the mainstay of the economy, tobacco exports rising from £14 million in the 1670s to £100 million by the 1770s. Rice, indigo and grain were also produced for export. Development was most advanced in the **Tidewater**, where the population was densest. Population pressure and the constant search for higher profits ensured that the **backcountry** was filling rapidly.

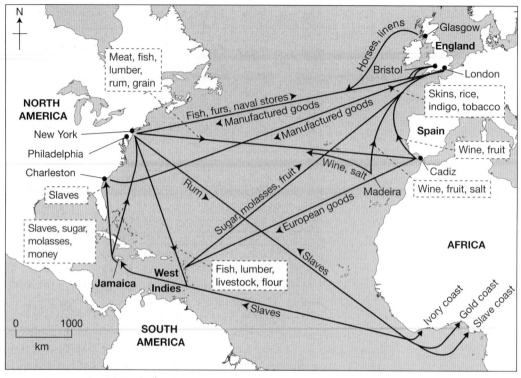

Figure 1.4: Colonial overseas trade.

Mercantilism

In the seventeenth and eighteenth centuries most European governments believed in **mercantilism** and **economic self-sufficiency**. Mercantilists assumed that colonies existed to serve the interests of the mother country, to supply her with raw materials, absorb her manufactures and provide employment for her shipping.

Between 1651 and 1673 the English Parliament put these ideas into practice in a series of Trade and Navigation Acts designed to establish an English monopoly of the colonial carrying trade, the colonial market and certain valuable colonial products:

- All cargoes to or from the colonies were to be carried in ships built and owned in England or the colonies and manned by predominantly English crews.
- Certain **enumerated commodities** – sugar, cotton, indigo, dyewoods, ginger and tobacco – could only be exported directly from the colonies to England even if their ultimate destination lay elsewhere.
- European goods bound for America had, with few exceptions, to be landed first in England and then reshipped.

English/British colonial policy remained strictly mercantilist through the early eighteenth century. The list of enumerated commodities was steadily extended until by 1763 it included practically everything the colonies produced except fish, grain and lumber. Laws were also passed to check colonial manufacturing:

Key terms

Mercantilism
The belief, widely held in Europe in the seventeenth and eighteenth centuries, that economic self-sufficiency is the key to national wealth and power.

Economic self-sufficiency
The situation when a country or a community produces all it needs for itself and is not dependent on others.

Enumerated commodities
Listed items which were affected by the Trade and Navigation Acts.

- The Woollen Act (1699) forbade the export of woollen yarn and cloth outside the colony in which it was produced.
- The Hat Act (1732) prohibited the export of colonial beaver hats.
- The Molasses Act (1733) placed high duties on sugar and molasses imported into the colonies from French, Spanish and Dutch possessions in the Caribbean.
- The Iron Act (1750) banned the export of colonial iron outside the Empire.

The effects of the mercantilist system

> **Key question**
> What were the effects of mercantilism?

British mercantilist policies affected colonial economic development less than was once thought. Few Americans complained about mercantilist regulations in the early eighteenth century.

The mercantilist system was not well enforced. While most of the Navigation Acts used stiff duties to compel what they required, not many officials were appointed to collect the duties. Nor was the character of the officials sent to America calculated to promote imperial interests. The chief posts in the colonial customs service came to be **sinecures**, filled by men who remained in Britain and who sent deputies to perform their duties. The ill paid deputies could easily be bribed, ensuring they often turned a blind eye to infractions of the trade laws. The laxity of control particularly prevailed during British Prime Minister Robert Walpole's long ascendancy (1721–42). Calculating that strict enforcement of the mercantilist laws would simply limit colonial purchases from Britain, Walpole deliberately relaxed them. Although Halifax, as president of the Board of Trade (1748–61) tried to tighten imperial control, the colonies were able to avoid most of the trade laws and smuggling was a fact of colonial economic life.

> **Key terms**
>
> **English/British**
> England and Scotland signed the Act of Union in 1707. Thus it is correct to term policy British (rather than English) after 1707.
>
> **Sinecure**
> An office without much, if any, work: in other words, a cushy job.

The few laws restricting colonial production had little effect. The Woollen Act had a limited impact because sheep and wool did not exceed local demand. The Hat Act affected an industry of minor importance. The Molasses Act, which threatened New England's profitable rum industry, was evaded almost at will. The prohibitions of the Iron Act were openly disregarded. Moreover, the Iron Act was not wholly restrictive. Though designed to check the expansion of the iron-finishing industry, it aimed to encourage crude-iron production and allowed colonial bar and pig iron to enter Britain free of duty. By the 1770s the colonies had outstripped Britain as producers of crude iron.

Economic benefits

On balance the mercantilist policies benefited the colonies:

- American products enjoyed a protected market in Britain and the rest of the Empire.
- Parliament granted generous subsidies to producers of some colonial commodities, such as indigo.
- The American shipbuilding industry profited by the exclusion of foreign ships from colonial trade. By the 1760s one-third of British merchant ships were built in the New England colonies.

As the eighteenth century progressed, colonial trade played an increasingly important role in the British economy. By the 1760s a third of British imports and exports crossed the Atlantic. The major exports of the colonies were tobacco, flour, fish, rice and wheat. The colonies in turn imported a host of British manufactured goods. Trade brought prosperity to British and colonial merchants, shippers, planters and bankers.

Colonial society
The elite

Key question
How different were the colonial and British societies?

In every colony a wealthy elite – great landowners, **planters** and wealthy merchants – had emerged whose pre-eminence was evident in their homes, possessions and lifestyles and in their control of politics. The elite copied the behaviour and social values of the English aristocracy, building opulent houses, having their portraits painted, indulging in high-stake gambling, and educating their sons at American and British universities. The Virginia planters sat prominently in church, served as JPs, rode to hounds and even had family coats of arms. The Penns, with almost 40 million acres, were the largest landed magnates. They dominated Pennsylvania with the governorship descending from one member of the family to another just as an earldom might descend in Europe. Several landowners received returns from their lands rivalling the incomes of the great British landed families. By 1770 the richest one per cent owned fifteen per cent of American wealth.

Planters
Southern landowners who owned more than 20 slaves.

Key term

Yet the colonial elites lacked the titles, privileges and often the possessions that gave automatic social prestige and political authority to the British aristocracy. The American elite were hard-working capitalists, intensely and of necessity absorbed in land speculation and in the business of marketing commercial crops. Since their capital was largely tied up in land (and slaves in the South), their liquid assets were not impressive by European standards. Indeed, many were embarrassingly in debt.

The professionals

Below the elite were the professionals – ministers, lawyers, doctors, schoolmasters. Although not enjoying the wealth of those above them – and upon whom they often depended for their livelihoods – these were men who could achieve elite status by hard work or good fortune. Respected in their communities, they often held positions of public responsibility.

Farmers

Eighty per cent of free American males were farmers and most owned and (with the help of their families) worked their own land – usually between 50 and 500 acres. For almost all of them the great goal in life was the possession of enough land to support their families and to guarantee the future of their children.

Artisans

In the towns, two-thirds of the population were self-employed craftsmen.

The property-less

Below the property holders were those who laboured for others. This was a diverse group, ranging from sons of property holders (who could expect to inherit land) to African slaves. Approximately thirty per cent of land was farmed by tenants who rented rather than owned the land. Some parts of the colonies, especially the Hudson Valley in New York, seemed almost **feudal**. The tenants might have to work a few days a year on the fences and roads of the land owner. However, the availability of cheap frontier lands limited the numbers of tenants and prevented the growth of a large class of landless agricultural workers. Only about a fifth of adult white males were landless labourers. Many were recent immigrants who had arrived as indentured servants.

In the towns, the property-less included apprentices, sailors, servants and labourers. There was a growing number of poor. In Philadelphia one in ten men received some sort of public aid. Nevertheless, pauperism in the towns was not the problem that it was in England.

Slavery

Black slaves were at the bottom of the social structure. Slavery was the usual condition for African Americans. Although slavery existed in every colony, over ninety per cent of the slaves lived and worked in the South. Slaves were subject to the will of their owners and could be bought and sold. While some slaves were used as domestic servants, most worked on plantations producing tobacco, rice and indigo. (Cotton was not produced to any great extent until the 1790s.) Within the structure of slavery, there was huge variety. A house servant in New York had a very different lot to a slave growing rice in the Carolina lowlands.

A middle-class world?

According to historian Richard Hofstadter, colonial America was 'a middle-class world'. The groups at the top and bottom of the British social pyramid – the nobility and the poor – were under-represented in America. The availability of land meant that, unlike Britain where farm tenancy was the norm, the vast majority of colonial farmers tilled their own soil. In the cities, **artisans** capitalised on their scarcity value by demanding and getting higher wages.

Nevertheless, American society was hierarchical and there were huge differences between rich and poor. While society may have been more mobile than that in Britain, the notion of widespread social mobility should not be exaggerated. A few individuals did rise from humble beginnings to wealth and power. But most of the colonial elite came from families of substance.

Key terms

Feudal
Describing the system of social organisation prevalent in most of Europe in the Middle Ages, in which powerful land-owning lords granted degrees of privilege and protection to lesser subjects (holding a range of positions) within a rigid social hierarchy.

Artisans
Skilled manual workers.

Families

The basic social unit of eighteenth-century American life was the family. At its head was a white male. As head of the family, he had responsibility for all members of the household, including servants. Households were hierarchical. Children were subordinate to elders, females to males, servants to family, blacks to whites. Although the structure and functions of the family were the same as in Europe, American conditions tended to loosen family ties and undermine parental authority. The easy availability of land encouraged young people to leave the household in order to set up on their own. This weakened the ability of fathers to influence marriage choices by withholding their sons' inheritance.

While it has been claimed that the preponderance of males among early American settlers helped to raise the status of women, this seems doubtful. Irrespective of wealth or condition they were assigned a subordinate role and were denied the political and civil rights enjoyed by men. Wives, for example, had no legal right to property.

American culture

By the 1760s Americans could boast their own cultural and intellectual achievements.

Education

In the New England colonies education was strongly encouraged and even small towns established elementary and high schools. New Englanders were thus a highly literate people. Education provision was less good elsewhere, especially in the South where the dispersal of population increased the difficulty of establishing schools. Nevertheless, by 1763 75 per cent of white male American adults were literate, compared with sixty per cent in England. There was less concern over women's education and none over that of black slaves.

Harvard College, the first institution of higher learning in the colonies, was founded in Boston in 1636. By the late 1760s there were eight other colleges and universities including William and Mary (1693), Yale (1701) and Princeton (1746). The colonial intellectual elite were greatly influenced by the **Enlightenment**, the ideas of which permeated every branch of thought from religion and science, to economics and literature. By the mid-eighteenth century Americans could boast their own intellectual achievements. Learned organisations were founded in America, most notably the American Philosophical Society (1743). Colonial Americans gained international notice for their work in natural history and in physical sciences.

The rising levels of education had extensive ramifications. Printing presses and booksellers were common. Several towns had chartered libraries and over 30 newspapers were in circulation by 1763.

Enlightenment
This is the name given to a school of European thought of the eighteenth century. Those influenced by the Enlightenment believed in reason and human progress.

Key term

Profile: Benjamin Franklin (1706–90)

1706	– Born in Boston: apprenticed as a youth to his half-brother, a printer
1722	– Published his 'Silence Dogwood' essays, the first essay series in American literature
1725–26	– Apprenticed in the printing trade in London
1729	– After returning to Philadelphia, he purchased the *Pennsylvania Gazette*
1751–64	– Sat in the Pennsylvania Assembly
1757–62	– Pennsylvania's colonial agent in London
1763–64	– Returned to America
1764–75	– Again represented Pennsylvania in London
1775	– Chosen as a delegate to the Second Continental Congress
1776	– Sat on the committee that drew up the Declaration of Independence
1776–85	– Worked successfully for American interests in France, helping bring France into the War of Independence
1787	– Helped draft the Constitution

Benjamin Franklin was the most famous American intellectual and one of the eighteenth century's most original scientists. A self-made man, he was a many-sided genius who succeeded in everything he tried – journalism, business, invention, politics and diplomacy. Largely self-educated, he prospered as owner of a printing business in Philadelphia and as editor of the *Pennsylvania Gazette*. He was a prolific pamphleteer on politics, economics, religion and other topics. His passion for learning and civic improvement led him to play a leading role in founding, among other things, a subscription library, a city hospital, the American Philosophical Society and the College of Philadelphia. Elected to the Pennsylvania Assembly, he served as deputy postmaster general of the colonies (1753–74) and represented Pennsylvania and other colonies as an agent in London.

Franklin became famous in America and Europe as a result of his inventions, including the lightning rod and bifocal spectacles, and still more for his scientific researches into the nature of electricity. In all his endeavours Franklin displayed a faith in reason and in progress, a passion for freedom and a humanitarianism that were characteristic of the Enlightenment.

Religion

Church membership was high, especially in New England. The vast majority of Americans were Protestants, a fact that shaped their cultural, social and political attitudes as well as defining their theological principles. However, in contrast to most European states, there was no dominant religious denomination in the colonies as a whole or even within most individual colonies. The tendency towards religious division, together with the immigration

Table 1.1 Estimated religious census: 1775

	Number	Chief locale
Congregationalists	575,000	New England
Anglicans	500,000	N.Y., South
Presbyterians	410,000	Frontier
German churches		
(incl. Lutherans)	200,000	PA
Dutch reformed	75,000	NY, NJ
Quakers	40,000	PA, NJ, DE
Baptists	25,000	RI, PA, NJ, DE
Roman Catholics	25,000	MD, PA
Methodists	5,000	Scattered
Jews	2,000	NY, RI
Total membership	1,857,000	
Total population	2,493,000	
Percentage church members	74%	

of sectarians from different countries, produced a multiplicity of denominations – **Congregationalists**, Presbyterians, Quakers, Baptists, Anglicans, Lutherans, German and Dutch Reformed and Methodists. There was an established church in nine colonies: Rhode Island, Pennsylvania, Delaware and New Jersey were the exceptions. The Congregational Church was the established church in Massachusetts and other New England colonies. The Anglican Church was established in Virginia and other Southern colonies. Established churches enjoyed certain privileges, including support from taxation, but by no means everyone belonged to them.

The plethora of diverse religious groups forced Americans to acknowledge a degree of religious tolerance. Tolerance, however, was largely confined to other Protestant groups. Most Americans were strongly anti-Catholic. Maryland was the only colony to possess a substantial Roman Catholic minority, partly because it had been founded in the seventeenth century as a Catholic refuge and partly because it had subsequently received a large number of Irish Catholic indentured servants.

The Great Awakening

A wave of religious revivals known as the Great Awakening began in the Middle Colonies in the 1720s and swept through the rest of the colonies in the next two decades. Preachers like William Tennent and Jonathan Edwards emphasised the individual's personal relationship with God and the necessity of salvation through conversion. Religious ferment was further stimulated by the arrival in 1739 of the English evangelist George Whitefield, whose preaching tours drew enormous crowds.

The Great Awakening led to controversy and division. Conflicts arose between laymen and clergy, between different denominations and within existing religious organisations. When congregations

Key term

Congregationalists Members of a church that has a form of government in which each congregation is independent in the management of its affairs.

Key question
How important was the Great Awakening?

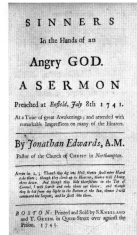

Jonathan Edwards and the title page from 'Sinners in the hands of an Angry God' – his famous sermon warning the wicked of the terrible punishments awaiting them in Hell.

found that the organised clergy was trying to put an end to the religious revival, they frequently voted out of church office men who had grown used to ruling. Not infrequently the result was schism and the increasing fragmentation of religious sects.

It has been claimed that the Great Awakening aroused an egalitarian and democratic spirit as all souls were now considered eligible for salvation. By implying that the elite were morally no better than their social inferiors, it may have made the lower orders increasingly reluctant to submit unquestioningly to a hierarchical social order. However, the levelling tendencies of the Great Awakening may have been overstated by historians. While it tended to undermine the position of the established clergy, it did not develop into a general challenge to traditional forms of authority.

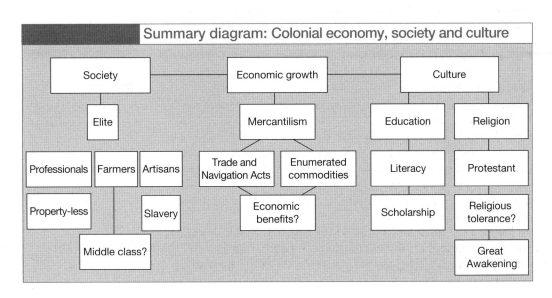

Summary diagram: Colonial economy, society and culture

4 | The Struggle with France

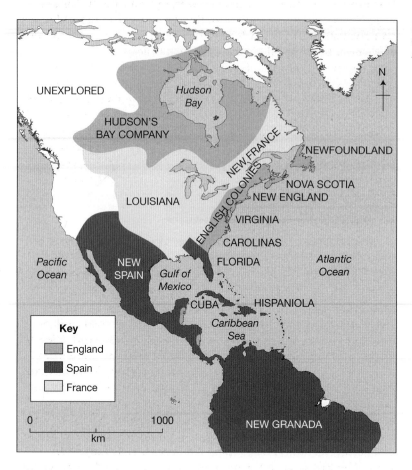

Figure 1.5: European control of North America in 1713.

Warfare was a fact of colonial life in the seventeenth and eighteenth centuries. To secure their foothold on the American continent the early colonists had to overcome resistance. Towards the end of the seventeenth century warfare between colonists and Indians merged with a larger international struggle between Britain and France for control of North America. France controlled Canada and Louisiana at the mouth of the Mississippi River.

The wars
Between 1689 and 1763 England and France fought four wars:

- the War of the League of Augsburg (1689–97)
- the War of Spanish Succession (1702–13)
- the War of Austrian Succession (1744–48)
- the Seven Years' War (1756–63).

The first three began in Europe – and were essentially about the balance of power within that continent. The wars then spread across the Atlantic. That the colonists viewed them essentially as foreign wars in which they became embroiled only as subjects of

> **Key question**
> What were the main results of the British–French struggle for control of North America?

the English crown was evident from the labels they attached to the first three of them: King William's War, Queen Anne's War and King George's War. Nonetheless, they were eager to defeat French and Spanish neighbours whose Catholicism was anathema to them and whom they regarded with fear and suspicion.

In the first three wars, Britain was too absorbed in Europe to send much help to the colonists. Most of the fighting was left to the colonial militia. The English-speaking colonists outnumbered the French fifteen to one but intercolonial disputes and French alliances with Indian tribes largely offset the English advantage. The colonists' greatest military achievement was the capture of Louisbourg in 1745. Proud of their victory the colonists were appalled when the Treaty of Aix-la-Chapelle (1748) handed Louisbourg back to France.

The Albany Congress

As far as America was concerned, the 1748 peace was simply a truce. No sooner had it been signed than British and French colonists redoubled their efforts to control the Ohio Valley. In the spirit of salutary neglect, there were only about 500 British troops in America. The Board of Trade recognised that Indian support could be vital in the coming struggle against the French. It thus called upon the colonies from Virginia northward to send delegates to a meeting at Albany to discuss joint Indian policy. The Albany Congress (June 1754) failed to secure an alliance with the Iroquois, the tribe best disposed towards the British. However, the Congress did adopt a scheme, drawn up by Benjamin Franklin, for a permanent intercolonial confederation. Franklin's Plan of Union envisaged an elected colonial Parliament with authority over Indian affairs and defence and with power to levy taxes to support an army. The British government might well have vetoed the proposal since it went much further than it had intended. But the colonial assemblies saved it the trouble by either rejecting or ignoring the Plan of Union.

Fort Duquesne

In 1753–54 a group of Virginia planters organised the Ohio Company and secured from the British government a grant of some 200,000 acres in the trans-Allegheny region. When the French began to build a chain of forts between Lake Erie and the Allegheny River, a Virginian force, led by George Washington, was sent to forestall them. But Washington found that the French were already in possession of the key site – the forks of the Ohio River (present-day Pittsburgh) where they were busy constructing Fort Dusquesne. In the fighting that followed Washington was forced to surrender (July 1754). Although war was as yet undeclared, Britain sent General Braddock and 2000 troops to America. On his way to Fort Dusquesne, Braddock blundered into a French–Indian ambush. He was killed and his army routed (July 1755). Over the next two years Indian war parties devastated scores of frontier settlements.

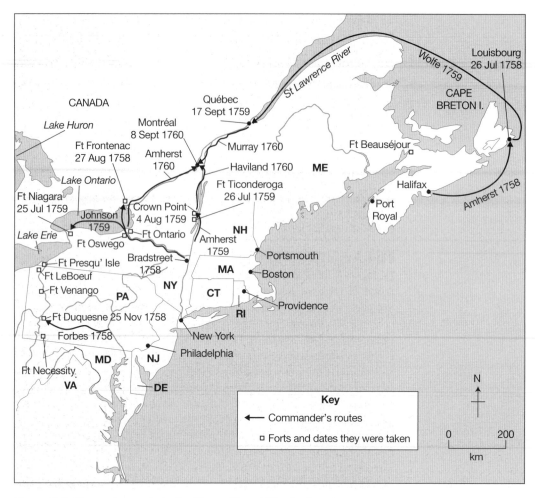

Figure 1.6: The main events in the Seven Years' War in America.

The Seven Years' War

In 1756 Britain finally declared war on France. The Seven Years' War – or the French–Indian War as it was known in America – developed into a worldwide conflict. There was fighting in Europe, the West Indies, Africa and India as well as in North America. At first things went badly for the British. The French General Montcalm captured Fort Oswego on Lake Ontario in 1756 and Fort William Henry at the southern end of Lake George in 1757. These reverses reflected the inability of the Earl of Loudon, the British commander, to induce the colonists to unite in their own defence. Miserly colonial assemblies, dominated by men from the secure seaboard, were unperturbed by the threat to remote frontiers.

But once William Pitt was recalled to power in Britain in 1757 the tide begin to turn. Determined to expand Britain's imperial power, Pitt judged that defeat of the French in North America was the key to ultimate victory. He thus sent 25,000 troops to America under the command of Jeffrey Amherst and James Wolfe, and paid

Key dates

The French–Indian (or Seven Years') War: 1756–63

Britain captured Québec: 1759

William Pitt (the Elder), Britain's successful war leader in the Seven Years' War.

for raising a further 25,000 American colonists. As never before, the British government was preoccupied with the American colonies. The war proved an economic bonanza for the colonies. They were paid good money to support the British forces.

Meanwhile Pitt provided subsidies to Frederick the Great of Prussia to preoccupy the French in Europe. The strategy worked brilliantly. In 1758 British forces captured Louisbourg and then cut the link between Canada and the Mississippi Valley by taking Fort Frontenac on Lake Ontario. This led to the fall of Fort Dusquesne, renamed Fort Pitt. Meanwhile Robert Clive won a series of victories in India while Frederick the Great defeated the armies of France, Russia and Austria in Europe.

The greatest triumphs came in 1759 – the year of victories:

- Admiral Hawke smashed a French fleet at Quiberon Bay, south-east of Brest, thereby preventing France sending reinforcements to Canada.
- In the West Indies Britain captured Guadaloupe.

- The British launched a three-pronged attack on Canada from the mouth of the St Lawrence, Lake Ontario and Lake Champlain. General Wolfe's defeat of Montcalm on the Plains of Abraham (12 September 1759) ensured the capture of Québec and effectively destroyed French power in Canada.

In 1760 Amherst took Montréal, and the capture of Canada was complete. While Pitt wanted to continue fighting, the new king George III wanted peace. Pitt resigned in October 1761 when the cabinet refused to extend the war to include Spain. Peace was eventually agreed. By the terms of the Peace of Paris (1763):

> **Peace of Paris: 1763** — Key date

- Britain received Canada and all the French possessions east of the Mississippi.
- Britain acquired most of France's West Indian islands (although Guadaloupe and Martinique remained French).
- Britain acquired Florida but returned the Philippines and Cuba to Spain.
- France ceded Louisiana to Spain.

Other results of the Seven Years' War
- Britain was now the world's greatest imperial power. She controlled North America, the Caribbean and much of India.
- The war gave training to Americans who later became the senior officers of the Continental Army.
- There was mutual contempt between some American and British soldiers. General Wolfe wrote in 1758: 'Americans are in general the dirtiest, the most contemptible, cowardly dregs that you can conceive. There is no depending upon them in action.' The Americans, in turn, considered British officers haughty and incompetent.
- Ironically the British triumph prepared the ground for the American Revolution. By eliminating France from North America, Britain had weakened the colonists' sense of military dependence on herself.

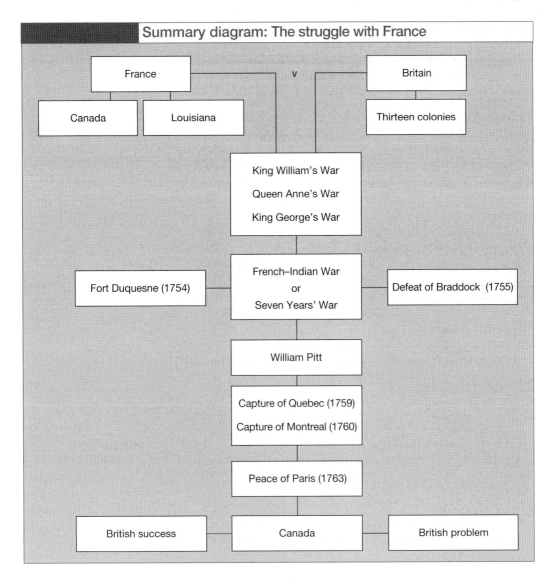

Summary diagram: The struggle with France

France — v — Britain

Canada | Louisiana

Thirteen colonies

King William's War

Queen Anne's War

King George's War

Fort Duquesne (1754) — French–Indian War or Seven Years' War — Defeat of Braddock (1755)

William Pitt

Capture of Quebec (1759)

Capture of Montreal (1760)

Peace of Paris (1763)

British success — Canada — British problem

Key question
How strong was Britain in 1763?

5 | Britain by 1763

In 1763, to most contemporaries, Britain seemed a state of modernity, combining economic growth, political maturity and imperial strength.

The economic situation

Britain had a steadily rising population – 7.5 million in 1760. Her economy was expanding. Although more than half the British people were connected with farming, the **Industrial Revolution** was beginning to take effect, principally in the production of textiles, iron and steel. Cities like Birmingham and Manchester were rapidly growing. London, with 700,000 people, was the largest city in the world.

Britain's success lay in world trade, especially with her own colonies. The jewels in the imperial crown were the West Indies, with their sugar plantations. But the thirteen American colonies were a good market for British manufactured goods, especially textiles, weapons and household utensils.

The social situation

British society was hierarchical. Great landowners dominated society and politics. The nobility and their relations filled most of the high offices, whether in the ministerial departments, church, navy or army. Although nobles themselves could sit only in the House of Lords, many of their family members were in the House of Commons.

Britain's rising middle class was vital to the growth of the economy and to Britain's social flexibility and stability. The middle class, diverse in both wealth and economic activity, was not a coherent grouping. There was a large gap, for example, between the great merchants, who often married into the aristocracy, and the small tradesmen and craftsmen who represented the backbone of commercial England.

At the bottom of society there were large numbers of landless agricultural labourers. There was also widespread urban poverty.

The political situation

Britain was a parliamentary monarchy. While the Glorious Revolution had reduced the monarchy's power, all government was – in theory – the king's. From the lowest official in the parish to the greatest minister of state, service undertaken was in the name of the monarch. George III (1760–1820) took an active part in government. Within limits, he chose the ministers who served him – the limits being essentially their ability to command parliamentary support.

Parliament

This consisted of the House of Lords and the House of Commons:

- The Lords contained 222 members in 1776 – 26 bishops, 16 representatives of the Scottish peerage and 180 hereditary English and Welsh nobles.
- The Commons comprised 558 MPs. Its control of financial matters meant it had ultimate power.

Britain was not democratic:

- In the 1761 election only 215,000 adult and reasonably wealthy (usually landowning) males were entitled to vote.
- Most of the growing cities were not represented in the Commons.
- Wealthy landowners usually determined who would stand as candidates and who would be elected. Over half the MPs owned large estates. Twenty per cent were younger sons of wealthy landowners.
- Few MPs were independent. A half owed their seats to patrons. Nearly a third held offices or honours under the government. They thus usually voted as the government directed.

Key term

Industrial Revolution
The economic and social changes arising out of the change from industries carried on in the home with simple machines to industries in factories with power-driven machinery.

Key date

Accession of George III: 1760

Parliament did very little with regard to public policy. This was largely because most MPs believed the best form of government was the least form of government.

The Cabinet

The inner cabinet usually consisted of the prime minister, the chancellor of the Exchequer, the two secretaries of state, and the president of the Privy Council. Its members came from either the Lords or Commons and had responsibility for initiating and directing a legislative programme.

The political parties

In the early eighteenth century there were two major political parties – the **Whigs** and **Tories**. After the Hanoverian succession in 1714, George I (1714–27) and George II (1727–60) were strongly committed to the Whigs, suspecting the Tories of links with the Jacobites. Thus the Whigs – or rather a few great Whig families – dominated government and the Tory party remained in the wilderness for more than 40 years. Between 1722 and 1762 there were only seven years in total in which the Whig **oligarchy** failed to provide Britain with stable and generally successful government. Politics after 1720 was dominated first by Sir Robert Walpole and then by the Pelhams – Henry Pelham and his brother the Duke of Newcastle. Walpole and the Pelhams were adroit managers of the House of Commons, using government patronage to skilful effect.

The Whig party in the late seventeenth and early eighteenth centuries had stressed government by consent of the people, resistance against arbitrary rule, and the inviolability of the individual's fundamental rights. However, by 1760 Whiggism – indeed the Whig party – had little real meaning. Everyone who mattered politically was a Whig. The Whigs were less a party than a broad-based political establishment with the great traditional Whig families at its core. The Tory party had effectively disintegrated with many of its ambitious members joining Whig factions. In 1761 only 113 MPs were accounted Tories. In the absence of the Whig–Tory framework, which had given shape to politics for so many decades, politics became factionalised. Several powerful political leaders – Bute, Bedford, Grenville and Newcastle – battled for control. Given the Whig feuding, ministries found it hard to command majorities. There was a constant shifting of support from one faction to another. Moreover, the death or ill-health of many experienced politicians led to the emergence of a new generation of political leaders. The result was political instability in the 1760s.

The situation 1757–63

The Duke of Newcastle, in every government since the days of Walpole, proved to be a poor war leader. In 1757 he was forced to take William Pitt into his government and make him co-equal. Pitt had popular support and was a great orator. After 1757 he controlled military, naval and foreign policy while Newcastle

Key terms

Whigs
Members of the Whig party – one of the great English political parties in the late seventeenth and eighteenth centuries. The party usually upheld popular rights and opposed royal power.

Tories
Members of the Tory party – the great English political party in the late seventeenth and eighteenth centuries. The party usually opposed change.

Oligarchy
Goverment by a small (usually wealthy) exclusive class.

looked after finances and government patronage. Despite Britain's success in the Seven Years' War, the Newcastle–Pitt coalition broke down in 1761. The cabinet, concerned at mounting costs, voted against declaring war on Spain and Pitt resigned. Newcastle continued as prime minister. John Stuart, the Earl of Bute, George III's former tutor and 'dearest friend', replaced Pitt. He sought peace. In 1762 Newcastle resigned, in protest against the proposed peace terms. Bute now became prime minister. Bute, a Scottish peer, had little political experience. Having made enemies among the great Whig families, he soon realised he was out of his depth and resigned in 1763.

Porphyria
A physical condition affecting the nervous system, inflicting huge pain and symptoms which can sometimes be taken for insanity.

Key term

Profile: George III (1738–1820)

1738	– Born, grandson of George II: he was the first Hanoverian king to be born and brought up in England
1760	– Became king
1761	– Married Princess Charlotte of Mecklenburg Strelitz: they had fifteen children
1765	– Suffered his first attack of **porphyria** (not diagnosed until the 1930s!)
1788	– Suffered another attack of porphyria
1811	– Became permanently incapacitated: his son George became regent
1820	– Died

In 1760, influenced by his former tutor, the Earl of Bute, George hoped to inaugurate a new era in politics by breaking the dominance of the Whigs and by ending the exclusion of the Tories from government, court and other office. This naturally offended some Whig leaders who accused George of plotting to enhance the power of the Crown and reduce Parliament to subservience. There is no evidence that Bute infected the future king with authoritarian intentions. Far from planning to reduce the powers of Parliament, George III wanted to protect the constitution from the Whigs and the corruption which he imagined they employed to reinforce their power. George had no wish to be a despot. Nevertheless, he was determined to rule as well as reign. He thus did what he could to influence government policy.

He has generally had a bad press. In the early twentieth century historian Sir George Otto Trevelyan wrote that 'he invariably declared himself upon the wrong side in every conflict'. Historians today are somewhat kinder but most agree he was headstrong and obstinate. His political prejudices helped cause the ministerial instability in the 1760s. If he had had greater perception or intelligence he might have steered Britain away from the disastrous policies of confrontation with the American colonies.

Summary diagram: Britain by 1763

Economic situation — Britain

Social situation — Political situation

King — George III

Cabinet

House of Lords — Parliament — House of Commons — Despotic ambitions?

Whigs v Tories

Whigs v Whigs

Newcastle and Pitt

Bute

6 | The Key Debate

To what extent were there signs in 1763 that the colonies were likely to break their ties with Britain?

Signs of a weakening relationship

It can be argued that by 1763 the thirteen colonies were developing so rapidly that it was only a matter of time before they broke their ties with Britain. In all parts of America, argues historian Robert Middlekauff, there were tendencies at work that pointed to autonomy rather than to colonial dependency. The colonies' populations were rapidly growing and by 1763 colonists were aware of being something other than Britons. The mixing of diverse peoples in the colonies helped forge a new identity. 'The standard culture retained its English cast but the presence of large bodies of non-English populations eroded its English texture', thinks Middlekauff.

A sense of independence was being established and by 1763 the colonies pretty well ran their own affairs. Even the proprietary colonies were scarcely ruled by the proprietors, as the Penn family found in Pennsylvania. British governors complained throughout the early eighteenth century that they were dealing with an incipient or even fully matured spirit of independence. Unless Britain asserted its rights, they were likely simply to drift away from British control. But if Britain tried to assert its rights, this was likely to cause ructions. According to historian Bernard Bailyn, the colonists' ideological outlook predisposed them to be acutely sensitive to all threats, perceived or real, to their liberty.

The colonists were also aware of their considerable economic strength and economic ties were beginning to pull the colonies together. British mercantilism, although not strictly enforced, rubbed the colonies up the wrong way.

In foreign affairs things had also begun to shift. The peace settlement of 1763 boded ill for future American–British relations. Josiah Tucker, a prolific essayist, wrote in 1774 'that from the moment in which Canada came into possession of the English an end was put to the sovereignty of the mother-country over her colonies. They had then nothing to fear from a foreign enemy.'

Signs of a strong relationship

However, it is also possible to argue that the colonies' relationship with Britain appeared strong in 1763. For all the apparatus of regulation and control, the British imperial system was in practice easygoing. No other colonising nation conceded to its colonial subjects the degree of autonomy the inhabitants of the thirteen colonies enjoyed. There were strong bonds of affection between Britain and the colonies, much of which stemmed from the colonists' pride in their British heritage and rights. Most Americans were loyal to the British Empire and during the Seven Years' War some 25,000 Americans had joined militias to fight alongside the British.

It is also true to say that it was this relationship with Britain which united the colonies at the time, rather than any inner unity. The only common institutions were those derived from Britain – notably the monarchy, common law, the English language and British culture. Moreover, Britain and the colonies were held together by a real community of economic interests within the mercantile system. In contrast, the colonies had different governments, different laws and different interests. There was a good deal of intercolonial jealousy and squabbles over boundaries and land claims.

Pre-1763 the colonies showed no desire to attain unity. The people of the separate colonies did not think of themselves as one people. The word 'American' was mainly a geographical expression. People's loyalties were confined primarily to their own colony and then to Britain. Many customary features of nationhood were missing. The army, customs service and post office were British, and there was no single legal or monetary system.

In 1763 virtually no American colonist sought or predicted the likelihood of independence from Britain. There was nothing inevitable about American independence. The argument that distance, population growth and nationalism would sooner or later have made separation inevitable is conjecture: the same factors did not make Canada in 1775 or later fight a war for independence.

Some key books in the debate:
Edward Countryman, *The American Revolution*, Hill and Wang, 1985.
Robert Middlekauff, *The Glorious Cause: The American Revolution, 1763–1789*, OUP, 1982.
Harry M. Ward, *The American Revolution: Nationhood Achieved 1763–1788*, St Martin's Press, 1995.
Esmond Wright, *The Search for Liberty: From Origins to Independence*, Blackwell 1995.

Study Guide: AS Questions
In the style of AQA
(a) Explain why Britain was successful in the war against the French in North America, between 1757 and 1763. (12 marks)
(b) 'In 1763, the relationship between Britain and the North American colonies was strong.' Explain why you agree or disagree with this view. (24 marks)

Exam tips

(a) To answer this question you will need to assemble a range of reasons to explain British success and you should try to present your reasons in a logical order, so as to emphasise the links between them and show which you consider the most important. You will need to refer to the contribution of Pitt and his diplomatic strategy and the importance of 'money' as well as the military and naval strategy employed by the British. Try to show some judgement in your conclusion.

(b) Always ensure you write a short plan for a question like this. You need to think of points which agree and others which disagree with the statement. Before you begin to write, decide whether, on balance, you agree or disagree and try to maintain your view through the answer so as to arrive at a substantiated judgement in the conclusion. You will need to comment on the nature of Britain's imperial system, the allowance of some autonomy, the shared institutions, the community of economic interests and the underlying level of loyalty that cut through the differences between individual colonies. These should be balanced against the rapid development and independent behaviour of the colonies, their economic strength and the disappearance of a common enemy which might unite them to Britain.

In the style of Edexcel

How far do you agree that by 1763 the ties between Britain and the American Colonies were already strained?   (30 marks)

Exam tips

The cross-references are intended to take you straight to the material that will help you to answer the question.

This question asks you to explore the relationship between Britain and the American colonies. The words 'already strained' suggest that the ties between them were threatened. You need to consider evidence that the ties remained strong and evidence of attitudes or situations which weakened those ties.

For evidence of weakening ties see:

* the effects on American attitudes of the colonies' involvement in Britain's conflicts with European powers (pages 20–21)
* the weakening of colonial dependence on Britain as a result of the elimination of France from North America (page 24)
* the growing sense of independence in the colonies (page 29)
* resentment of Britain's mercantilist polices (pages 12–13). But note (pages 13–14) that there is a debate here.

For evidence that ties remained strong, even if there were matters of disagreement, refer to (pages 29–30):

* the bonds of affection between the colonies and Britain
* the considerable colonial autonomy that already existed
* the degree of intercolonial rivalry
* the virtual non-existence of pressure for independence from Britain.

In coming to your overall conclusion, note the comment at the end of this chapter. Beware of assuming, with the benefit of hindsight, that the relationship must already have been seriously threatened simply because the colonies achieved their independence twenty years later.

---

2 The Causes of the War of Independence

POINTS TO CONSIDER

In 1763 Americans seemed closely bound to Britain by ties of interest and affection. British actions brought about the War of Independence. American colonists vigorously resisted British efforts to tighten control over the colonies. · Americans saw the British measures as a deliberate attempt to subvert their freedom. Twelve years of controversy culminated in armed revolt and the Declaration of Independence in 1776. This chapter will examine the causes of the War of Independence by examining the following themes:

- The situation in 1763–64
- The Stamp Act controversy
- The Townshend crisis
- The years of calm: 1770–73
- The impact of the Boston Tea Party
- The outbreak of war
- The Declaration of Independence

Key dates

1763		The Proclamation Line
1764		The Sugar and Currency Acts
1765		The Stamp Act
1766		Repeal of the Stamp Act
1767		Townshend duties
1770	March	The Boston Massacre
	April	Repeal of Townshend duties
1773	May	The Tea Act
	December	The Boston Tea Party
1774	Spring	The Coercive Acts
	September	First Continental Congress
1775	April	The Battle of Lexington and Concord
	May	Second Continental Congress
	June	The Battle of Bunker Hill
1776	January	Publication of *Common Sense*
	July	The Declaration of Independence

1 | The Situation in 1763–64

Key question
Why did Britain try to strengthen its control over the American colonies?

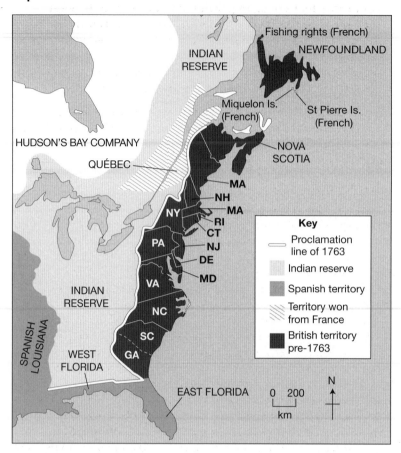

Figure 2.1: North America: 1763.

Within the map:

Fishing rights (French)

NEWFOUNDLAND

INDIAN RESERVE

Miquelon Is. (French)

St Pierre Is. (French)

HUDSON'S BAY COMPANY

QUÉBEC

NOVA SCOTIA

MA
NH
MA
NY
RI
CT
PA
NJ
DE
MD
VA
NC
SC
GA

INDIAN RESERVE

SPANISH LOUISIANA

WEST FLORIDA

EAST FLORIDA

Key

— Proclamation line of 1763

Indian reserve

Spanish territory

Territory won from France

British territory pre-1763

0   200
km

N

In 1763 Britain emerged from the Seven Years' War with a vastly increased empire in North America and a vastly increased national debt which had risen from £72 million in 1755 to £137 million by 1763. The cost of the war in America had very much contributed to the debt. For the most part, the colonies had escaped paying for the war, although they greatly benefited from the defeat of France.

Stronger imperial authority

It seemed essential to most British politicians in 1763 that imperial control over the newly extended North American empire should be tightened:

- Defence was a major concern. As the colonial boundaries moved westwards, there was the likelihood of Indian attacks. It was also possible that France might launch a revenge attack on Canada.
- Government had to be provided for 80,000 French Canadians, alien in language and religion and unfamiliar with British law and political institutions.
- A coherent Western policy was needed to reconcile the conflicting needs of land settlement, the fur trade and the Indians.

- During the Seven Years' War it had become apparent to British authorities that smuggling, with both Europe and the West Indies, was big business in America. The colonists had even traded with the enemy during the war, thus damaging the war effort.
- Some politicians were angry that colonial governments had done little to contribute to their own defence during the war.

In February 1763 the new prime minister, the Earl of Bute, announced that 10,000 British troops were needed as a permanent army in North America and that the Americans should contribute something to the expense.

George Grenville

In April 1763 Bute resigned. He was succeeded as prime minister by George Grenville, an experienced, hard-working politician who had served ably in various ministries since 1744. Like Bute, Grenville owed his elevation to high office solely to the king. In his rise to power he had broken with his brother-in-law William Pitt and with the main Whig leadership. Lacking a major base of political support, Grenville's ministry was certain to be weak.

Grenville's main concern was the expansion of the national debt. The annual interest on the debt alone was £4.4 million at a time when the government's income was only £8 million per year. Grenville had little option but to increase taxation and try to reduce expenditure. The cost of colonial administration and defence was a major concern: it had risen from £70,000 in 1748 to £350,000 in 1763 and still more money would be needed to maintain 10,000 troops in America. Grenville enthusiastically supported the notion that Americans should contribute to the cost of their own defence. According to one estimate the average American paid only sixpence a year in taxes while the average

Prime Minister George Grenville. What were his motives in introducing policies that instigated colonial resistance to British rule?

Briton paid 25 shillings – the Americans were therefore paying 50 times less. Grenville also believed that it was time to impose more order on the thirteen colonies. His purpose was not to establish tyranny but mainly to deal with the results of the Seven Years' War.

Pontiac's rebellion

Angered by the frauds of British traders and fearing (with good cause) further encroachments on their lands by white settlers, the Ohio Valley Indian tribes, led by the Ottawa chief, Pontiac, rose in revolt in May 1763. They destroyed every British post west of Niagara, except Detroit, killing or capturing hundreds of settlers in the process. Indian success was short-lived. In August British forces lifted the siege of Detroit. British officials used bribes to detach most of the Iroquois from Pontiac and to persuade the southern tribes to remain neutral. Although fighting continued into 1764, the serious Indian threat was over. The Indians were defeated by British regular soldiers paid for by Britain, not by the colonies. The Western situation seemed to confirm the view already held in London that the colonies were unable or unwilling to provide for their own defence and that there was thus need for British troops, deployed as a permanent peacetime force in America.

Key question
To what extent did Grenville's Western policies alienate Americans?

The 1763 Proclamation

In October Grenville's ministry issued the Proclamation of 1763. This tried to provide for the government of the new American territories:

Key date

The Proclamation Line: 1763

- The Proclamation created two new provinces in East and West Florida.
- The new colony of Québec was established in Canada to administer the recent acquisitions.
- More controversially, the boundary of white settlement was to be a line running along the crest of the Alleghenies. All land claims west of the boundary were to be nullified (see Figure 2.1).

The British regarded the 'Proclamation Line' as a temporary measure to reassure the Indians, minimise white–Indian conflict, and allow time for a comprehensive policy to be worked out. The intention was not to curb white expansion permanently but to ensure that it was gradual and controlled.

The Plan of 1764

The Plan of 1764 placed the fur trade directly under royal control. Only licensed traders could obtain furs. Commissaries were to be appointed to supervise the exchange of furs between whites and Indians at designated sites. Northern and southern Indian departments took over the conduct of Indian relations from the individual colonies.

The results of British Western policy

British Western policies were unpopular:

- The check on Western settlement outraged many **frontiersmen** and land speculators.
- The Proclamation went against the claims of some colonies, especially Virginia, to Western lands.
- Most Americans viewed the Proclamation as pro-Indian.

Nevertheless, British policies did not spark serious discontent. It was one thing for British politicians to draw a line on the map and proclaim that Indians should remain on one side and settlers on the other. It was quite another to enforce it. At least 30,000 American settlers ignored the restriction and moved west in the five years after 1763. By 1768 Britain had accepted the breakdown of the Proclamation Line and abandoned most of the features of the Plan of 1764.

Grenville's anti-smuggling measures

Grenville hoped to use the trade laws to extract more revenue from the Americans. The problem was that the colonial customs service was inefficient: smuggling was rife and the customs officers were frequently corrupt. Americans thus evaded most of the customs duties. The Customs Board estimated that the total duties obtained from America in 1763 would be a paltry £1800, which would cost more than £7000 to collect. The Board of Trade estimated that, in contrast, £700,000 of goods were being smuggled into the colonies annually without any duty being collected.

In 1763 Britain introduced a series of measures intended to lay the foundation for a more aggressive customs policy in America. In March Grenville, then first lord of the Admiralty, sponsored a bill approving the use of the Royal Navy to collect customs revenue and suppress smuggling. In October Grenville, now prime minister, introduced an **order-in-council** intended to increase customs' revenue in the colonies. This required colonial customs officials to reside at their stations rather than remaining in Britain and delegating their duties to a colonial deputy – a common practice. To counter the notorious leniency of colonial juries towards smugglers, Grenville transferred jurisdiction in revenue cases from colonial courts to a vice admiralty court where the judge alone would hand down the verdict. This would sit at Halifax, Nova Scotia, far from local interferences.

The Sugar Act

Under the terms of the Sugar Act of 1733 Americans should pay a duty of 6d (six old pence or half a shilling) per gallon on molasses and sugar imported from non-British colonies in the West Indies. This duty, largely ignored by American merchants and British customs officials, had yielded only £21,652 over 30 years. Grenville's Sugar Act, passed in April 1764 reduced the duty on foreign molasses from 6d a gallon to 3d. The Board of Customs commissioners advised Grenville that the revised duty, strictly enforced and rigorously collected, would yield £78,000 per year.

The purpose of the 1733 Sugar Act had been to protect the interests of British West Indian planters. The purpose of the 1764 Act was essentially to raise revenue for maintaining troops. There was virtually no opposition to the Act in Parliament. Most British MPs were complacent about and indifferent to the situation in the American colonies. There was no sustained American pressure group in Parliament and very few Americans: only five sat in the Commons between 1763 and 1783. Few British politicians anticipated much resistance to the measure. After all, it lowered duties. Moreover, it affected primarily just one region – New England.

As part of the legislation associated with the Sugar Act, Grenville added products (including wine, silk and coffee) to the list of enumerated commodities which, according to the Navigation Acts, would be subject to increased duties if not traded via Britain. Among the new regulations of the Sugar Act and its companion legislation any customs official convicted of accepting a bribe was subject to a £500 fine and disqualification from serving in any government post.

The Currency Act

The 1764 Currency Act placed a ban on colonial paper money. No future paper money could be used for private debts and paper money already in circulation had to be returned. The Act, aimed largely at Virginia which had issued a large amount of paper money during the Seven Years' War, appeased British merchants who insisted that colonial debts be paid in a more acceptable currency.

The American reaction

Grenville's measures angered many colonists and kindled their suspicions. In 1763–64 the American view was that the imperial system wasn't broken and didn't need fixing.

The new controls were all the more unpopular because past British policy had been so lax. The Currency Act could not have been passed at a worse time as far as the colonists were concerned. An economic depression had hit the colonies as the war came to an end and orders for supplies for the forces fell off. The **deflationary** effects of the Currency Act threatened some Americans with economic ruin.

New England merchants were especially aggrieved:

- The Sugar Act reduced the incentive to smuggle, thus obliging many American merchants to pay the duty for the first time.
- The extension of the list of enumerated items and stricter customs enforcement threatened to curtail other – illegal – trade.
- The enforcement of the new legislation by vice admiralty courts represented a challenge to the colonial legal system.

Key question
Why did many Americans oppose Grenville's 1764 measures?

Key term

Deflationary
The situation resulting from a decreasing amount of money in circulation. People have insufficient money to buy goods or to invest.

American suspicions

Britain's right to regulate colonial trade had long been accepted as normal practice. However, the Sugar Act represented a fundamental revision in the relationship between Britain and the colonies. By imposing duties to raise revenue, Britain was essentially taxing Americans who were unrepresented in the British Parliament. Once it was accepted that Parliament could tax the colonies at will, where would it end? Moreover, Americans were aware that Parliament sought to tax the colonies further. In 1764 Grenville informed all colonial governors that he intended to introduce a stamp tax in America. Colonial autonomy suddenly seemed under threat.

By the mid-eighteenth century, the colonists regarded themselves as good Whigs. Their Whiggism, however, was not the same as the Whiggism prevalent in mid-eighteenth-century Britain. American Whiggism was that of the first English Whigs who had come to prominence when England seemed to be sliding towards despotism under Charles II and James II. American Whiggism in the 1760s was still concerned with the old Whig issues of resisting **arbitrary power**, upholding popular rights and defending the integrity of representative institutions. The writings of a spate of early eighteenth-century British radical Whigs, who attacked the conduct of nominally Whig ministers, enjoyed wide support in the colonies. Pamphleteers, like John Trenchard, argued (in the 1720s) that England's constitution was being subverted by a sinister conspiracy of the king's ministers. Ministers, it was claimed, were using corruption to gain control over the other branches of government and establish a tyranny.

Americans took these views seriously. Accordingly, many were convinced of the need to guard against attempts to expand executive power by stealth. The early years of George III's reign seemed to provide cause for alarm, not least the position of influence attained by George's ex-tutor, the Earl of Bute. Although Bute was no longer prime minister, many Americans (and Britons) feared he was still a power behind the throne. There was also the fact that a large peacetime British army was being stationed in North America. The colonists had not asked for that army and many were suspicious of it. Standing armies had long been seen as a potential threat to liberty.

Historian Bernard Bailyn, who spent many years studying American political pamphlets, thought that what distinguished them was 'the fear of a comprehensive conspiracy against liberty throughout the English-speaking world – a conspiracy believed to have been nourished in corruption and of which, it was felt, oppression in America was only the most immediately visible part'.

The influence of John Wilkes

Many Americans identified with John Wilkes, a radical British MP and co-editor of the journal *North Briton*. Wilkes demanded freedom of the press and a more democratic Parliament. In 1763, after he had criticised the king and accused his ministers of being 'the tools of despotism and corruption', Wilkes was arrested on a **general**

Key term

Arbitrary power
Power that is not bound by rules, allowing a monarch to do as he or she wishes.

warrant and imprisoned. Although Wilkes was soon released, he was subsequently convicted of libel and fled to France. Wilkes became an American as well as a British hero. The British government seemed to be trampling on British – as well as American – liberties.

American opposition in 1764

The Massachusetts assembly defended its right to levy its own taxes and asked the other colonial assemblies to unite behind its stance. By 1765 nine colonies had sent messages to London all arguing that by introducing the Sugar Act Parliament had abused its power. While conceding Parliament's right to regulate trade, they did not accept its right to tax for the purpose of raising revenue in America.

It was not only the assemblies that objected to the Sugar Act. Some Americans took up their pens. James Otis, for example, a member of a prominent Massachusetts family, published an influential pamphlet in 1764, *The Rights of the British Colonies Asserted and Proved*, in which he criticised Parliament's new aggressiveness towards the colonies and asserted that there should be no taxation in America without the people's consent.

Despite the objections of assemblies and pamphleteers and the grumbling of colonial merchants, most Americans complied with the Sugar Act. Few were directly affected by it. This compliance gave Grenville the confidence to proceed with the Stamp Act.

Key term

General warrant
A warrant that allowed the government to make an arbitrary arrest for a political offence. A general warrant did not name an accused individual but merely specified the crime.

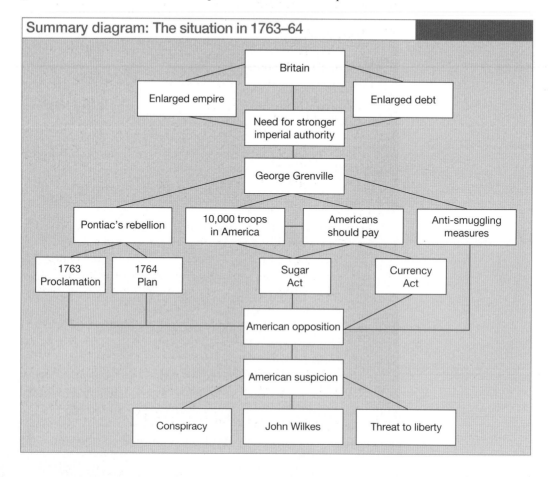

Summary diagram: The situation in 1763–64

Key question
Why did the Stamp
Act provoke such a
violent reaction in the
colonies?

2 | The Stamp Act Controversy

In March 1764 Grenville let it be known that he was planning to bring in a stamp duty in America. He added, however, that he would canvas colonial opinion before introducing the measure. In May he met the American agents in London and told them he wished to listen to their opinions 'to have the sense of the colonies themselves upon the matter, and if they could point out any system or plan as effectual and more easy to them, he was open to every proposition to be made from the colonies'. But it seems he was already determined to introduce a stamp bill and was merely expecting the Americans to suggest the rate of duty.

It was possibly a mistake to give Americans a year's warning of the Stamp Act. The measure might have created less controversy had it been brought in more quickly. As it was the colonies had time to prepare their opposition. By late 1764 protests from the colonial assemblies began arriving in London. In early 1765 Grenville again met with the colonial agents to discuss the Stamp Act before he presented it to Parliament. When some of the agents suggested that the colonies offer financial requisitions in lieu of the stamp duty, Grenville said this was unacceptable. In the wake of colonial protests, Grenville seems to have viewed the stamp measure not only as a source of revenue but as an assertion of parliamentary sovereignty over the colonies.

Key date

The Stamp Act: 1765

The Stamp Act

On 6 February 1765 Grenville introduced the stamp bill to Parliament. The bill required stamps to be affixed to almost anything formally written or printed in the colonies. Fifty items, ranging from newspapers, legal documents, commercial bills, insurance policies, tavern and marriage licences, articles of apprenticeship, even playing cards, would be affected. By its very pervasiveness – the tax would impact on virtually all Americans – the measure differed in important ways from all previous imperial legislation. Stamp-tax officers would be appointed in each of the colonies and these officers would be empowered to open sub-offices in towns and villages.

The stamp duties in America would not be a particularly heavy burden. They were much lighter than those in England, where they had been levied for over 70 years. The Treasury estimated that the new duty would raise about £60,000 in its first year. The money would be spent entirely in the colonies. It would be only a quarter of the sum needed for colonial defence.

There was some opposition to the stamp bill in the Commons – from William Pitt, Edmund Burke and Isaac Barre – but not enough to challenge the measure seriously. Most MPs agreed with Grenville that Parliament had the right to tax the colonies and that the Americans should contribute something to their own defence. The bill was adopted by the Commons by 245 to 49 and given royal assent on 22 March. It was to take effect on 1 November 1765.

The American reaction

News of the Stamp Act arrived in the colonies in April 1765. By the summer, it had produced an extraordinarily widespread and intense reaction. Whereas the Sugar Act had affected only New England merchants, the Stamp Act applied universally, antagonising some of the most influential groups of colonists – lawyers, printers and tavern-keepers. The first direct tax levied by Parliament upon the colonies, it was condemned as a dangerous and unjustified innovation. It again raised the issue of whether the colonists could be taxed by a body in which they were not represented. Determined to prevent the implementation of the Act and to convince Parliament to repeal the measure, the colonists pursued three main strategies:

- They protested through their assemblies and printing presses.
- They exerted pressure through popular actions.
- They applied economic pressure.

The Virginia Resolves

Virginia, the most populous state, led the way. On 29 May 1765 Patrick Henry introduced in the House of Burgesses (the Virginia assembly) seven resolutions attacking the Stamp Act. Henry, a 29-year-old frontier lawyer, had been a member of the House for just nine days. His resolves were put forward at the very end of the legislative session when most of the burgesses had left for home. Only 39 of the 116 remained. On 30 May the 39 burgesses, by no means unanimously, adopted the five mildest of Henry's resolutions:

- The colonists possessed the rights of Englishmen.
- Their rights were guaranteed by royal charter.
- They could be taxed only if they had proper representation.
- Colonists had the right to give their consent to their laws.
- The House of Burgesses had the sole right to tax Virginians.

The House rejected the two most radical resolutions:

- Virginians were not obliged to obey any laws designed to tax them without their consent.
- Those who supported such taxes were enemies of the colony.

Since Henry's resolutions were printed and circulated in their entirety in many colonial newspapers, the impression was given that Virginia had rejected the Stamp Act and sanctioned open resistance if Britain tried to enforce it.

Most of the colonial assemblies had finished their spring sessions by the time the news of the Virginia Resolves arrived. It was not until the autumn, therefore, that they discussed the Stamp Act. However, by the end of 1765 eight other colonial assemblies had passed resolutions condemning the Act and denying Parliament's right to tax the colonies. Most drew up petitions to the king and Parliament appealing for the Act's repeal.

Key question
Why was the Stamp
Act Congress a threat
to Britain?

The Stamp Act Congress

In June, the Massachusetts House of Representatives suggested
that an intercolonial meeting be held in order to draft a set of
resolutions which expressed a common colonial position.
Accordingly, a Stamp Act Congress met in October in New York.
Twenty-seven delegates from nine colonies attended – all men of
high social standing. New Hampshire did not participate but later
endorsed the Congress' work. Virginia, North Carolina and
Georgia were unable to send delegates because their governors
refused to call their assemblies into session in order to send
delegates. The representatives spent two weeks drafting a set of
fourteen resolutions – a 'Declaration of Rights and Grievances' –
which set out the colonial view on the Stamp Act and the
relationship between the colonies and Britain. The delegates
denounced the Stamp Act as having 'a manifest tendency to
subvert the rights and liberties of the colonies' and claimed that
only their own legislatures could impose taxes upon them. It was
the duty of the colonies to seek the repeal of the Stamp Act, the
abolition of vice admiralty courts and 'of other late Acts for the
restriction of American commerce'.

Key question
Why did the
Americans oppose
parliamentary
taxation?

The ideological debate

Similar views were expressed in scores of pamphlets that issued
from American presses during 1765. The colonists were not
prepared to accept taxation without representation. This was a
right that Americans, as Englishmen, believed was enshrined in
the English Constitution. To raise money by parliamentary
taxation was to deny Americans control of their property. Once
they lost that control they became in effect slaves – an emotive
term to Americans. Direct American representation in Parliament
was thought impracticable by most colonists because of the
distance involved. A handful of American MPs, some colonists
feared, would be worse than none. Their presence at Westminster
would simply give Parliament the excuse to levy higher taxes on
the colonies. The only proper way to raise money in America, the
colonists maintained, was through the colonial assemblies.

Many Americans saw the political world in terms of an
unending struggle between liberty and its enemies. They also
believed that government was by its nature oppressive, and that
only constant vigilance could check its tendency to encroach on
individual rights. Accordingly, the notion that the Stamp Act was
evidence of a conspiracy to deprive the Americans of their liberties
was widely disseminated.

But who was conspiring? The ministry? Parliament? The king?
Were they all in league against the Americans? No one suggested
that they were. Indeed, George III was still seen as the 'the best
king in the world'. Parliament furnished the model of the
colonists' own representative assemblies. Thus the ministers – first
Bute and now Grenville – were seen as the real villains. While the
fears of covert designs against colonial liberty were misconceived,
they seemed eminently reasonable to many Americans. Why did

the British need a standing army in America unless it was to be used to force Americans to yield to such oppressions as unconstitutional taxes?

Popular protest

Colonial leaders could not have challenged British policy successfully without popular support. It was people in crowds who turned the situation from a debate into a movement. Crowd action was a fact of life in the eighteenth century. However, the sustained popular militancy that developed in most American towns in 1765 was something very new.

The Loyal Nine

The street protests began in Boston. The popular initiative to resist the Stamp Act originated among a group of artisans and shopkeepers known as the Loyal Nine. The group included a printer, Benjamin Edes, who published the *Boston Gazette*. Its most important leader, however, was Samuel Adams, a Harvard graduate. Fuelled by economic stagnation, resentment grew. It was particularly focused on purported supporters of the Stamp Act. These included Andrew Oliver, a rich merchant and the designated Massachusett's stamp distributor, the Chief Justice (and Oliver's brother-in-law), Thomas Hutchinson, and Governor Francis Bernard.

The Loyal Nine turned to the North and South End gangs for support. These gangs, comprising unskilled workers, sailors and apprentices, had fought each other for years, usually on 5 November – Guy Fawkes' day. After the fight of 1764, in which a child had been accidently killed, the leader of the South Enders, Ebenezer MacIntosh (a cobbler), assumed leadership of both gangs. Persuading MacIntosh and his followers to take action against the Stamp Act was not difficult. Instead of the opposing mob, Oliver and other 'traitors' became the enemy.

Mob action

On 14 August, effigies of Oliver and Bute (see Chapter 1) were hung from the **Liberty Tree** in Boston. Men stood by the tree throughout the day to collect a mock stamp duty from every passer-by. When Hutchinson ordered the sheriff to cut down the effigies, a crowd prevented the order being put into effect. Towards nightfall, Oliver's effigy was carried by the mob towards the wharves where Oliver had an office, rumoured to be the place from which stamps would be distributed. The crowd tore down the building and then used the timbers to start a bonfire by Oliver's house. He was not at home but Hutchinson appeared and tried to reason with the crowd. Hutchinson's presence simply infuriated the mob. He was forced to flee in a hail of stones and the crowd proceeded to destroy Oliver's house. On 15 August Oliver resigned from the stamp distributor post.

On 26 August another Boston crowd inflicted serious damage on the houses of two British officials. The goal was the same: to

Key term

Liberty Tree
An actual (but also symbolic) tree in Boston, representing freedom from tyranny.

force the officials to resign. (One rapidly did.) The crowd then went on to attack Hutchinson's mansion. As the place was torn apart, he was lucky to escape with his life. There was, as historian Edward Countryman recognises, an element of class resentment in the destruction. Oliver and Hutchinson were unpopular, not just because they were seen as British minions, but also because they were wealthy. Social discontent was a latent ally of political rebelliousness. Indeed, many rich Bostonians feared that popular resentment at the Stamp Act had turned into an attack on property by the 'rabble'. Consequently Governor Bernard, to his surprise, had no difficulty raising the **militia** and for several weeks was able to maintain order.

As news of events in Boston spread, so did crowd action. By the end of October stamp distributors in Rhode Island, New Hampshire, Pennsylvania, Delaware, Virginia and Connecticut, fearing for their lives and property, had resigned. On 1 November a New York City crowd copied Boston, first raising effigies, this time of the devil and Lieutenant Governor Colden (the stamp distributor) and then breaking into Colden's carriage house and burning his carriages and the effigies. Then it marched to a mansion occupied by Major James, a British officer, and destroyed it. The New York stamp distributors resigned or fled. So did those in Maryland and North Carolina. Only in Georgia did a stamp man briefly take office before he was forced to resign.

The Stamp Act had been nullified by mob action. If no one was prepared to be a stamp distributor, the stamp duties could not be levied. Britain would have to use force if it was to maintain its authority. Britain had 10,000 soldiers in America but most were stationed in Newfoundland, Nova Scotia and on the Western frontier. In 1766 only a few hundred men were garrisoned in New York and Philadelphia. Moreover, the army could only be called out to deal with civil disobedience if the civil authorities made a formal request to the military commander. No governor did so.

The Sons of Liberty

By the autumn of 1765 the men directing the crowd action were known as the Sons of Liberty. The first Sons originated in New York. Committed radicals, they called on like-minded men to establish similar groups elsewhere. Groups like the Loyal Nine in Boston soon took the name 'Sons of Liberty'. Operating as a semi-secret society, the Sons were committed to rousing the public, forcing the stamp distributors to resign and preventing the use of stamps. The Sons included members of the elite. However, they also comprised a host of new men – small merchants, artisans and dissident intellectuals like Sam Adams. Although the Sons established useful channels of communication and helped keep political consciousness high, the influence of the organisation can be exaggerated:

• It was by no means a united organisation. Each group operated in its own way within its own community.

Key term

Militia
A force, made up of all military-aged civilians, called out in times of emergency.

- Many rich Americans, fearing social upheaval, opposed the Sons.
- The Sons had limited influence in the Southern colonies.
- The Sons were an urban movement. But townspeople made up less than five per cent of America's population.

Economic sanctions

As the crisis deepened, the Sons of Liberty appealed to the public not to buy British goods. On 31 October 1765, 200 leading merchants in New York signed an agreement not to import goods from Britain until the Stamp Act was repealed. The boycott soon spread to Boston and Philadelphia. Merchants formed non-importation associations to boycott British goods. Elsewhere non-importation was adopted as a tactic without resort to formal agreements. Many colonial craftsmen supported the boycott because their own products would face less competition.

The repeal of the Stamp Act

Grenville was determined to see the authority of Parliament upheld. Had his ministry remained in office, an attempt would have been made to collect the stamp tax. This might well have led to armed conflict. However, in July 1765 Grenville was replaced by a new ministry led by the inexperienced Marquis of Rockingham. Like Grenville, Rockingham wanted to see Parliament's authority upheld. But while Grenville thought Parliament's right to tax the colonies had to be boldly asserted to avoid being lost, Rockingham believed that it was best not to exercise some rights, or at least to exercise them with discretion.

British opinion, inside and outside Parliament, was divided. When the parliamentary session began in December 1765, many MPs, horrified by the mob violence in America, were against repealing the Stamp Act, convinced that this would seem an act of weakness. They did not accept the American argument that because they were unrepresented Parliament could not legislate for them. The colonies were no more unrepresented than many British towns. There were MPs willing to speak for America just as there were MPs who could speak for Manchester and Birmingham. Most MPs believed they represented not the interests of certain communities but the whole 'Commons of Great Britain' – and that included the Americans who were British subjects. However, British merchants and manufacturers, alarmed by the colonial boycott, organised a national campaign for repeal of the Stamp Act.

By December Rockingham's government had a choice between making concessions to the colonists or attempting to coerce them into complying with the Stamp Act. General Thomas Gage, commander-in-chief in the colonies, declared that the Stamp Act could not be enforced without far greater military force than he possessed. Rockingham, influenced by the merchants' petitions, resolved to repeal the Act.

The Commons debated the issue in January 1766. William Pitt, pro-American, declared that 'this kingdom has no right to lay a tax upon the colonies'. Grenville, anti-American, defended his

Key question
Why did Britain repeal the Stamp Act?

Key date
Repeal of the Stamp Act: 1766

measure, asserting that taxation was part of the sovereign power. He wanted a motion to declare the colonies in a state of rebellion. Pitt responded by praising American resistance to the Stamp Act. 'I rejoice that America has resisted. Three millions of people, so dead to all the feelings of liberty, as voluntarily to submit to be slaves, would have been fit instruments to make slaves of the rest.' But some MPs wondered why anyone should expect Americans ever to pay taxes again if they escaped this one. Benjamin Franklin, appearing before a Commons committee, did his best to ease those fears. He made a distinction between internal and external taxes. The colonies, Franklin said (not quite correctly), objected only to internal taxes: they would willingly pay external duties on trade in return for the protection of the Royal Navy. The Stamp Act was finally repealed in March 1766 by 275 votes to 167.

The Declaratory Act

The reason why the majority of British MPs did vote for repeal was not because they thought it was the right thing to do. They acted because they feared the colonies' ability to damage Britain's economy. Nor did they wish to incite rebellion. The British government, while abandoning a measure it could not enforce, did not surrender the constitutional principle of parliamentary sovereignty. At the same time as it repealed the Stamp Act, Parliament passed the Declaratory Act. This asserted that the colonies were subordinate to the 'Crown and Parliament of Great Britain' and that Parliament had full authority to make laws 'to bind the colonies and people of America … in all cases whatsoever'.

The effects of the crisis

In America the news of the repeal was rapturously received. Non-importation was abandoned. The Sons of Liberty virtually disbanded. As the colonial legislatures convened throughout 1766 they declared their pleasure over the repeal and most sent addresses of gratitude to the king.

Nevertheless, the Stamp Act crisis marked a crucial turning point in British–colonial relations. As Grenville had recognised, there was more at stake in the controversy than revenue. The fundamental issue was Parliament's sovereignty over the colonies. In denying Parliament the right to tax them, the Americans were implicitly denying Parliament's right to govern them. In 1765, most Americans still believed the Stamp Act was the problem, not British rule itself. The Americans were not yet demanding independence in principle but they were demanding independence – or at least self-rule – in practice. They ruled out all British – in practice parliamentary – interference in American internal affairs and recognised a connection only with the king. This stance arose from the need to find a reason to deny Britain the right to impose a fairly modest tax. The response seemed out of all proportion to the provocation.

The British had been caught unawares. British assumptions that the colonies were too self-interested to act together had been swept away. The Stamp Act had brought the American colonists closer together than they had ever been before.

In several colonies the Stamp Act crisis resulted in important shifts of power. Those factions who could be charged with supporting the Stamp Act lost control of the colonial assemblies. In Massachusetts, for example, the Otis faction had no trouble in discrediting Governor Bernard and Thomas Hutchinson for supporting British policy. Consequently, in 1766, Bernard's supporters took a drubbing at the polls.

Americans and Britons learned important lessons from the crisis:

- Americans believed they must be vigilant in defence of their liberties.
- The crisis had shown that British authority could be defied if there was colonial unity of purpose.
- Many British politicians felt that they must reassert authority over the obstreperous colonies or they would become independent by default.

Summary diagram: The Stamp Act controversy

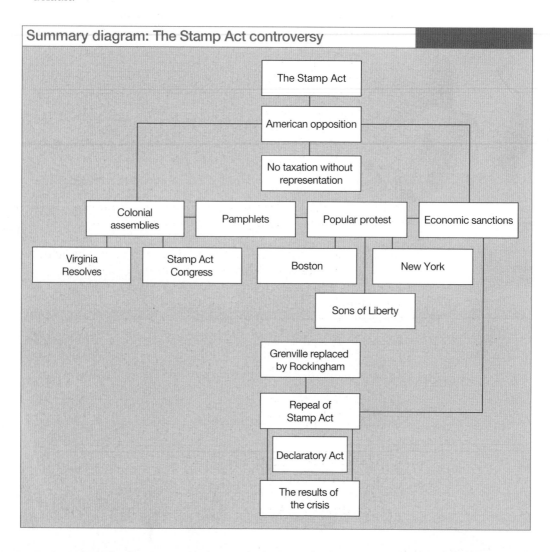

Key question
Why did Townshend
introduce his duties?

3 | The Townshend Crisis

In July 1766 the Rockingham ministry fell. Rockingham was replaced by the great national hero, 57-year-old William Pitt. He believed passionately in the British Empire and did not want to see it undermined by provocative measures like the Stamp Act. However, as a result of poor health (he seems to have had a nervous breakdown), Pitt – who was now created Earl of Chatham with a seat in the Lords – took little active interest in the administration. The Duke of Grafton, aged 31, took over as head of government. Unfortunately Grafton was a lightweight with little political experience.

Townshend's duties

In this situation, Chancellor of the Exchequer Charles Townshend dominated proceedings. According to the writer Horace Walpole, Townshend 'had almost every great talent … if he had had but common truth, common sincerity, common honesty, common modesty, common steadiness, common courage and common sense'. Gifted but erratic in private and public conduct, Townshend, an ex-president of the Board of Trade, had extensive experience in colonial administration. Concerned that royal officials in America were dependent on colonial opinion, he was determined that they should be paid directly by Britain, not by the colonial assemblies. Nevertheless, he also believed that the American colonies should shoulder the burden of this expense.

Key date

Townshend duties:
1767

In May 1767, Townshend introduced new duties on colonial imports of glass, wine, china, lead, paint, paper and tea. During the Stamp Act crisis some Americans (like Franklin) had drawn a distinction between internal and external taxes, denying Parliament's authority to impose the former upon them but conceding its right to regulate trade, even if such regulation produced a revenue. Since Townshend's new duties were unquestionably external, he reasoned that the colonists could not logically object to them. Given that the duties were relatively light, he hoped Americans would pay them. Some MPs realised that Townshend's measures, which would raise a paltry £40,000 per year, were a mistake. Edmund Burke pointed out that it no longer mattered to the Americans whether taxes were external or internal: if they were levied by Britain they would oppose them. Nevertheless, Townshend had gauged the strong anti-American mood in the Commons and his measures passed by a vote of 180 to 98.

To tighten the machinery of trade enforcement, Townshend established an American Board of Customs Commissioners. Stationed in Boston, it was to be directly responsible to Britain and would give American customs officials more powers.

The New York Restraining Act

Townshend also took steps to enforce the Mutiny (or Quartering) Act of 1765. Designed to remedy the shortage of military accommodation, the Act required colonial assemblies to make provision for quartering and supplying British troops. Most of the colonies had grudgingly complied but New York, the headquarters of the British army in America, had refused because the burden of the Act fell disproportionately on the colony. Faced with this defiance, Townshend brought in the New York Restraining Act (March 1767). Under its terms the New York assembly was prohibited from taking any legislative action until it complied with the Quartering Act. By suspending the assembly, Parliament had posed the problem of the constitutional standing of the colonial legislatures. Many disliked the notion that Parliament could suspend or change them at will. However, the New York assembly, lacking support from the other colonies, agreed to support the troops in June 1767.

Townshend's death

It was somewhat ironic that an administration at least nominally headed by Chatham, who was pro-American, approved Townshend's policies. It was also ironic that Townshend did not have to deal with the colonial response to his measures. He died suddenly in September 1767.

Colonial resistance

Colonial resistance to Townshend's measures developed more slowly than had been the case in 1765. Not all Americans were sure whether the new duties constituted a violation of colonial rights. Merchants and shopkeepers, enjoying a period of economic boom, had no wish for another trade war with Britain. Nevertheless, it was soon clear that American resentment was strong and widespread.

Key question
To what extent was American resistance between 1767 and 1770 similar to that in 1765?

The intellectual response

John Dickinson, a member of the Pennsylvania assembly, wrote the most influential attack on Townshend's measures. Dickinson penned twelve letters which first appeared in Pennsylvania. Reprinted in most colonial newspapers, the letters were then gathered together in a pamphlet – *Letters of a Pennsylvania Farmer* (1768). Dickinson, a wealthy lawyer, was no rabble-rouser. He accepted that the colonies were part of the British Empire and that Parliament had the right to preside over the whole. Nevertheless, he strongly opposed what he considered to be liberty-threatening changes from Britain. He argued that while Parliament could regulate the colonies' trade, it did not have the right to tax them without their consent, either through internal taxes or external duties. He also condemned the Mutiny Act for being an attempt at direct parliamentary taxation, and attacked the suspension of the New York assembly as a blow to colonial liberty.

Other writers suggested that Townshend's measures would strengthen the executive and make colonial governments less accountable. Americans particularly feared that the new position of customs official would become a rich field of **patronage** at the disposal of the executive. Many feared that patronage power would in time corrupt a majority in the assemblies, making their members mere creatures of the British government.

Patronage
The right of bestowing offices – offices usually given to supporters, family or friends.

Key term

In fact, there was little that was original. Most writers (like Dickinson) merely applied arguments that had been used against the Stamp Act.

The political response

Over the winter of 1767–68 the Massachusetts assembly discussed the Townshend duties. In February 1768 the assembly sent out a **circular letter**, largely the work of Samuel Adams and James Otis. The letter denounced the Townshend duties for violating the principle of 'no taxation without representation' and appealed to the other colonies for common action. The document was no call to revolution: its tone was moderate. Nevertheless, Governor Bernard branded it seditious and other governors tried to prevent assemblies from endorsing it – with limited success. Seven colonial assemblies quickly approved the letter.

Key term

Circular letter
A letter of which copies are sent to several persons.

Profile: Samuel Adams (1722–1803)

1722	– Born in Boston
1740	– After graduating from Harvard, he was apprenticed to a merchant who soon decided he had no aptitude for business
1748	– On the death of his father, he took over – not very successfully – the family malt business
1756	– Elected tax collector in Boston. Although inefficient, he held the job for nine years
1765	– Helped co-ordinate the Stamp Act resistance in Boston
1768	– Secured passage of the circular letter
1772	– Helped form the committees of correspondence
1773	– Helped plan the Boston Tea Party
1774	– Led the opposition to the Coercive Acts
1774–81	– A member of the Continental Congress
1794–97	– Governor of Massachusetts

A radical idealist, Sam Adams was a fanatical, unscrupulous man, skilled in propaganda and a great opportunist. The puritanical Adams hated what he saw as the corruption of the British ruling elite. In his view, this justified any misrepresentation which might shed the worst possible light on Britain. He was the man who sculpted the protest movement in Massachusetts, influenced resistance elsewhere and both openly and behind the scenes led the first Congress to embargo Britain and the second towards independence. More agitator than statesman and more prominent in Massachusetts than nationally, this may explain why he is not regarded as one of the great revolutionary figures. Nevertheless, he was a pre-eminent early rebel leader. Thomas Jefferson described him as 'truly the man of the revolution'.

The Virginia House of Burgesses went further. Armed with petitions from Virginia's counties against the suspension of the New York assembly, as well as against parliamentary taxation, the House issued a circular letter of its own (in May), advocating joint measures by the colonies against any British actions which 'have an immediate tendency to enslave them'.

At a lower level, the Sons of Liberty movement was revived throughout the colonies in order to co-ordinate opposition.

Economic resistance

In 1768 the colonists organised another economic boycott similar to the one organised against the Stamp Act. Boston led the way. Other towns and states followed, albeit slowly in some cases. The non-importation agreements adopted in various colonies differed greatly in their implementation. Many merchants and Southern planters opposed non-importation so the boycott was never totally watertight. Nevertheless, by late 1769 every colony except New Hampshire had organisations pledged to boycott British goods. Complementing the non-importation agreements were decisions by individuals not to purchase British products. American housewives, for example, stopped serving British tea. As in 1765, non-importation spurred home manufacturing as an alternative to boycotted British goods.

Non-importation provided considerable scope for popular activity because it touched the lives of ordinary people, offering them a means of effective action. Unofficial bodies, usually called committees of inspection, were set up in most colonies to enforce non-importation. Those who broke the boycott were threatened with being named and shamed. Merchants who did not comply had their warehouses broken into and their goods damaged. Violators also faced the threat of violence, not least being **tarred and feathered**.

As well as putting economic pressure on Britain, non-importation also strengthened the moral resolve of the colonists. Some Americans were delighted to stem the tide of British luxury goods that were thought to be undermining the simplicity, virtue and independence of colonial life. 'The baubles of Britain,' says historian T.H. Breen, 'were believed to be threatening American liberty as much as were parliamentary taxation and a bloated customs service.'

> **Key term**
>
> **Tarred and feathered**
> Victims were stripped naked, covered with hot tar and then rolled in goose feathers.

The situation in Boston

Placing the American Board of Customs Commissioners in Boston had been a major error. From the time they arrived in November 1767 the commissioners were targets of popular wrath. Charged with tightening up the customs service, they faced an impossible task. There were far too few customs men to stop smuggling. Unable to carry out their duties, the commissioners sought help from the Royal Navy. In June 1768, the 50-gun warship *Romney* sailed into Boston harbour. Emboldened by this reinforcement, the commissioners seized the *Liberty*, a small vessel belonging to John Hancock, one of Boston's richest merchants and a leading radical.

A mob of Bostonians soon marched to the wharf and a scuffle began with the customs men. Sailors from the *Romney* boarded the *Liberty* and took the boat out into the harbour. However, in the face of threats, the customs officials were forced to take refuge in Castle William, on an island in Boston harbour. By the summer of 1768 the Sons of Liberty were in control of Boston.

The Wilkesite movement

In 1768, John Wilkes returned to England from France. He was promptly arrested, fined £1000 and sentenced to 22 months in prison. On 10 May 1768 some 30,000 people gathered near the prison in London where Wilkes was incarcerated, demanding his release. Troops fired into the crowd, killing six and wounding twenty. While in prison, Wilkes was elected to Parliament three times: on each occasion he was expelled for libel. On the fourth try, the Commons illegally installed a rival. Wilkes' treatment, which was well reported in colonial newspapers, suggested to Americans that the British government was pursuing a concerted programme to suppress liberty on both sides of the Atlantic. Subscriptions for Wilkes' relief were taken in several towns. In 1769 the South Carolina assembly donated £1500 to Wilkes' cause.

The Secretary of State for America

In January 1768, Grafton created a secretary of state for colonial and American matters. Unfortunately the Earl of Hillsborough, the first colonial secretary, lacked tact and political wisdom. One of his first acts was to order the Massachusetts' assembly to rescind the circular letter it had sent out upon penalty of dissolution. Any colonial legislature that voted approval of the letter was to be dissolved by the governor.

Unrest in Boston

In Massachusetts, Governor Bernard did his best to obey Hillsborough's orders. When the Massachusetts assembly voted 92 to 17 not to rescind the letter, he dissolved it. This only worsened matters. The Sons of Liberty now had another issue on which to campaign. To keep up popular enthusiasm, Otis and Adams organised marches and events while radical newspapers like the *Boston Gazette* carried on an endless campaign against the British government and its servants in Massachusetts. By 1768 Boston had a disciplined cadre of men who spent so much time and energy countering every British move, they were virtually professional revolutionaries. Not surprisingly, crowd trouble in Boston continued. Royal officials were threatened and the houses of customs commissioners' damaged. Bernard had little option but to ask for troops to try to restore order.

The announcement of the troops' coming increased tension. In September 1768 Boston called a convention of towns to consider the crisis. The convention opened with 70 representatives from 66 towns, including Sam Adams and John Hancock. The convention did little but petition the king for redress of grievances. But the fact that it had met at all marked an extension of defiance of royal authority.

In late September, 600 British troops arrived in Boston. Far from ending Boston's disaffection, they gave it another focus – themselves. The day-to-day presence of British troops became a constant aggravation:

- There were problems of barracking and quartering the troops.
- Bostonians, accustomed to leading their lives with a minimum of interference from government, were harassed by British patrols.
- Off-duty soldiers sought to improve their meagre incomes by taking part-time jobs. The fact that they were prepared to work for less money than Americans increased tensions.

Radicals like Sam Adams exploited civilian–military tensions. Boston newspapers almost daily reported – usually fabricated – stories of brutality and debauchery among British troops. The army, goaded by a hostile population, also had good cause to grumble. Brawls between troops and Bostonians were common. Troops resented the fact that they received severe treatment in the local courts.

Civil–military relations were bad in New York as well as Boston. In January 1770 a week of street fighting broke out between soldiers and civilians. Many people were wounded in the so-called Battle of Golden Hill.

The Boston Massacre

In Boston tension increased:

The Boston Massacre: March 1770

Key date

- On 22 February 1770, a suspected customs informer killed an eleven-year-old boy during a riot. The Sons of Liberty turned the funeral into a political demonstration: 5000 Bostonians attended.
- On 2 March workers at a rope factory attacked some **redcoats** seeking jobs and a pitched battle ensued.

Redcoats
British troops who wore red uniforms.

Key term

The climax came on 5 March. A small detachment of British soldiers guarding the customs house were attacked by a mob hurling hard-packed snowballs. The troops opened fire, killing five Bostonians. Although the soldiers had fired under extreme provocation, Samuel Adams' political machine, operating from the Green Dragon pub, gave the impression that there had been a massacre – a version of events that was accepted by most Americans. The funerals of the dead were occasions for mass political demonstrations. The American cause now had martyrs. Henceforward 5 March became a patriotic holiday in Boston.

Eight of the soldiers were eventually brought to trial. Six were acquitted after a skilful defence by their counsel John Adams, a cousin of Sam. Two, found guilty of manslaughter, were released after being branded on the thumb.

Paul Revere's engraving of the Boston Massacre. Why was this a masterful piece of colonial propaganda?

The situation by 1770

- 'The Americans,' wrote Edmund Burke, 'have made a discovery, or think they have made one, that we mean to oppress them. We have made a discovery, or think we have made one, that they intend to rise in rebellion against us … we know not how to advance, they know not how to retreat … some party must give way.'
- Many British officials, aware they were being manipulated by agitators and provincial assemblies, did know what to do about it. There were not enough troops to impose a full crackdown.
- By 1770 relations between British authorities and the leaders of the colonial legislatures had broken down.
- However, colonial unity was not total. Conservatives were alarmed at the resort to mob action. There was also resentment at the fact that non-importation was not being uniformly observed. Indeed, by 1770 the boycott of British goods had started to collapse.

The repeal of the Townshend duties

The British government was seriously concerned by events in the colonies. The Townshend duties, which had stirred up such a hornet's nest, made little financial sense. Not only were they failing to raise a significant revenue, they were also penalising British exports to the colonies. In 1769 the Grafton cabinet decided that the duties should be repealed. When Grafton resigned in January 1770 the task of overseeing the repeal fell to the new prime minister, Frederick, Lord North. North supported repealing the duties: they were, in his view, 'teasing the Americans for a trifle'. On the same day as the Boston Massacre, North secured the repeal of all the duties save that on tea. The decision to retain the duty on tea was taken in cabinet by a single vote, that of North himself. He saw the duty 'as a mark of the supremacy of Parliament'.

North's action divided conservative merchants from more radical agitators. New York quickly abandoned non-importation. As other ports followed suit, the crisis ended.

Repeal of the Townshend duties: April 1770

Key date

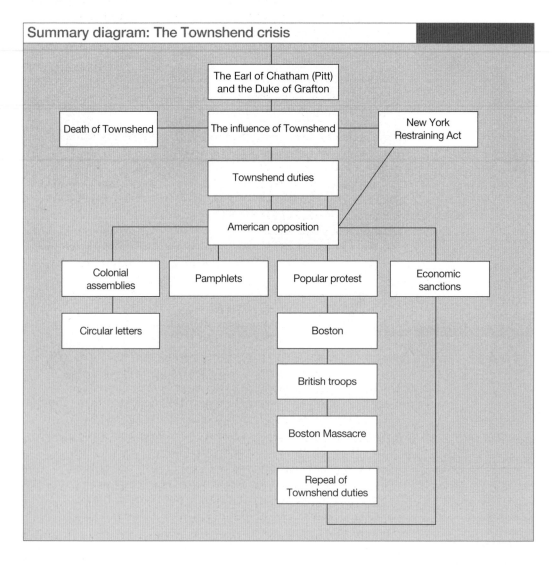

Summary diagram: The Townshend crisis

Key question
How far were the years 1770–73 a period of calm?

4 | The Years of Calm: 1770–73

There followed three years of comparative calm. Anglo–American trade resumed at a high level. Between 1771 and 1774 the colonies' imports from Britain reached £9 million – almost double what they had been between 1768 and 1770. There was a vigorous economic recovery in the early 1770s, both in Britain and in the colonies. As prosperity returned in the colonies there was something of a conservative reaction against the radicals. In 1772 Hillsborough resigned as secretary for the colonies and was succeeded by the Earl of Dartmouth who believed in accommodation rather than confrontation.

Lord North

An efficient, popular and skilful politician, North was not closely aligned with any particular faction. George III trusted North and having found a minister who had managed to create a durable administration and who was capable of governing, the king wanted nothing better than to let him get on with it. North led the ministry from the Commons and led his team well. He was by no means a cipher under the control of an autocratic monarch.

Anglo–American problems

There was still enough provocation and controversy to sustain a resistance movement:

- Congregationalists and other non-Anglicans were worried by rumours that the Church of England intended to appoint an American bishopric. They feared that the Anglican Church might grow at the expense of their own congregations. Radicals were concerned that a strong Anglican Church might provide support for royal authority in the colonies.
- In Boston, there was anger that the Massachusetts assembly, on the orders of Bernard, had been moved to Cambridge. The new governor, Thomas Hutchinson, kept it there until 1772.
- In 1772 Hutchinson revealed that he and the senior Massachusetts' judges were to receive their salaries direct from the Crown, payable from the tea duties. Some saw this as evidence of a British design to impose arbitrary rule.

Committees of correspondence

In September 1771 the **Boston town meeting**, at Sam Adams' behest, created a committee of correspondence which was to communicate colonial grievances to all the towns of Massachusetts, as well as to people throughout the thirteen colonies. By mid-1773, 50 Massachusetts towns had their own committees and other colonies followed suit. The movement was so successful that in 1773 the Virginia House of Burgesses recommended that each colony establish a committee of correspondence to ensure the rapid dissemination of information and a unified response in the event of another crisis. By February 1774 every colony except Pennsylvania and North Carolina had its own committee. Although

Key term

Boston town meeting
The town council of Boston.

the committees did not do a great deal pre-1774, they at least kept in touch with each other and were a focus for radical activity in each colony. Governor Hutchinson described the Boston committee as composed of 'blackhearted fellows whom one would not wish to meet in the dark'.

The *Gaspee* incident

Illegal trade persisted. Colonists smuggled in foreign tea rather than pay the duty on British tea. Customs officers continued to find it hard to enforce the law. In June 1772 the revenue cutter *Gaspee* ran aground off Rhode Island, pursuing a suspected American smuggler. Eight longboats boarded the *Gaspee*. The captain and crew were put ashore (violently) before the boat was burned. A royal commission investigated the incident and was instructed to send any persons accused to England for trial. The commission, lacking co-operation from the local populace, found insufficient evidence for prosecution. Dartmouth avoided confrontation over the affair.

American disunity

From Britain's point of view, the good news was that the colonists were far from united. Indeed at times in the 1760s and early 1770s they seemed more intent on quarrelling among themselves than with Britain:

- There were still disputes between colonies over boundaries and land claims, not least that between New York and New Hampshire over what (eventually) became Vermont.
- There were social tensions between rich and poor in some colonies.
- Divisions between Tidewater and backcountry (see page 11) continued in the South. In 1768 the so-called Regulator movement began in North Carolina and spread to South Carolina. Most of the participants were backcountry farmers who protested against the oppressions and corruption of Tidewater officials. After a period of virtual civil war the Regulators were crushed in 1771 at the Battle of Alamance by eastern militia forces. Some 300 Regulators were killed.

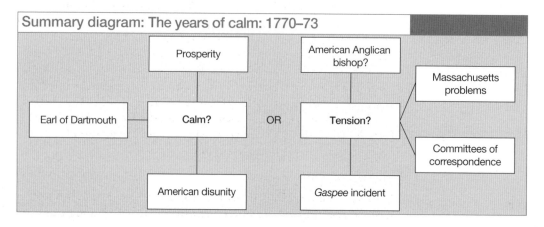

Summary diagram: The years of calm: 1770–73

Earl of Dartmouth — Calm? — Prosperity / American disunity — OR — Tension? — American Anglican bishop? / Gaspee incident — Massachusetts problems / Committees of correspondence

Key question
What caused the
Boston Tea Party?

Key dates

The Tea Act: May
1773

The Boston Tea Party:
December 1773

5 | The Impact of the Boston Tea Party

The 1773 Tea Act

In 1773 the British government reopened old wounds by introducing a Tea Act. The Act was designed to save the near bankrupt East India Company rather than assert parliamentary sovereignty over the colonies. It aimed to relieve the financial stresses of the company by permitting it to export tea to the colonies direct and retail it there, using its own agents. The Tea Act abolished British duties on the company's tea while obliging Americans to continue paying the duty levied under Townshend's legislation. Nevertheless, the tea sold by the company would be so cheap that it could undercut tea that was traded legitimately by American merchants and foreign tea that was smuggled in, usually by the same merchants. It seemed all parties would benefit:

- The American consumer would gain as tea would drop in price.
- The East India Company would benefit as hopefully it would sell its vast stocks of tea in America at a healthy profit.
- Britain would profit from increased duties.

But North had miscalculated. The Tea Act was certain to antagonise Americans:

- By threatening colonial merchants with monopoly and the smuggling rings with extinction, it united two powerful interests in opposition.
- Radicals opposed the retention of the import tax on tea on constitutional grounds. Taxation without representation remained the key issue.

It should have been clear to North that the colonists would not buy the tea until the duty was lifted. For a few pounds – the tea imported into America had netted only £400 in 1772 – North was risking the export of £2 million of tea and antagonising the Americans into the bargain.

The American reaction

Most Americans were convinced that the Tea Act was another attempt at parliamentary taxation and the destruction of the independence of their legislatures. The measure was bitterly attacked in newspapers and pamphlets. Philadelphians set the tone of the opposition and gave it direction in ways made familiar in the crises over the Stamp Act and the Townshend duties. Artisans soon threatened violence against those merchants importing East India Company tea. The tea sent to Philadelphia and New York was rejected and sent back to England. The tea sent to Charleston was landed but popular pressure prevented it from being offered for sale. In all the major ports the tea agents, facing severe intimidation, were forced to resign.

The Boston Tea Party

On 28 November 1773 the ship *Dartmouth*, bearing 114 chests of East India Company tea, entered Boston harbour. Among the

merchants to whom the tea was consigned were two sons of
Governor Hutchinson. Hutchinson was determined that the tea be
disembarked. The *Dartmouth* thus tied up. According to law it had
twenty days to make its customs entry, pay the duty and unload.
Meanwhile, Bostonians demanded that the ship depart and
thousands gathered daily to prevent the tea from being unloaded.
On 2 December the *Eleanor* joined the *Dartmouth*. The *Beaver*
arrived on 15 December. Two weeks of discussion between
Hutchinson and the patriots resulted in deadlock. The ships could
not sail without customs clearance and that would not be granted
until the status of the tea was cleared up.

On 16 December 60 Sons of Liberty men, crudely disguised as
Mohawk Indians and directed by Sam Adams, boarded the three
tea ships and threw their cargoes – 342 tea chests worth about
£10,000 – into the harbour. A huge crowd watched in silence.
Admiral Montagu, the Royal Navy commander in Boston, could
have ordered his nearest warship, anchored only a few hundred
metres away, to open fire. Fearing that this might worsen the crisis,
Montagu did nothing. Nor did the troops stationed at nearby
Castle William.

The Tea Party was an act of revolutionary defiance. John
Adams, who had come late to radical politics, wrote in his diary:
'This destruction of the tea is so bold, so daring, so firm, intrepid
and inflexible, and it must have so important consequences and so
lasting, that I cannot but consider it as an epocha in history.'

What is happening – and has happened – to the excise collector in this
British cartoon? Printed in 1774.

The British reaction

News of the Boston Tea Party reached London in January 1774. The reaction was anger and outrage. In 1766 and 1770 colonial protest had brought about a reversal of British policy. But now, confronted with colonial defiance for a third time, North's government determined to take a hard line. North declared in Parliament, 'The Americans have tarred and feathered your subjects, burnt your ships, denied obedience to your laws and authority; yet so clement and so forbearing has our conduct been that it is encumbent on us now to take a different course … If they deny our authority in one instance, it goes to all. We must control them or submit to them.' He was convinced, as was British opinion generally, that Britain faced a fundamental challenge to its imperial and constitutional system, a challenge which could not be ignored without imperilling national prosperity and security. Parliament was either the supreme authority in the Empire or it was not. Even staunch friends of the colonists in Britain refused to defend the Tea Party. Chatham said it was 'criminal'.

Key date

The Coercive Acts: Spring 1774

The Coercive Acts

Concluding that Boston was at the centre of colonial troubles, North's ministry decided to isolate and punish it. Thus in early 1774 Parliament passed four Coercive (dubbed by the colonists 'Intolerable') Acts:

- The port of Boston was to be closed to all ocean-going trade from 1 June until the destroyed tea had been paid for.
- The Massachusetts Government Act revised the Massachusetts charter of 1691, allowing the royal governor to appoint and remove most civil officials. Town meetings could not be held without the governor's permission.
- The Impartial Administration of Justice Act provided for the transfer to England of murder trials in law-enforcement cases.
- A new Quartering Act gave broader authority to military commanders seeking to house their troops.

Chatham and Edmund Burke spoke against the measures, warning of the consequences. Their eloquence had no effect. All passed with large majorities. Meanwhile, the commander-in-chief in America, General Gage, was made the new governor of Massachusetts.

The Québec Act

Colonial sensibilities were further inflamed by the passage of the Québec Act in June. This statesmanlike but ill-timed effort to solve the problem of governing the French inhabitants of Canada was seen by the older colonies as confirmation of evil British designs. The Act placed authority in the hands of a governor without an elected assembly, left French civil law in force and limited trial by jury. This suggested to Americans that Britain intended to put the whole of North America under authoritarian forms of government. Recognition of the privileged position of the Roman Catholic Church in Canada seemed to 'smell strong of popery'. Moreover,

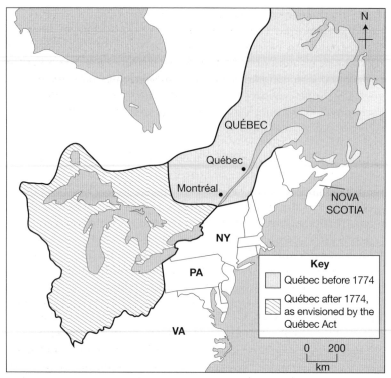

Figure 2.2: The expansion of Québec.

the extension of the Québec boundary south and west to the Ohio and the Mississippi invalidated all land claims in that region and looked like a deliberate attempt to check westward expansion by the thirteen original colonies.

The American reaction

While the Coercive Acts were intended to punish and isolate Massachusetts, especially Boston, most Americans believed the measures were a threat to all the colonies. If Massachusetts could be dealt with in this way, no colony was secure. People in other colonies rallied to Boston's support, sending food and money to help the town's poor.

In March 1774 New Yorkers found East India Company tea on board the *Nancy*. They set out to follow the Bostonians' example. While a party of 'Mohawks' prepared themselves, the main crowd surged on to the ship and disposed of the tea.

The economic response

On 13 May the Boston town meeting asked all the colonies to boycott British goods until the Boston Port Act was repealed. The Boston committee of correspondence drafted a Solemn League and Covenant (5 June) calling for the non-consumption of British goods. Many communities held special town meetings to endorse the document. However, not all merchants were convinced that this was sensible. In Boston over 100 merchants signed and published a protest against the Solemn League. The Boston merchants, like merchants elsewhere, perceived that the boycott would probably harm America more than Britain. The previous non-importations had shown that boycotts were difficult to enforce and that some merchants had made money from trade with Britain at the expense of others. Rich merchants, fearing civil disorder, tried – with some success, especially in New York – to prevent radical elements from dominating the protest movement.

The political response

Colonial assemblies, town and country meetings, newspapers, clergymen and other men of influence denounced the actions of the British government. Radical propaganda, disseminated by the committees of correspondence, persuaded the colonists of the need for common action to defend American liberties.

Royal governors prorogued or dissolved assemblies that seemed ready to denounce the Coercive Acts and to support an economic boycott. Undeterred, the Virginian House of Burgesses passed a resolution condemning the Coercive Acts on 24 May. Two days later Governor Lord Dunmore dissolved the House. Virginia now led the way in forming an extra-legal body to function in place of its assembly. On 27 May, 89 of the 103 burgesses met at the Raleigh Tavern in Williamsburg. This body proceeded to adopt a non-importation agreement, pledged non-consumption of tea and denounced the Boston Port Act. It declared that 'an attack, made on one of our sister colonies, to compel submission to arbitrary taxes, is an attack on all of British America and threatens the ruin of all'. Accordingly, it proposed that an intercolonial congress be called to seek redress of American grievances.

During the summer of 1774 seven other colonies, where the royal governors had forbidden the regular assemblies to meet or conduct formal elections, set up extra-legal provincial conventions. Meeting in open defiance of British authority, they assumed the role of government. Usually they were simply the assemblies meeting without sanction, although in some colonies the conventions had a broader membership than the old assemblies.

Newspapers and pamphlets

By 1775 there were 42 colonial newspapers, mainly concentrated in New England. All but two or three were radical in emphasis, their language incendiary and strident. Numerous pamphlets were also published defending the rights of the colonies. In 1774 Thomas Jefferson, elected to Virginia's first revolutionary convention, published *A Summary of the Rights of British America*. In Jefferson's opinion the British Parliament had no right to exercise authority over the Americans. There was no reason why 160,000 electors in Britain should give laws to millions of Americans, 'every individual of whom is equal to every individual of them'. Jefferson viewed the Empire as a network of separate states, held together because the states shared the same constitutional monarch. Even the king's power was for the people's 'use and consequently subject to their superintendence'.

What ultimately united most colonists by the 1770s was the view that British policy constituted a threat to American liberties. In 1774 George Washington declared, 'The crisis is arrived when we must assert our rights, or submit to every imposition that can be heaped upon us, till custom and use shall make us tame and abject slaves, as the blacks we rule over with such arbitrary sway.' The existence of black slavery perhaps made white Americans more determined to protect their own liberty. Ironically, many of the champions of American freedom, like Washington, were slave owners (see Chapter 5).

By 1774 some pamphlets and newspapers openly discussed – and some supported – colonial independence. For example, John Adams, under the pseudonym Novangulus, published twelve essays between January 1774 and April 1775 in the *Boston Gazette*. In one he declared, 'America is not any part of the British realm or dominions'.

The Continental Congress

In September 1774 all the colonies except Georgia sent at least one delegate to Philadelphia to the first Continental Congress 'to consult upon the present unhappy state of the colonies'. The total number – 56 – was large enough for diversity of opinion but small enough for genuine debate. Most of the delegates were lawyers, merchants or planters who had played prominent local roles in opposition to Britain over the previous decade. John Adams declared: 'There is in the Congress a collection of the greatest men upon this Continent in point of abilities, virtues and fortunes.'

First Continental Congress: September 1774 — Key date

Given that many of the delegates were chosen by extra-legal conventions, those who supported Britain were not represented. Otherwise the membership of the Congress was probably a fair cross-section of American opinion. John Adams thought the Congress was almost equally divided between radicals and moderates. The most prominent radical figures were Richard Henry Lee and Patrick Henry of Virginia, and John and Sam Adams of Massachusetts. Leading moderates included John Dickinson and Joseph Galloway of Pennsylvania. Radicals and moderates held widely differing views on the relationship between the colonies and Britain:

- Radicals accepted that the colonists owed allegiance to George III but believed that Parliament could not exercise legitimate authority over the American colonies, which had historically been governed by their own assemblies.
- The moderates, by contrast, insisted that the Congress should acknowledge Parliament's supremacy over the Empire and its right to regulate American trade.

While accepting the need for concerted action, the congressmen were divided on its form. Moderates favoured a scheme for imperial federation put forward by Galloway. His Plan of Union would have tied the colonies together by creating an all-colony Grand Council which would have a president appointed by the Crown, to share power with Parliament over colonial matters. Debate was close. A procedural vote to postpone consideration effectively killed the proposal but this was passed by only six colonies to five. (The Congress had agreed on one vote for each colonial delegation.)

Instead, Congress supported the radicals, endorsing the Suffolk Resolves (17 September). These declared the Coercive Acts null and void and called upon Massachusetts to arm for defence. Congress also called for non-importation of all British goods starting on 1 December 1774, unless Parliament repealed the Coercive Acts. A total ban on exports to Britain would start on 10 September 1775 (allowing planters time to sell their crops raised in 1774). To promote the trade embargo Congress called on colonists everywhere to form a Continental Association. Unlike previous boycotts, non-importation would be a united colonial effort rather than a mix of local initiatives.

On 14 October Congress agreed on a Declaration of Rights and Grievances. While acknowledging allegiance to the Crown, the declaration denied that the colonies were subject to Parliament's authority. While Parliament could regulate trade for the good of the whole empire, it could not raise revenue of any kind from the colonists without their consent. It also proclaimed the right of each colonial assembly to determine the need for troops within its own province.

By the time the First Continental Congress came to an end (on 26 October) the congressmen were no longer strangers. 'They knew who among them was hot, who was tepid, who was cool', says historian Countryman. The 'cool' ones, for example Galloway, were already losing their influence. The 'hot' ones, for example John Adams, favoured cutting America's ties with Britain. Although the Congress had no coercive or legislative authority, it provided a useful unifying purpose. Another Congress was called for May 1775.

The trade boycott

The ban on British imports had serious economic effects. Nevertheless, the ban also boosted the radical cause by encouraging local production and pride in frugality. Indeed, non-importation and non-consumption again became the basis for a drive for moral regeneration in which the rejection of luxury items and a return to a simple rustic life played an important part. Even wealthy planters felt obliged to temper their aristocratic lifestyles so they were in tune with ordinary Americans.

Committees of safety

In late 1774 committees of inspection (or safety) were established across the colonies in accordance with the Continental Association. Some of these committees were organised by the old elite. Others involved new men – ordinary Americans. These committees had a mandate to enforce the boycott. But many went much further than this, acting in place of the defunct local government. By the spring of 1775 some 7000 colonists were serving either on local committees or in the extra-legal colonial conventions. There were no fewer than 160 town committees in Massachusetts, involving some 1600 people. Thus ordinary Americans were directly involved in politics, often for the first time. The committees had considerable powers. As enforcers of the Continental Association, they functioned as quasi-courts, investigating suspected Tories. Persons found not abiding by the association faced physical intimidation.

The situation in Massachusetts

By late 1774 British authority had broken down completely in Massachusetts. In outlying areas those officials who were still loyal to Britain were terrorised by mob action and forced out of office. Outside Boston, effective authority resided in the Provincial Congress and a host of committees. As well as stopping trade with Britain, these bodies took upon themselves the organisation of military resources. Across Massachusetts, militia units began to prepare for war.

The newly appointed military governor General Gage found that his power extended only as far as British troops could march. Effectively besieged in Boston where his relatively few troops were concentrated, all Gage could do was ask the British government for 20,000 extra troops. He was all for teaching the rebels a bloody lesson but had insufficient force to do so.

The situation in other colonies

By early 1775 in most colonies the extra-legal conventions and committees had taken over and all but expelled traditional authority. By 1774–75 the local committees in Virginia were, as Governor Dunmore observed, the government of Virginia. Throughout the colonies arms and ammunition were stockpiled and militias drilled. In December 1774 Rhode Islanders seized the cannon in Fort George and conveyed them to Providence. In the same month, New Hampshire militiamen stormed Fort William and Mary in Portsmouth, overpowered its garrison and seized the arms and munitions stored in the fort.

However, not all Americans were united in the rebel cause. While some areas were united against Britain, other places remained predominantly loyal – not least New York. Most Americans continued to hope that a solution to the troubles could be found within the framework of a continuing Anglo–American connection. Even now relatively few Americans actively sought independence.

Prime Minister, Lord North. To what extent was he to blame for the War of Independence?

Key question
Why was the British government determined to stand firm?

British determination

In November 1774 Gage wrote to North recommending the temporary suspension of the Coercive Acts. But neither North nor the king had any intention of backing down. George III told North, 'the line of conduct now seems chalked out … the New England governments are in a state of rebellion, blows must decide whether they are to be subject to this country or independent'.

By Christmas 1774 all of Britain knew there was a fully fledged rebellion in America. Most MPs in the new House of Commons – North had won a large majority in the November 1774 general election – were determined that Britain should assert its authority over the colonies. North told Parliament that more troops were being sent to Massachusetts. Nevertheless, his military measures were remarkably lax:

- Four thousand extra troops were not enough to help Gage.
- In December North announced a reduction in army and navy recruiting.

Britain had failed to protect its officials – stamp distributors, customs collectors, tea consignees – from attack. It now failed, when it was ready to invoke the use of force, to make sufficient force available. British ministers did not appreciate the scale and difficulty of the military task facing them in America until it was too late. They continued to assume that Boston was the key to breaking American resistance and that the other colonies would not support Massachusetts.

Some politicians tried to persuade the government to make concessions to the Americans. In January 1775 the Earl of Chatham asked the House of Lords for a resolution to request the Crown to remove troops from America: the motion failed by 77 votes to 18. On 1 February Chatham introduced a bill proposing repeal of the Coercive Acts and the non-levying of taxes on the colonies by Parliament, except by common consent in their colonial assemblies. Chatham's bill was rejected by 61–32. Edmund Burke, in the Commons, offered repeal of all legislation offensive to the Americans. His proposal was defeated by 270 votes to 78.

North did introduce a Conciliation Plan but it yielded little of substance. It promised merely that Parliament would 'forbear' to tax any colony paying the cost of its own civil administration and making a satisfactory contribution to imperial defence. Many MPs thought North had conceded too much. The opposition, probably correctly, claimed that North's offer was an attempt to break the united front of the colonies by tempting the moderates to come to terms. North's Conciliation Plan failed. Americans were no more inclined to accept his carrot than to bend to his stick.

On 9 February 1775 Parliament declared Massachusetts in a state of rebellion. Thus the legislation prohibiting the trade of Boston was extended to all of Massachusetts. In March the New England Restraining Act limited the commerce of New England with Britain and the British West Indies. In April this restriction was extended to all the other colonies except New York, Georgia and North Carolina.

Meanwhile, in March Dartmouth finally despatched a letter telling Gage to move against the rebellion and to arrest 'the principal actors and abettors'. Concerned that Gage lacked firmness, the government sent three new generals to Boston – William Howe, Johnny Burgoyne and Henry Clinton.

Summary diagram: The impact of the Boston Tea Party

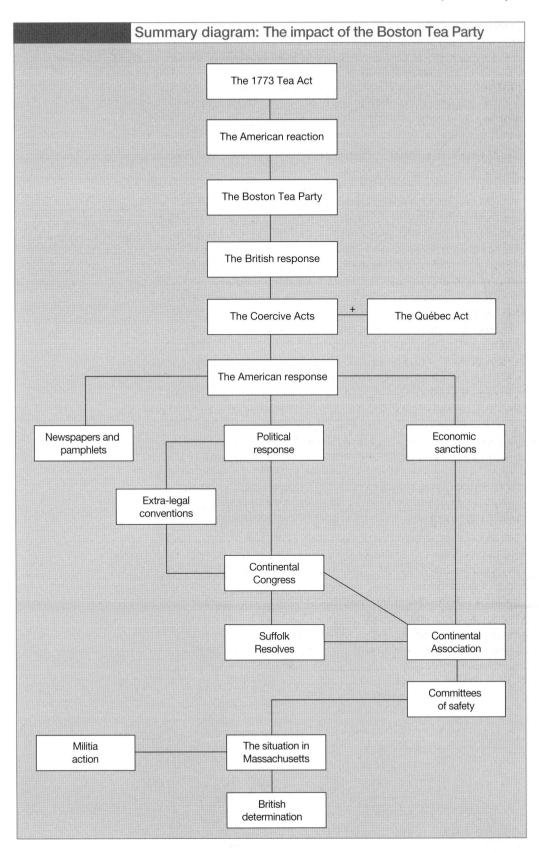

6 | The Outbreak of War

Over the winter of 1774–75 General Gage sent spies through Massachusetts to assess the strength of colonial resistance and to discover where the rebels had stockpiled their weapons. In February 1775 he sent troops to Salem to seize munitions. Denied entry to the town and outnumbered by hundreds of militiamen, the troops were forced to withdraw. Americans now not only defied parliamentary laws, they openly resisted British soldiers performing their duty.

Lexington and Concord

Gage received no help from Britain and no instructions until 14 April when Dartmouth's letter instructed him to arrest the leaders of the Provincial Congress and authorised him to use force to disarm the population. Gage, for so long patient and conciliatory despite serious provocation, was ready to act. On the evening of 18 April 1775 he sent 700 men from Boston under Colonel Smith to seize rebel powder and arms stored at Concord 26 km (16 miles) away. The troops were also to arrest members of the Provincial Congress which met at Concord. Unfortunately for Gage, the Massachusetts militia were informed of British intent by Paul Revere, William Dawes and Dr Prescott – all members of the Boston committee of safety.

On 19 April the British troops found their path barred by a body of 70 **minutemen** at Lexington. Shots were fired – it is still not clear who fired first – and eight militiamen were killed. The British pushed on to Concord. Here they encountered a larger militia force and there was a heavy exchange of fire. After destroying the military stores but failing to arrest the members of the Provincial Congress, Smith's troops turned back to Boston. On the return they were assailed on all sides by steadily swelling American forces firing from the cover of stone walls and woods.

Key question
Why were the colonists successful in 1775–76?

Key dates

The Battle of Lexington and Concord: April 1775

Second Continental Congress: May 1775

The Battle of Bunker Hill: June 1775

Key term

Minutemen
Men who were pledged to rush to America's defence at a minute's notice.

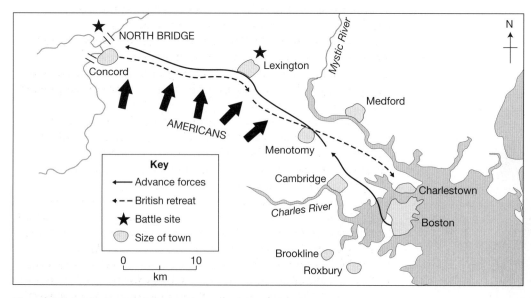

Figure 2.3: Lexington and Concord.

Smith's troops would probably have been forced to surrender had it not been for the timely arrival of a relief force under Earl Percy. Percy's brigade held the militiamen at bay at Lexington, allowing Smith's men time to regroup. The British then resumed the retreat to Boston, galled all the way by rebel forces. By the time they reached Boston, the British had suffered 273 casualties (73 killed). The Americans, who had lost only 49 dead and 43 wounded or missing, now besieged Boston. Within a week some 20,000 militia, from all the New England colonies, had gathered round the city.

The results of Lexington and Concord

The events of 19 April transformed the political dispute between the colonists and Britain into a military struggle. Lexington and Concord galvanised military preparations throughout the colonies. New York now threw itself behind Massachusetts and even the conservative Pennsylvania assembly voted to raise 4300 men.

A group of militiamen, led by Ethan Allen and Benedict Arnold, seized Fort Ticonderoga (see Figure 2.5 on page 75) on 10 May, capturing 45 men and 78 cannon. Crown Point, with a garrison of just nine men, fell two days later.

The Second Continental Congress

On 10 May the second Continental Congress met in Philadelphia. Sixty-five delegates attended from all thirteen colonies. Fifty had served in 1774, ensuring there was an important degree of continuity. Newcomers included John Hancock of Massachusetts, James Wilson and Benjamin Franklin from Pennsylvania and Thomas Jefferson of Virginia. The first Continental Congress had been summoned to express and co-ordinate colonial opposition to the Coercive Acts. The second Congress had little choice but to take charge of the conduct of the war. It quickly resolved that the colonies 'be immediately put into a state of defence', assumed responsibility for the army around Boston and impressed a quota on each colony sufficient to raise a Continental Army of 20,000 men. In mid-June Congress voted to issue $2 million in paper money to finance the force. Denomination of the issue in Spanish dollars (which circulated widely in the colonies) was an indication of future developments in the American currency.

Congress unanimously appointed George Washington to command the Continental Army. Washington at least looked the part. Six feet three inches tall and with natural aristocratic manners, he had worn his militia colonel uniform at all the Congressional meetings, reminding congressmen of his military experience in the Seven Years' War. Washington was crucially from Virginia. Placing a Southerner in command of what was still a predominantly New England army was expected to help cement colonial unity. Moreover, the choice of a wealthy planter – Washington reputedly owned 35,000 acres – would allay fears of radicalism. Washington refused to take pay for his service (but was meticulous in keeping account of what he was due in expenses).

While the exigencies of war compelled Congress to adopt the attributes of a national government, some of its members were reluctant to accept such a role. Most colonial conventions had instructed their delegates to seek reconciliation with Britain. Parliament, not the king, was seen as the enemy. The minority who favoured a complete break from Britain did not yet admit that independence was their objective.

On 6 July Congress adopted a Declaration of the Causes and Necessities of Taking up Arms. Drafted by Dickinson and Jefferson, it listed the colonial grievances since 1763. While asserting that Americans would rather die than be enslaved, it disclaimed any intention of 'separating from Great Britain and establishing independent states'. Congress also adopted the Olive Branch Petition (8 July) drawn up by Dickinson. Professing attachment to George III, it begged him to prevent further hostile measures so that a plan of reconciliation might be worked out. The petition's purpose was to convince conservatives within Congress, and Americans generally, that Congress did not intend to pursue independence except as a last resort. John Adams described the Olive Branch as giving 'a silly cast to our whole doings'. In his view, the time for petitioning was past. 'Powder and artillery are the most efficacious, sure and infallible conciliatory measures we can adopt.'

George III was not inclined to hear appeals from an illegal body which was waging war against his troops. He refused to receive or consider the Olive Branch Petition. On 23 August he declared the colonies to be in a state of open rebellion and called upon all civil and military officials as well as his loyal subjects to help in suppressing the rebellion.

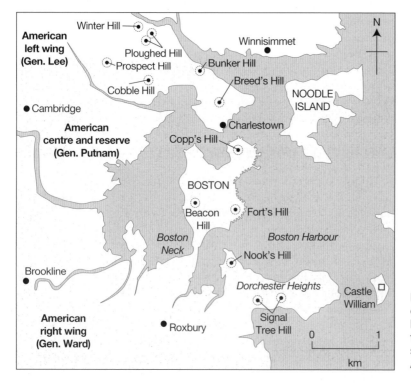

Figure 2.4: The Siege of Boston. The British held Boston but, as the map shows, were surrounded by American forces.

The Battle of Bunker Hill

On 26 May British generals Howe, Clinton and Burgoyne arrived in Boston with a few thousand British troops. Gage now had a force of 6500 men. On 12 June, acting on instructions from Dartmouth, he issued a proclamation declaring Massachusetts in a state of rebellion and establishing martial law. However, he promised amnesty 'to all who shall lay down their arms and return to the duties of peaceable subjects', except for John Hancock and Sam Adams.

Gage felt he had to do something, particularly as American forces looked set to occupy Bunker Hill which commanded Boston from the Charlestown peninsula. When a rebel force of 1500 men occupied the neighbouring Breed's Hill by mistake, Gage determined to dislodge them. Rather than getting the Royal Navy to convey men behind the American positions, General Howe launched a frontal attack on the rebel defences. Howe dislodged the Americans but only after three frontal assaults and at a fearful cost. More than a 1000 of Howe's 2500 men became casualties (226 killed: 828 wounded). The Americans lost fewer than half that number.

The battle (which is always called Bunker rather than Breed's Hill) was the bloodiest engagement of the entire war. One-eighth of the British officers killed in the war died in the battle. Gage wrote to Dartmouth, 'the rebels are not the despicable rabble too many have supposed them to be, and I find it owing to a military spirit encouraged amongst them for a few years past, joined with an uncommon degree of zeal and enthusiasm'. One politician remarked that 'if we have eight more victories such as this there will be nobody left to bring news of them'.

The Battle of Bunker Hill. Do you think this is a British or American representation? Why?

Washington takes command

Washington assumed command of the Continental Army on 2 July. He was not impressed by what he found. Fifteen thousand poorly trained, poorly equipped and poorly disciplined troops were present and fit for duty. The army had fewer than 50 cannon, hardly any powder, and few trained gunners. Far worse, in Washington's view, was the fact that the army lacked any kind of military order. The officers, most of whom had been elected by the men, failed to inspect their troops or supervise their food and quarters. Washington, who had never before commanded more than 2000 men, realised that he must transform what was essentially a militia force into a professional army, similar to that of the British. Improving the officer corps seemed essential. Convinced that sharp distinctions of rank were imperative, he determined to curb the democratic excesses of the army. Incompetent officers and those guilty of misconduct were removed. Those who remained were distinguished from ordinary troops by special insignia. Washington also set about imposing discipline on the men. Discipline, he believed, was 'the soul of an army'. Offences from card playing to desertion were punished by flogging.

Boston 1775–76

Washington was eager to attack Boston but was restrained by politicians who feared the destruction of the town. He was also discouraged by the strength of the British fortifications, by his own shortage of arms and gunpowder and by the fact that many of his men went home to their families. By mid-winter, the American army, suffering from dysentery, typhus and typhoid fever, had fallen in numbers so much that the British, now substantially reinforced, outnumbered their besiegers. But Howe, who had replaced Gage in October, did nothing. The Americans undoubtedly benefited from having the main British army – 9000 men – bottled up in Boston, taking no effective action. As historian Jeremy Black says, 'It is not difficult … to feel that opportunities were missed and that the British failed to make adequate use of their sea power' in 1775–76. British inaction gave the rebels time to consolidate their hold in other colonies.

The invasion of Canada

In 1775 Congress decided to invade Canada. It hoped that the French population would join the rebellion and assist in overthrowing the small British garrison. In June 1775 Congress ordered General Philip Schuyler to seize Montréal. While Schuyler advanced from Ticonderoga, a second force under Benedict Arnold was to march through Maine, joining Schuyler in an attack on Québec.

Schuyler's army headed north without Schuyler who fell ill. Richard Montgomery, a former British officer, took command of the 1200-strong force. Having advanced up the Champlain waterway (see Figure 2.5), Montgomery's army besieged Fort St John from 16 September until its surrender on 2 November. The dogged defence

Figure 2.5: The invasion of Canada, 1775–76.

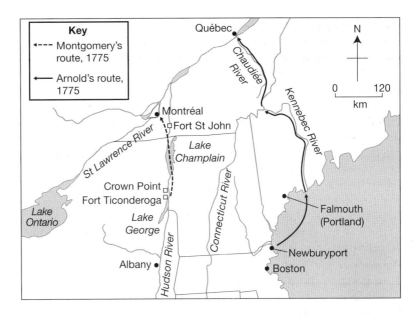

of Fort St John probably saved Canada. Montgomery had used up valuable weeks that he could ill afford to lose. Nevertheless, he went on to capture Montréal, whose 150-man garrison surrendered on 13 November. Meanwhile, Arnold's 1000-strong force had marched through Maine. Fewer than 700 exhausted, hungry and sickly men arrived opposite Québec in November. In early December 300 soldiers under Montgomery arrived from Montréal. Since most American enlistments expired at the end of the year, an attack on Québec had to be made quickly.

General Guy Carleton, the British commander, had 1800 men – French Canadian militia, seamen and marines from British ships and about 100 regular soldiers – to defend Québec. The American assault, made in a heavy snowstorm on 31 December was a costly failure: Montgomery was killed and Arnold wounded. Over 400 Americans surrendered. Arnold pulled back a mile from Québec. Over the next few weeks his men suffered from lack of supplies and smallpox. Many deserted. The arrival of 10,000 British reinforcements in the spring ended the siege. Montréal was abandoned as the Americans retreated from Canada in disorder.

Britain's other colonies

Britain's other colonies in America remained loyal:

- There were few settlers in East and West Florida and these colonies posed no serious problems.
- The West Indian islands, dependent on Britain for protection from France and Spain, remained loyal.
- Nova Scotia and Newfoundland benefited from British commercial protection.

Virginia

Lord Dunmore, with a band of 500 loyalists and the assistance of several warships, launched raids on Virginian coastal towns for several months. In November, he issued a proclamation promising freedom to any slaves who fled their rebel masters and aided the British war effort. This was anathema to most white Southerners, solidifying rebel support in Virginia.

The South

For much of 1775 Britain ignored the Southern colonies. Then intelligence from the royal governors suggested that co-ordinated operations by loyalists and (minimal) British forces could quickly put an end to the rebellion in the South. North Carolina was selected as the starting point. Backcountry settlers, many of whom had supported the Regulator movement (see page 58), resented the Tidewater elite and were ready to support Britain. But Carolinian loyalists, mainly Scots and Scots-Irish, acted too quickly and suffered a crushing defeat at Moores Creek in February 1776. General Clinton, with 1500 troops, did not sail south from Boston until February. He was supposed to meet a British fleet carrying 2500 troops under Cornwallis at Cape Fear. Clinton arrived in early March but the fleet carrying Cornwallis did not arrive until five weeks later. Finding little support along the North Carolina coast, Clinton sailed to South Carolina and tried – unsuccessfully – to take Charleston. The British force then sailed to New York.

The evacuation of Boston

By the spring of 1776 Washington had overcome some of his difficulties around Boston. Thanks to the efforts of ex-bookseller Henry Knox, artillery from Ticonderoga was transported by sledge, boats and wagon more than 480 km (300 miles) to Boston, arriving in February. On 4 March the rebels – 17,000 strong – captured Dorchester Heights which overlooked Boston. As the rebels set about placing their heavy guns, it was clear that the British position was untenable. On 17 March Howe's army, accompanied by more than 1000 loyalists, began evacuating Boston, sailing to Halifax, Nova Scotia – Britain's main naval base. Thus Britain relinquished, for the time being, its foothold in the thirteen colonies.

The situation in Britain

Despite the early setbacks most Britons supported the American war. Although a few highly placed army and naval officers resigned their commissions rather than fight the Americans, the loyalty of the armed forces as a whole was never in question. In Parliament, some notable politicians, not least Chatham, criticised the policy of force. But most of North's opponents were no more willing than North himself to abandon Parliament's right to legislate for the colonies, still less entertain the notion of an independent America. Thus, once war had begun only a handful of radicals continued to champion the American cause.

On 22 December 1775 the Prohibitory Act declared the rebellious colonies to be outside the protection of the Crown. It forbade commerce with the colonies and made their ships forfeit to the Crown.

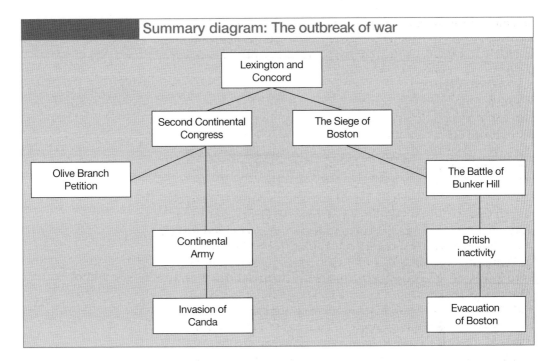

Summary diagram: The outbreak of war

7 | The Declaration of Independence

Key question
Why did Congress not declare independence until July 1776?

Although American and British forces were now at war, relatively few Americans talked of independence until early 1776.

Loyalty to Britain

Americans had long thought of themselves as Britons overseas. Severing the emotional, political, economic and intellectual ties with Britain was no easy matter. By no means all Americans were convinced that their interests would be best served by independence. A large minority remained loyal to Britain. Others continued to protest their loyalty to the Crown while believing that it was acceptable to engage in armed self-defence of colonial rights. Moderate delegates in the Continental Congress affected to believe that coercion was the policy of an evil British ministry and hoped for a conciliatory royal gesture.

But by early 1776 all hopes of reconciliation had faded:

- It was clear that George III, no less than his ministers, was bent on subjugation. He returned no answer to the Olive Branch Petition.
- Several months of fighting weakened the British–American ties.
- Support for separation in the South was strengthened when Governor Dunmore offered slaves their freedom.

By early 1776 the political tide had begun moving towards independence. In the 1760s most Americans had blamed evil ministers for conspiring to destroy American liberty. But by 1775–76 many believed the conspiracy included Parliament and the king. Some were convinced that the British people had become so corrupt that they could not save themselves from their rulers.

Common Sense

Thomas Paine's 47-page pamphlet *Common Sense* expressed the developing mood. It may also have helped to convince waverers of the necessity of separation from Britain. The 37-year-old Paine had only arrived in America in November 1774, quickly involving himself in radical politics. In England he had failed at everything – corset making, tax collecting, teaching, shopkeeping and marriage (twice: his second wife paid him to leave her home). *Common Sense* was far from a failure. Published in January 1776, it quickly sold 120,000 copies and had the greatest influence of all the hundreds of pamphlets published during the 1770s.

Written in forceful, straightforward prose, *Common Sense* was readily accessible to most Americans. Paine believed that events made independence a foregone conclusion. Blood had been spilled and with its loss American affection for Britain had drained away. 'Reconciliation is now a fallacious dream.' He savagely attacked the British constitution, not least the king – 'the royal brute' – and the whole concept of hereditary monarchy and aristocratic privileges. Rather than fear independence, Americans should welcome the opportunity to sever their ties with an oppressive system of government which had no basis in scripture or natural law. Paine called on Americans to establish a republic, based on a broad franchise and annual assemblies.

Publication of *Common Sense*: January 1776

Key date

The situation in early 1776

There was a growing conviction in Congress that foreign aid was vital to the American cause but that this would not be forthcoming so long as Americans shrank from independence. In November 1775 Congress had established a committee of secret correspondence to carry on diplomacy with foreign nations. It also sent Silas Deane to France to obtain military supplies.

By the spring of 1776 all royal governors had been replaced by makeshift rebel governments. Congress exercised sovereign powers – making war, issuing money and preparing to negotiate treaties. 'Is not America already independent?' Sam Adams asked in April 1776. 'Why then not declare it?'

Moves towards independence

The Continental Congress would have to be the body to declare independence formally. Those who favoured independence realised the need for a unanimous vote. However, the delegations within Congress were bound by instructions from their provincial conventions: they could not declare their colony's independence without prior authorisation. Therefore the political momentum for independence had to originate at local level in the colonies. Between April and July 1776 various bodies and institutions debated the merits and risks of independence. Thus independence was not foisted on the American people by a small group of radical congressmen. Rather, throughout early 1776 local organisations urged Congress to declare independence.

Some bodies effectively declared independence before Congress made its decision. On 4 May, for example, the Rhode Island legislature repealed legislation imposing new officials to take an oath of allegiance to the Crown and expunged all references to the king from its charter and laws.

In April 1776 the North Carolina assembly authorised its Congressional delegation to concur if other delegations voted in favour of independence. In May Virginia was the first colony to instruct its delegation to propose that independence be adopted. Other colonies followed suit. However, the Pennsylvania, Delaware, New Jersey, New York and Maryland legislatures instructed their delegates not to agree to separation from Britain.

On 7 June Richard Henry Lee introduced the resolution of the Virginia provincial convention 'that these united colonies are, and of right ought to be, free and independent states'. The following day Congress debated the proposal. Although the moderates had given up hope of achieving reconciliation with Britain, their leaders argued that the time was not yet right for a declaration of independence because the Middle Colonies had not yet pronounced in favour. Recognising the need for unanimity, Congress decided to delay a decision by three weeks. In the meantime, a committee was set up to work on a draft declaration in the event Congress agreed on independence in July. The committee, appointed on 11 June, consisted of Thomas Jefferson (Virginia), John Adams (Massachusetts), Benjamin Franklin (Pennsylvania), Roger Sherman (Connecticut) and Robert Livingston (New York).

Jefferson, a 33-year-old Virginian planter, did most of the work. He was an extraordinarily gifted man of many interests – architecture, music, politics, law, history and science. He did not have to come up with new ideas or arguments. He drew from principles set forth by John Locke and other Enlightenment writers, and from Virginia's Declaration of Rights. The case against the king he derived from two documents he had previously written – the 1774 *A Summary View of the Rights of British America* and the 1776 draft of a Virginia Constitution – along with the petitions and declaration of Congress. Jefferson worked on the declaration of independence for two weeks, consulting with Adams and Franklin on its content. His draft was then discussed and approved by the full committee.

In mid-June, Delaware instructed its delegates to support independence. In New Jersey, radicals ousted Governor William Franklin (son of Benjamin) and sent a new delegation to Congress with instructions to support independence. In Pennsylvania the conservative assembly was overthrown by a radical committee of safety on 14 June. This committee, which set about organising new elections based on a broad franchise, authorised Pennsylvania's delegates to vote for independence. The Maryland delegates received similar instructions on 28 June. Despite pressure, the New York provincial assembly refused to instruct its delegates to vote for independence, preferring to wait until Congress had made a decision on the issue before deciding.

Jefferson submitted the draft declaration to Congress on 28 June. When Congress considered the question of independence on 1 July the momentum seemed to favour the radicals. However, when the vote was taken on the motion for independence, the radicals were disappointed. Nine colonies voted in favour but four did not. South Carolina and Pennsylvania voted against. The two-man Delaware delegation was split while the New York delegates were prohibited by their instructions from participating. Realising that nine was not sufficient, Congress decided to return to the question the next day. After a night of frantic lobbying the radicals finally got the vote they wanted on 2 July:

- A third Delaware delegate rode through the night to Philadelphia to support independence.
- The South Carolina delegates changed their minds.
- Pennsylvanians John Dickinson and Robert Morris, who opposed independence, did not attend the session, while James Wilson changed his vote.

Consequently, on 2 July twelve of the thirteen colonies voted in favour of independence: New York abstained. (Its provincial assembly endorsed Congress' decision a week later.) It was the 2 July vote, rather than the adoption of the Declaration of Independence on 4 July, that proclaimed the birth of the United States. Thus, for over 200 years Americans have been celebrating their country's birthday on the wrong day!

This painting of the Declaration of Independence by John Trumbell shows, standing in the centre from left to right: John Adams, Roger Sherman, Robert Livingston, Thomas Jefferson and Benjamin Franklin.

Declaration of
Independence: 4 July
1776

The Declaration of Independence

Having decided to declare independence, Congress turned its attention to the declaration itself. On 3 July it discussed the draft declaration. Congressmen made a series of changes, eliminating a quarter of the original draft. Although Jefferson claimed Congress had 'mangled his manuscript', the final declaration was considerably improved by Congressional editing.

The purpose of the declaration was to furnish a moral and legal justification for the rebellion. The preamble, a lucid statement of the political philosophy underlying the colonists' assertion of independence, was the most significant part of the document.

> We hold these truths to be self-evident, that all men are created equal; that they are endowed by their creator with certain unalienable rights; that among these are life, liberty and the pursuit of happiness. That, to secure these rights, governments are instituted among men, deriving their just powers from the consent of the governed; that, whenever any form of government becomes destructive of these ends, it is the right of the people to alter or to abolish it, and to institute new government, laying its foundation on such principles, organising its powers in such form, as to them shall seem most likely to effect their safety and happiness.

Just what Jefferson meant by the celebrated phrase 'all men are created equal' still bemuses historians. Few think he was advocating an equality of wealth or social condition. What he may have had in mind was equality of rights and opportunity. The phrase came to have very different meanings to later generations of Americans.

Having asserted that the American people had a right to change their government if it violated their rights, the Declaration presented a list of the wrongs committed against the colonists since 1763 – charges ranging from interfering in colonial government to waging war against the colonies. All the charges were laid squarely, if somewhat unfairly, at the door of George III who was accused of seeking to establish an 'absolute tyranny over these states'.

The Declaration of Independence was formally adopted by Congress on 4 July. Over the next few weeks the document was read before troops and public gatherings throughout the colonies. But it was one thing to declare independence; it was another thing to win it. While Congress was in the process of declaring independence, Britain was deploying 32,000 troops off New York in preparation for a major assault. The British Empire was about to strike back.

Summary diagram: The Declaration of Independence

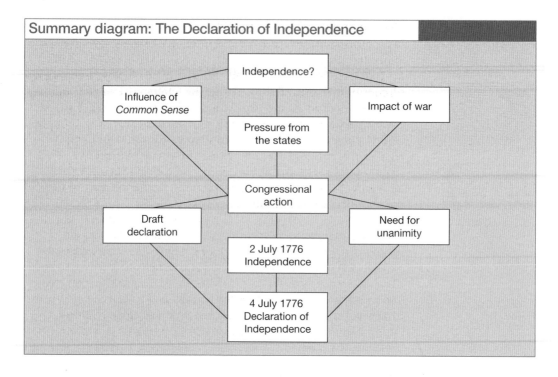

8 | The Key Debate

What caused the American Revolution?

In 1763 the vast majority of white colonists considered themselves
loyal British subjects. By 1775–76 most sought to end the
relationship with Britain. What had brought about this change?

How important were economic factors?

Historians like Charles Beard and Merrill Jenson once emphasised
the importance of economic factors in bringing about the
American Revolution. They stressed the irksome Trade and
Navigation Laws, oppressive customs duties and the drain on
colonial finance. But the evidence suggests that commercial issues
were not a major cause of the Revolution. Trade grievances were
mentioned only once in the Declaration of Independence.
Americans were aware that they benefited from the mercantilist
system. Indeed, trade relations were a factor pulling Britain and
the colonies together rather than dividing them. Nor was the
Revolution caused by high taxes. Americans were among the most
lightly taxed peoples on earth. The unpopular taxes/duties,
proposed by Britain in the 1760s and 1770s, were low and the
colonists could easily afford to pay them. Principle, not economic
hardship, was the cause of opposition to the taxes/duties.

How important was ideology?

Most historians today stress the importance of ideology in bringing about Revolution.

American leaders had developed a political ideology to provide a philosophic basis for their actions. This philosophy was derived from many sources – classical ideas, Puritanism and Enlightenment thinking. However, American ideology owed a great deal to English constitutional thought which emphasised the rights and liberties of free-born Englishmen and the limitations of royal power. Repeatedly the colonists insisted they were Englishmen, entitled to all the rights granted by the English constitution. If Englishmen could not be taxed without their consent, as given by their representatives in Parliament, the same applied to Americans. Influenced by early eighteenth-century English radical writers, many Americans came to the (misconceived) conclusion that a small clique of evil British ministers aimed to destroy American liberties. This view was sufficiently strong among influential Americans in the decade before 1775 to invest almost every British action with a sinister intent. The 'acts and measures ... adopted since the last war', complained the first Continental Congress, 'demonstrate a system formed to enslave America'.

Who led the American cause?

The traditional social and political elite led the resistance to Britain. While new men of relatively humble background (like Sam Adams) did emerge and play important roles, in general, the elite managed to hold on to leadership.

Why did so many Americans resist British rule?

Leaders need followers. Tens of thousands of ordinary Americans actively resisted British demands. Why?

- New taxes served to concentrate all American minds on the constitutional status of the colonies within the British empire.
- Ordinary Americans were politicised by town and country meetings and committees which sprang up and by local churches and newspapers which claimed that British measures were a threat to liberty.
- Peer group pressure played a role.

Ordinary Americans did not simply follow. Their concerns helped persuade public bodies to act against Britain.

How important was the mob?

Crowd or mob action was central to the way that British power in America came to an end. From 1765–75 the main story of the Revolution was acted out in towns. Crowds, often orchestrated by the Sons of Liberty, made it impossible to enforce the British legislation. But perhaps the significance of urban radicalism should not be exaggerated. The great majority of Americans were farmers who did not take part in mob action. Occasionally violent mob action frightened the American elite as well as British officialdom.

To what extent were British policies to blame?

Independence was not inevitable. British policy made it so. After 1763 the French threat had gone and the old colonial system, with its lax enforcement of the trade laws, was supplanted by more definite policies. These policies brought Britain into conflict with the colonies. In the 1760s various short-lived British ministries devised a series of irritations which propelled the colonies towards independence. In 1764, 1765, 1767 and 1773 British governments forced the issue of Britain's power over the colonies. Parliament's first attempt (1764) was ambiguous and so was the American response. But on the other three occasions the result was confrontation. Twice Parliament backed down, first repealing the Stamp Act and then the Townshend duties. By bowing to American pressure, Parliament undermined its claim to exercise control over the colonies. With each crisis, colonial resistance grew in strength and authority. After the Boston Tea Party, North's ministry chose to stand firm.

North's government thought that by defeating the wicked few, the loyal majority would revert to their traditional respect for Crown and Parliament. North expected that a show of force would be sufficient to subdue the rebellious people of Massachusetts. But what began as a police operation quickly became a major military effort. North's government took too long to appreciate the seriousness of the challenge. Thus it had too few forces on hand at the start to overawe the rebels. Possibly the colonists would not have been so headstrong if Gage had had 24,000 troops rather than 4000.

In defence of British policies

It is possible to blame a blundering generation of British politicians for causing the war. To historians like Basil Williams British policy made no sense. The Stamp Act was never expected to bring in more than £100,000 and tea only £30,000. The war was to cost the British Treasury £128 million.

But in fairness to the politicians:

- It is understandable that Britain failed to anticipate that the colonists, freer than any other at the time, would rebel against the nation that had nurtured the liberty they prized so highly.
- In 1765 there was little indication of the anger to be aroused by the Stamp Act. Even Benjamin Franklin misread the omens.
- Britain came to be demonised by Americans without good cause. The notion that British ministries were bent on reducing the colonies to a state of slavery was nonsense. With the possible exception of Townshend, no British minister had any deliberate wish to diminish American liberty or impose authoritarian rule on the colonies.

- Successive British ministries acted in a manner consistent with their understanding of the British constitution, in which Parliament was the supreme governing body in the empire. If Parliament was sovereign then it must have the power to tax. Giving up the right to tax was to surrender Parliament's supremacy – the equivalent to recognising American independence.
- Britain's determination to hold on to the American colonies was understandable. If the colonies won independence, other parts of the Empire would go their own way. Moreover, America was a valuable source of raw materials and a major market, taking over a third of British exports in 1772–73.
- Although the Americans talked lofty principals, there was a sordid side to what occurred. Many of the rebel leaders were unsavoury characters, acting ruthlessly to enforce their control – beating, tarring and feathering and publicly humiliating their opponents.

Some key books in the debate:

T.H. Breen, *The Marketing of Revolution: How Consumer Politics Shaped American Independence*, OUP, 2005.

Edward Countryman, *The American Revolution*, Hill and Wang, 1985.

Samuel B. Griffiths, *The War for American Independence: From 1760 to the Surrender at Yorktown*, University of Illinois, 2002.

Robert Middlekauff, *The Glorious Cause: The American Revolution, 1763–1789*, OUP, 1982.

Harry M. Ward, *The American Revolution: Nationhood Achieved 1763–1788,* St Martin's Press, 1995.

Study Guide: AS Questions

In the style of AQA

(a) Explain why there was widespread colonial opposition to the 1765 Stamp Act. (12 marks)

(b) 'Between 1766 and 1770 the American colonies became united in their opposition to Britain.' Explain why you agree or disagree with this view. (24 marks)

Exam tips

(a) The answer should focus on a variety of reasons for colonial opposition and you should not spend too long explaining what the Stamp Act was. Both long- and short-term factors will need to be included, so do not spend too long discussing each one. Instead, concentrate on identifying what you consider to be the most important reason. You should assess the effect of Grenville's anti-smuggling measures and the opposition to the Sugar Act and Currency Act to explain the disputes over taxation and 'arbitrary power'. You should also consider the short-term factors linked to the Stamp Act itself: the year's warning; the debate over 'parliamentary sovereignty'; the breadth of people affected and nature of the demand and the organisation behind official and popular opposition. Try to offer a judgemental conclusion.

(b) The key words here are 'became united'. You are being asked to assess the extent to which the American colonies showed unity in their opposition in this period and while you should be able to find a number of points to support unity, you will also need to remember that there is evidence which does not support it. In agreement with the quotation, you will need to refer to the 'united' opposition to the Stamp Act in defence of American 'liberties', the colonial resistance to Townshend's measures, the activities of the Sons of Liberty, the economic boycott and the effect of the Boston Massacre. In disagreement with the quotation you might mention the continuing quarrels between colonies over boundaries and land, the social tensions between rich and poor and the political divisions within the colonies. You should decide which way you are going to argue before you begin and your essay should progress logically to a well substantiated conclusion.

(a) Explain why the incident known as the 'Boston Tea Party' occurred in December 1773. (12 marks)

(b) 'It was only the way the British Government acted in the years 1774 to 1776 which provoked the American colonies to sign the Declaration of Independence.' Explain why you agree or disagree with this view. (24 marks)

Exam tips

(a) You will need to explain briefly what the Boston Tea Party was, but the focus of your answer should be on the reasons for it and the way those reasons are inter-linked. It would be helpful to think of long- and short-term factors here. The long-term factors are rooted in the dissatisfaction that had built up in the American colonies about the way they were treated by the British government. You might refer (briefly) to the troubles over the Stamp Act, Townshend's measures and more particularly to the Sons of Liberty, the Boston Massacre and the setting up of the committees of correspondence from 1771. The immediate cause of the 'Tea Party' was, of course, the Tea Act of May 1773 and the specific actions of the Bostonians and Sons of Liberty in November/December 1773. Try to reach an overall judgement in your conclusion.

(b) In this longer answer you will need to assess British actions towards the colonies in this period and contrast their importance with other factors encouraging colonial independence. The crucial word here is 'only'. In History, it is very unlikely that there is 'only' one cause for an event, so this invites a challenge! In support of the quotation you will need to consider the British reaction to the Boston Tea Party and the Coercive Acts and Québec Act of 1774. Lord North's determination to stand firm and the half-hearted conciliation plan should also be assessed. However, in disagreement with the quotation, it could also be argued that much of the damage had been done before 1774 by the Stamp Act, the Townshend duties and the way the British had repeatedly backed down under pressure. You might choose to argue that the Declaration of Independence was less the product of British failure than of American determination. The ideology which inspired the American leaders and the issues, particularly of taxation, which allowed for the politicisation of the ordinary American people are important factors too. In your conclusion you might consider whether, after 1774, the Declaration of Independence would have taken place even if the British government had acted in a more conciliatory fashion.

In the style of Edexcel

How far do you agree that the British were responsible for the serious deterioration of relations with the colonies in the years 1763–74? (30 marks)

Exam tips

The cross-references are intended to take you straight to the material that will help you to answer the question.

You only have 35–40 minutes to answer this question so you will need to be selective in what you cover here. It could become a very big answer. Also note the dates in the question and do not go beyond 1774 – the year in which the First Continental Congress met. You must also take care not to become involved in a narrative of events. Identify the main stages of the breakdown in relations and explore whether it was primarily the fault of the British that the situation was not resolved without relations being worsened. Ask yourself questions about Britain's handling of events and situations as you make your notes, but take into account whether the reactions of the colonists were unpredictable or unreasonable.

- Britain's Western policy after 1763 was unpopular – did it needlessly arouse resentment (pages 36–37)?
- Grenville's 1764 measures antagonised New England merchants: were they unreasonable (pages 37–38)?
- Was the Sugar Act an abuse of Parliament's power (page 39)?
- Was the Stamp Act a serious British mistake (pages 41–47)?
- Why did the Repeal of the Stamp Act not settle the problems (pages 46–48)? Were the Townshend Duties a serious British mistake and how badly did the British mishandle attempts to enforce them (pages 49–55)?
- Why did the repeal of the Townshend duties not settle the problems – what brought an end to the 'years of calm'? How serious a mistake was the Tea Act (pages 59–61)?
- Could the British have reacted differently to the Boston Tea Party? Were the Coercion Acts unwise?

And what is your overall conclusion? If you feel there were key stages which could have been differently handled by Britain then you will agree with the statement – but remember to make your judgement in the light of the values and attitudes of the time.

3 The War of Independence 1776–83

POINTS TO CONSIDER

The War of Independence was the USA's longest war until the Vietnam War (1963–73). The fact that it lasted so long suggests that its outcome was far from a foregone conclusion. Suppressing rebellions within the dominions of the British Crown was not a new problem for Britain's armed forces in the eighteenth century. Major risings in Scotland in 1715 and 1745–46 had been defeated. In 1775 George III and his ministers assumed that British victory in America was certain. Indeed, Britain arguably should have won the war in 1776. Did Britain eventually lose the war or did the Americans win it? How important was French help? Was the war actually winnable as far as Britain was concerned? This chapter will examine these (and other) questions by focusing on the following themes:

- The situation in 1776
- Military operations: 1776–77
- The extension of the war
- The war in North America: 1778–81
- Peacemaking

Key dates

1776	July	British forces landed in New York
1777	September	British forces captured Philadelphia
	October	British surrendered at Saratoga
1778		American alliance with France
1779		Spain joined the war
1781		British surrendered at Yorktown
1782		Resignation of Lord North
1783		Peace of Paris

1 | The Situation in 1776

British strengths

At the start of the war most Britons were confident of victory. Britain outnumbered the USA in population by more than three to one. Britain had eight million people: the colonies had 2.5 million of whom nearly 500,000 were slaves. Moreover, Britain had the support of at least 500,000 American loyalists (see page 94).

Britain possessed military superiority. In 1775 America had to build an army from scratch. Britain, by contrast, had an army of 48,647 officers and men. In 1775–76, having failed to hire 20,000 Russian soldiers, Britain hired 18,000 soldiers from the German principalities of Hesse-Cassel, Hesse-Hanau, Waldeck and Brunswick. Further treaties in 1777 added 3000 more. The **Hessians** provided Britain with trained troops who could immediately be sent to America. Britain also had the support of most Native Americans.

The Royal Navy, the premier branch of Britain's armed forces, ruled the waves in 1775–76. It had some 340 ships. The Americans had no navy worthy of the name. Eventually some 50 vessels were commissioned into the Continental Navy, and almost as many into state navies, but these were mainly converted merchantmen, not **ships of the line**. They posed no real threat to Britain. Congress never appointed an overall naval commander because there was no real navy to command. Naval superiority enabled Britain to reinforce and supply her forces, to move men along the American seaboard and to blockade and attack American ports. Given the fact that seventy-five per cent of Americans lived within 120 km (75 miles) of the sea, British naval strength was a crucial advantage.

Key question
Which side had the greater advantages in 1776?

Key terms

Hessians
German auxiliaries who fought for Britain.

Ships of the line
The great wooden battleships employed from the seventeenth to the mid-nineteenth centuries.

'Hessian' soldiers. Nearly 30,000 Germans served in America and 12,000 did not return home (5000 deserted).

Lord Sandwich, the first lord of the Admiralty, had ability and drive. He embarked on a prodigious ship-building programme that ensured that Britain retained command of the sea, even when France and Spain became involved.

Britain had much greater financial strength. America, by contrast, had huge financial problems. Unable to levy taxes and unsuccessful in inducing the states to comply with its requisitions, Congress could finance the war only by frequent issues of paper money. The states did just the same. As the quantity of paper money increased, its value declined and prices rose. Ordinary Americans became reluctant to accept American paper currency. The depreciation of the American currency affected economic and military activity.

Lord George Germain, who replaced Dartmouth as Colonial Secretary in November 1775, was given the task of co-ordinating the British war effort. An energetic and highly competent war minister, he sensibly gave his commanders in the field considerable latitude. Ironically, he had been convicted by court martial for disobedience at the Battle of Minden (1759) and sentenced never again to serve in the army.

Britain had a number of bases close to the thirteen colonies – Canada, Newfoundland, Florida, the West Indian islands – from which to launch attacks.

The Americans had a number of serious problems:

Key term

Continental Army
The main American army.

- They lacked unity. For the most part they remained thirteen distinct and separate states, each guarding its own interests.
- The **Continental Army** did not enjoy the support of a developed system for providing men and supplies. Filling the ranks of the army was a constant problem. Many states were slow to furnish their quota of troops. Moreover, many troops enlisted for only a short time. Washington's army never exceeded 20,000 men: much of the time he had barely 5000. The state militias were less impressive as a fighting force than most Americans hoped. Militiamen generally enrolled for only a few weeks and often went home before their terms expired.
- The Americans lacked an effective national government. The Articles of Confederation, adopted by the Continental Congress in 1777 but not ratified until 1781, conferred only limited powers upon the central government (see pages 142–3). Though empowered to make war, it was denied the means to wage it effectively.
- The American economy was gravely disrupted by the war. The demands of the various armies plus the British blockade meant there was a shortage of many goods, affecting both the army and civilians. Americans troops were desperately short of firearms and munitions in 1775–76. Throughout the war, the Continental Army was badly affected by inadequate provisions and poor clothing. By contrast, Britain's far greater manufacturing base enabled her to produce enormous quantities of war materials.
- Supply shortages, coupled with the fact that American soldiers' pay was often in arrears, caused serious morale problems.

American strengths

The American **patriots** did have some major advantages. First and foremost, Britain was fighting a war 4800 km (3000 miles) away from home. It took two to three months for reinforcements and supplies to cross the Atlantic. By the time they arrived the situation that they had been intended to deal with had often changed out of all recognition. To wage war in a huge, unfriendly territory was a formidable task for Britain. Co-ordinating land and sea operations over vast distances was particularly difficult. The terrain, and the problem of supplies, made it hard for British forces to go more than 24 km (15 miles) from a navigable river or the sea.

The British army was well below strength in 1775. Its real strength was more like 36,000 than its strength on paper of 48,000. The troops were scattered widely in Britain, Ireland, Gibraltar, Minorca, the West Indies and Africa. Only about 8000 were in America in 1775. Moreover, the army had not been seriously tested in action since 1763. A quarter of the infantry in 1775 was made up of men with less than a year's service.

The Royal Navy had been allowed to decay after 1763. Lord North was reluctant to provoke the French by a full-scale naval mobilisation. Not until October 1776, after reports that France was significantly increasing its naval forces, did North start putting the navy on a war footing. The age and decrepitude of many British ships were a problem. Moreover, Britain did not totally rule the waves. Congress and the states commissioned about 2000 **privateers**. These vessels initially inflicted heavy damage on British merchant shipping.

Most Americans were committed to the 'glorious cause', convinced that the struggle was one against tyranny and that there was a great conspiracy to undermine American freedom (although this was undoubtedly untrue). Although the Continental Army was relatively small, Washington could always rely on the militia turning out in large numbers in areas where the fighting took place. Despite the fact that Washington distrusted and criticised them, the militiamen played a vital role in the war. They served as a kind of political police, rounding up and intimidating people who were loyal to Britain. They also contributed as a fighting force, both in set-piece engagements and in guerrilla-type skirmishes. Over 100,000 Americans served at some time in the militias.

The presence of the Hessian troops, who brought with them a fearsome reputation for rapacity, convinced many neutral and even loyalist-inclined colonists to support the patriots. The Indians were also doubtful allies, spurring many Americans to oppose Britain.

There were a number of other British problems:

- Britain, seriously unprepared for war, lost the initiative both militarily and politically to the Americans in 1775.
- British requisitioning of supplies, seizure of property to accommodate troops and the harshness of martial law were always likely to alienate loyal and potentially friendly Americans.

Patriots
Americans who supported independence. They are sometimes called rebels.

Privateers
Privately owned vessels granted permission by a government to capture enemy ships.

Key terms

- North was not an inspired or inspiring war leader.
- There was always the likelihood that Britain's enemies France and Spain would join the war to settle old scores.

British strategy in 1776

Key term

Strategy
Long-term military planning.

British leaders, who had to find the right **strategy** to win the war, faced several problems. Firstly, British troops faced a generally hostile population. The British army was thus dependent on Britain for obtaining the bulk of its supplies. Crucially, the army had to protect the major American ports under British control, employing many troops in garrison duty. Thus only a part of the army was available for field operations. Secondly, there was no vital political or economic centre for British armies to capture. The occupation of territory by British forces brought no lasting advantage. The moment the British moved away from a town or subdued region, rebellion flared up in their rear. The task for British forces was, according to historian Eric Robson, like 'trying to hit a swarm of flies with a hammer'. From the British perspective the destruction of the Continental Army was more important than the possession of towns and territory.

Some British leaders favoured a seaboard strategy – a concentration of effort on gaining control of American ports and blockading the rest of the coast. They claimed this would minimise the problems of operating and fighting inland in difficult terrain. However, a fully developed seaboard strategy was not followed for several reasons:

- Such a policy would betray loyalists and lose loyalist support. With the help of British troops, loyalists might play a significant role in restoring British authority.
- The seaboard strategy had failed in New England in 1775 (see page 74).
- Canada needed to be defended.
- There was pressure in Britain for a speedy and decisive victory. A seaboard strategy would inevitably be long and drawn out.
- An effective naval blockade would be difficult to maintain given the 1900 km (1200 miles) of seaboard that needed patrolling.

British leaders hoped that military success would make possible the resumption of British rule. They realised, however, that they must achieve some kind of reconciliation with the Americans. The restoration of the colonies to royal control would serve little purpose if the embers of rebellion smouldered among a discontented population and a large army was needed to maintain order. This would simply result in a substantial tax burden that would have to be borne by the Americans or the British, both hazardous options. Given the need to reach a political solution, a war of unlimited destruction was ruled out. Finding the right blend of firmness and conciliation was no easy matter.

American strategy in 1776

The Americans could afford to fight a defensive war, wearing down the enemy. However, Washington feared that if he lost major towns or swathes of land without fighting a battle, it would damage American morale. He hoped that a major victory would help bind his new army together.

The loyalists

The War of Independence pitted Americans against other Americans as well as against Britons. John Adams estimated that one-third of the population were active rebels, one-third were loyalists (or Tories) and one-third were neutral. Most historians today suspect that two-fifths of the population were active rebels, one-fifth active loyalists and two-fifths sought neutrality. By either estimate, a majority of Americans did not support the rebellion. By 1783 some 19,000 Americans had enlisted in the British army. Thousands more joined loyalist militias.

Key question
To what extent was the war a civil war?

Who were the loyalists?

Far from being an upper-class phenomenon, as historians once believed, loyalism drew adherents from all ranks of society. Ownership of great estates or mercantile wealth provides no adequate guide to political allegiance. While some of the elite were loyalists, in Virginia the great planters overwhelmingly supported and led the patriot cause. Many loyalists possessed strong links with Britain, especially those who were recent immigrants, for example, the Scots of the Carolina backcountry. Loyalists also tended to be drawn from minority groups who had little in common with the majority patriot population. These groups included Southern backcountry farmers who resented the dominance of the Tidewater patriot elite, Anglicans in New England, and Germans and Dutch in New York.

The geographical distribution of loyalism was uneven. There were more loyalists in the Southern and Middle Colonies than in New England. In only a few areas (for example, New York City) did the loyalists comprise a majority.

Far more blacks fought for the British, in return for promises of freedom, than supported the patriot cause. Britain might have made more military use of blacks, a sixth of the population. However, British leaders were aware that large-scale recruitment of black troops would jeopardise white loyalist support.

Loyalist problems

The varied backgrounds and motivations of the loyalists meant that they did not constitute a coherent opposition to the patriots. While the rebels had a clear idea that they were fighting for independence and republican self-government, the loyalists knew only that they stood against these things. Often motivated by local concerns, they were unable to organise themselves on a national level. Instead, they relied on the British to provide them with leadership and protection. Thus, while Britain placed great hopes on loyalist assistance, significant loyalist activity required the presence of British forces. Once those forces departed, loyalists were left exposed and vulnerable to the wrath of their patriot neighbours. During the war tens of thousands of loyalists, real and suspected, were imprisoned, driven from their homes and deprived of their land and property by local committees of safety. A few were executed for treason.

The nature of the war

Key question
Was the War of Independence the first modern war?

Some historians, like Stephen Conway, regard the War of Independence as the first modern war, anticipating what happened in Europe in the French Revolutionary and Napoleonic Wars (1792–1815). Those who see the war as 'modern' claim:

- Unlike some early eighteenth-century wars, this was no dynastic war, waged for a strip of territory: it was a political struggle. Many of the soldiers were motivated by the political ideals embraced by the new republic.
- The war was one of the first instances of the nation-in-arms. The American army was a people's army. Nearly every free male of military age was eligible for service. By 1781 200,000 American males, from across the social spectrum, had engaged in some kind of military service – about one in three of the men of military age. The Continentals, both officers and privates, were essentially civilians and remained civilians even after they had learned to fight like professionals.
- To a much greater extent than any other army of the time, the Continental Army embodied the principle of careers open to talent. Officers, many of who had risen from the ranks, were often promoted according to merit, not birth.
- **Guerrilla war** was an important feature of the conflict.
- During the war, the Americans are thought to have made good use of the rifle, a weapon that was accurate at up to 200 metres, twice the range of the ordinary musket.

Key term

Guerrilla war
Warfare by which small units harass conventional forces.

- From Britain's point of view, this was not a traditionally limited eighteenth-century conflict. After 1778 Britain was involved in a world war and British resources were stretched to breaking point. One in seven or eight Britons of military age may have participated in the war – a higher mobilisation of manpower than in any previous war in which Britain had been engaged.

However, other historians, like Piers Mackesy, portray the contest as essentially traditional:

- Nationalism was well developed in early eighteenth-century Europe. Thus, soldiers often fought for ideological 'causes' well before the War of Independence.
- The notion of a nation of citizen soldiers putting aside their ploughs and picking up their guns was not really true. After an initial burst of enthusiasm, most people went back to their farms.

By no means all Americans chose to fight in the war. Most who did so fought in state militias, usually serving for a very limited term.

- The state militias were not very successful. The Continental Army did the bulk of the fighting. The officers and men of the Continental Army, like a traditional eighteenth-century army, came to think of themselves as a caste apart.
- Washington rejected the guerrilla option (urged by his second in command, Charles Lee) in favour of conventional European warfare. He realised that guerrilla warfare, by itself, could not defeat the British. He thus tried to create a traditional army, consciously emulating British methods.
- The Continental Army was similar to its European counterparts. Most of its officers were substantial landowners. The rank and file were drawn mainly from the poorest sections of white society.
- As the Continental Army fought essentially in the traditional manner, the British were not obliged to rethink their way of fighting.
- There was little innovation in the technology of war. It would be a mistake to exaggerate the importance of the rifle. A rifle took one minute to load and needed an expert to fire it. Most American and British soldiers were armed with the ordinary musket.
- The war was generally civilised by the standards of the time. (The only exceptions were the Indian war in the West and the fighting in the Carolinas in the early 1780s.) Most British officers tried to avoid a policy of large-scale destruction. This moderation is associated with pre-French Revolutionary warfare.

In historian Jeremy Black's view, the most that can be said is that the American war anticipated some of the features of the French Revolutionary War.

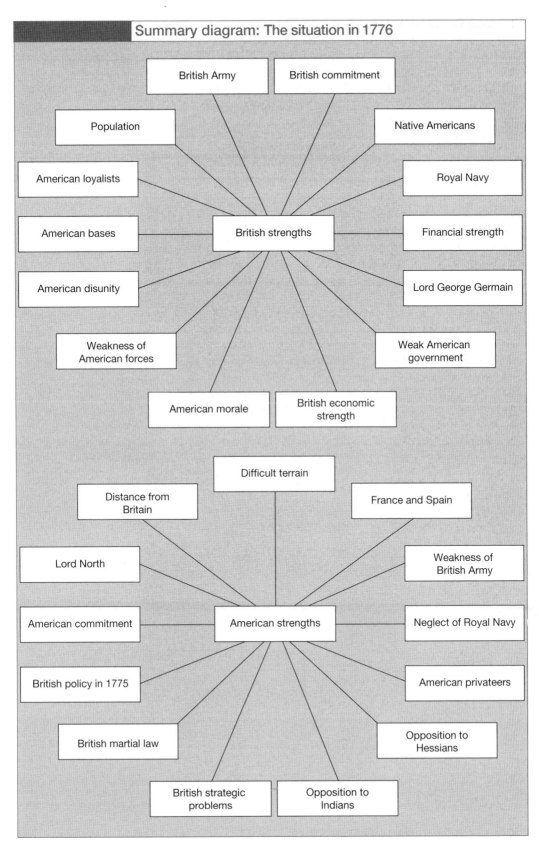

Summary diagram: The situation in 1776

British Army

British commitment

Population

Native Americans

American loyalists

Royal Navy

American bases

British strengths

Financial strength

American disunity

Lord George Germain

Weakness of American forces

Weak American government

American morale

British economic strength

Difficult terrain

Distance from Britain

France and Spain

Lord North

Weakness of British Army

American commitment

American strengths

Neglect of Royal Navy

British policy in 1775

American privateers

British martial law

Opposition to Hessians

British strategic problems

Opposition to Indians

2 | Military Operations: 1776–77

In 1776 British leaders hoped by mounting the largest trans-oceanic expedition ever sent from Britain they would overawe the rebels. Still convinced that the rebellion was the work of a few miscreants, they hoped that loyal Americans would rise up and kick out the rebels.

Key question
Why did Britain not win the war in 1776?

General William Howe

General William Howe, a second cousin of George III, commanded the British troops. He had fought with success in America in the Seven Years' War, helping Wolfe capture Québec. Howe, who had declared in 1774 that he was against a policy of coercion, was fond of Americans. His military role in America in 1776–77 is much debated.

Following his withdrawal to Halifax in March 1776, Howe planned an assault on New York City. All but surrounded by water,

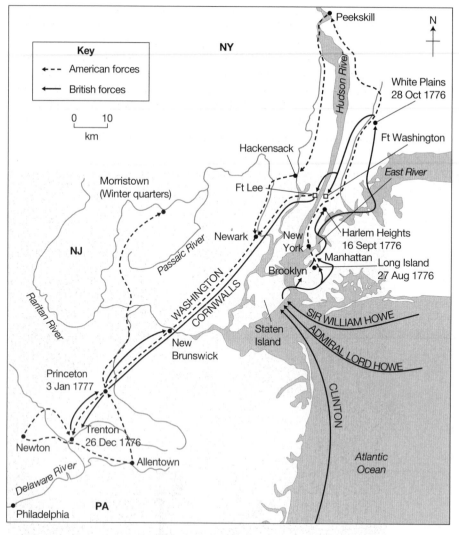

Figure 3.1: New York–New Jersey campaigns: 1776–77.

British forces landed in New York: July 1776

New York was an excellent potential naval base. Howe hoped to lure Washington into a decisive battle, defeat him and negotiate a peaceful end to the rebellion. After wasting several weeks awaiting reinforcements that did not arrive, he finally embarked for New York on 10 June, landing on Staten Island on 2 July. Howe's army was supported by a fleet commanded by his elder brother, Admiral Lord Richard Howe, who was in overall command in America. Like William, Richard had some sympathy with the Americans and favoured a policy of conciliation rather than coercion.

New York

By mid-August Howe commanded a 32,000-strong army. Washington, with only 20,000 men, would have been best abandoning New York. Given British command of the sea, the place was indefensible. But abandoning the city would have been bad for morale and bad politically. Washington had to fight for New York if only because Congress demanded he did so. Foolishly, he tried to defend the whole city, dividing his army between Long Island and Manhattan Island (see Figure 3.1). This deployment gave General Howe a great advantage. At the Battle of Long Island (27 August) Howe outflanked and heavily defeated the Americans who suffered 2000 casualties, six times as many as the British. Had Howe pressed on, he could have destroyed the American forces, trapped on the Brooklyn shore of the East River. Washington, under cover of a dense fog, managed to withdraw his army to the mainland on 29 August. Howe had missed a great opportunity to defeat the rebellion.

General William Howe. Why did Howe fail to destroy the Continental Army?

As well as being appointed to military and naval command, the Howes had also been appointed peace commissioners. Rather than continue the military momentum, they now sought to negotiate a peace agreement. On 11 September, Admiral Howe met representatives of Congress – Benjamin Franklin, John Adams and Edward Rutledge. The Declaration of Independence proved to be the stumbling block. Lord Howe was not empowered to discuss a treaty between Britain and an independent America. Thus the efforts at reconciliation failed.

On 15 September, 4000 of Howe's troops landed at Kips Bay in Manhattan, between the two halves of Washington's army. Howe's caution again gave Washington time to withdraw. For several weeks there was something of a stalemate. Rather than attack well entrenched positions, Howe set about turning the Americans' flank. Washington retreated slowly back across New Jersey. Explaining his strategy to Congress, he declared he was fighting a 'defensive' war and seeking to avoid a 'general action'.

American retreat

On 16 November British forces captured Fort Washington, taking nearly 3000 American prisoners and immense quantities of weapons and supplies. This was a shattering blow for Washington.

A romantic (but not very accurate) image of George Washington crossing the Delaware, Christmas Day, 1776, ahead of his victory at Trenton. It is the work of Emanuel Leutze who completed the painting in 1851. What was the artist's purpose?

For the next three weeks his army was in full retreat. To make matters worse, many militiamen returned home. When the Continental Army crossed the Delaware into Pennsylvania in early December, Washington's army had dwindled to 3000 men and the one-year enlistments would expire at the end of the month. It seemed that the Continental Army was about to collapse and with it the notion of a United States of America.

On 30 November Lord Howe issued a proclamation appealing for conciliation and offering all who would take an oath of allegiance to the king within the next 60 days a 'free and general pardon'. Thousands of Americans in New Jersey renounced their support for the rebels and applied for pardons. Given the size and strength of the British army, it seemed the prudent thing to do. On 8 December British forces seized Newport, Rhode Island – an excellent naval base. On 18 December a disconsolate Washington wrote, 'I think the game is pretty near up.'

Trenton and Princeton

Philadelphia was General Howe's for the taking. However, instead of marching on the American capital, he decided to go into winter quarters. Undoubtedly he faced serious logistical problems. But by not attacking Philadelphia, he threw away a great opportunity to destroy American morale.

The unexpected respite gave Washington time to regroup. Reinforced by militia from neighbouring states, his army grew to 6000. Recognising the importance of ending the campaign on a positive note – for Americans generally and for his army in particular – Washington tried to conjure up a victory. On 25 December he re-crossed the Delaware with 1600 men and fell upon the unsuspecting Hessian garrison at Trenton on 26 December, capturing over 1000 prisoners. American casualties were four wounded. Washington followed this up with a similar coup at Princeton on 3 January 1777, driving British forces from the town. These bold counterstrokes forced the British to relinquish most of their gains in New Jersey. More importantly, they breathed new life into the American cause, rekindling faith and hope.

Taking up winter quarters at Morristown, Washington was able to rebuild his army while keeping watch on British movements. For the next few months there was no major battle. However, there was considerable skirmishing as American **light infantry** tried – reasonably successfully – to prevent British detachments from foraging. British garrisons, short of food, suffered extreme hardship.

Key term

Light infantry
Foot soldiers who travelled with the minimum of equipment and were thus able to move quickly.

Profile: George Washington (1732–99)

1732	– Born to a Virginian planting family
1748	– Worked as a surveyor/speculator in the West
1753	– Sent by the governor of Virginia with a letter demanding that the French leave the Ohio Valley. Having made the dangerous journey, he received a polite rebuff from the French. Publication of the diary of his journey made him a hero throughout the colonies and in Britain
1754	– Led an unsuccessful military expedition into the Ohio country
1755–59	– Colonel of the Virginia militia, in charge of the Western frontier
1759	– Having failed to secure a British commission, resigned his post. Married Martha Custis, a wealthy widow
1759–74	– Managed his plantation and served in the House of Burgesses
1774	– Elected to the First Continental Congress
1775–83	– Led the Continental Army
1783	– Gave up his commission and returned to Mount Vernon (his home)
1787	– Served as president of the Constitutional Convention
1789	– Elected first president of the USA
1792	– Re-elected as president

Washington was by no means a military genius. He lost more battles than he won. In fairness to Washington, he struggled with a lack of supplies and men. He was sustained by his love for what he called the 'glorious cause' – the defence of American liberties. His greatest talent was somehow holding the Continental Army together. He learned from (bad) experiences and never gave up. Whatever his military failings, he did win the last major campaign, forcing General Cornwallis to surrender at Yorktown in 1781. Without his leadership, the Americans might well have lost the war. He was also the very model of the proper citizen soldier. He always acknowledged the supremacy of the civilian branch over the military, refrained from open criticism of Congress and kept Congress fully informed of his plans.

British plans in 1777

The situation for Britain in early 1777 was much better than it had been twelve months previously. Canada was secure. New York had been captured. Britain thus had great hopes of winning the war. In 1777 there were two large British armies in North America, one commanded by General Howe, the other by General Burgoyne. Howe's main concern was to capture Philadelphia, America's largest city. Burgoyne, who led a British army in Canada, aimed to drive down the Hudson Valley, isolating New England from the other colonies. Although Germain had instructed Howe to co-operate with

Key question
What were Britain's main military mistakes in 1777?

Burgoyne, Howe felt that he was not strong enough to guarantee any support. In the event, what was originally viewed from London as a co-ordinated operation to bring the war to an end became two very separate campaigns.

The capture of Philadelphia

Not until July 1777 did Howe commence his move on Philadelphia. Rather than march across New Jersey, he determined to move his 15,000-strong army by sea. Embarking most of his troops at New York, he sailed not to the lower Delaware but into Chesapeake Bay (see Figure 3.2). The soldiers endured nearly six weeks crammed on board transports. Eventually the sickly army landed at the head of Chesapeake Bay, barely 64 km (40 miles) closer to Philadelphia than it had been when it left New York. In effect, Howe did not open his campaign against Philadelphia until late August.

On 11 September Howe outflanked and defeated Washington at Brandywine Creek. The Americans lost 1200 men, the British only half that number. Howe again missed an opportunity to destroy

Key date

British forces captured Philadelphia: September 1777

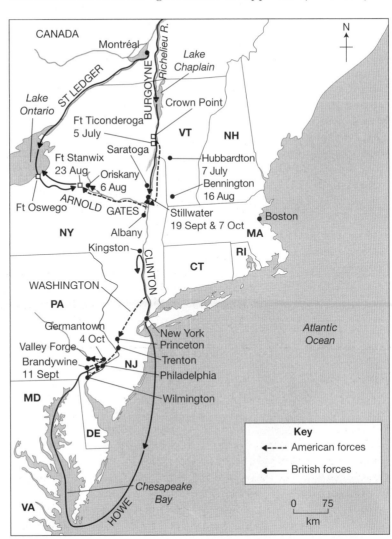

Figure 3.2: Saratoga and Philadelphia campaigns: 1777.

Washington's army. On 21 September Howe won another victory at Paoli and went on to capture Philadelphia on 26 September. This appeared a major triumph. However, Philadelphia's fall did not lead to the collapse of the rebellion. Congress simply fled to Lancaster. As long as Washington could keep his forces in the field, the rebellion would continue.

As American forts blocked the route up the River Delaware to Philadelphia, the British faced major supply problems. On 4 October Washington launched a surprise counter-attack at Germantown. His plan was too complicated and the Americans lost over 1000 casualties – twice as many as the British. In November Howe finally forced the Americans to evacuate the forts on the Delaware, allowing British naval access to Philadelphia. Washington now withdrew to the desolate plateau of Valley Forge, 32 km (20 miles) to the north-west of Philadelphia. If Howe had attacked at this point, he might well have destroyed the Continental Army. Instead, he prepared to spend the winter in the comfort of Philadelphia. He had again failed to win a decisive victory and not convinced American opinion that Britain was certain to triumph.

Burgoyne's plan

Key question
Why were the British defeated at Saratoga?

While Howe was focusing on Philadelphia, General Burgoyne planned a southward offensive from Canada. 'Gentleman Johnny' Burgoyne was a colourful character – MP, playwright and egotist. He gave the impression of confidence. On Christmas Day 1776 a bet was recorded in the wagers book at Brooks Club, one of London's most fashionable gambling clubs: 'General Burgoyne wagers Charles Fox one pony [£55] that he will be home victorious from America by Christmas Day, 1777.'

In February 1777 Burgoyne had presented to the king and to Germain his 'Thoughts for conducting the war from the side of Canada'. It was not a particularly original scheme. He aimed to lead a combined force of British regulars, Hessians, Indians,

General Johnny Burgoyne. To what extent was he responsible for the British defeat?

Canadians and loyalists south through the Champlain and Hudson Valleys to join with the main British forces in New York. This would cut off New England and help snuff out rebellion. Burgoyne's plan was over-optimistic about the likely response of the loyalists and minimised the logistical problems.

Although he later claimed otherwise, Burgoyne did not rely upon Howe's forces in New York advancing up the Hudson to meet him. He was confident he was strong enough to achieve his objective. When he left Canada in June 1777 he had over 8000 men. Had he known of the disarray of his enemy, he would have been even more optimistic. General Schuyler commanded the Northern Department but his hold was insecure. Most of his New England troops despised his aristocratic bearing and the fact that he came from New York.

The start of the campaign

Initially Burgoyne's campaign went to plan. His army floated down Lake Champlain in flat-bottomed boats and easily recaptured the strong fortress of Ticonderoga on 5 July, despite the Americans having had months to prepare its defences. Burgoyne's next problem was how to move to Fort Edward on the Hudson. The best method was to sail down Lake George and then follow a road already cut. Underestimating the difficulties of a wilderness campaign, Burgoyne chose instead to head due south through inhospitable terrain. Encumbered by an enormous baggage train – 30 vehicles were needed to carry Burgoyne's wardrobe and his stock of champagne – his army found movement increasingly difficult as patriot militia blocked roads, destroyed bridges and attacked stragglers. Consequently it took Burgoyne three weeks to cover the 37 km (23 miles) to Fort Edward.

Burgoyne's hope that loyalists would flock to his standard did not materialise. In fact, the presence of British forces did much to create rebels out of neutrally inclined Americans. Burgoyne's Indian allies did not help. Iroquois warriors, during the advance, attacked outlying farms, killing several families. Once Indians and whites came into conflict, political considerations took second place to racial enmity. One tragic incident in particular served to alienate those who had initially been sympathetic to Britain. Jane McCrea, who was engaged to a loyalist, was murdered and scalped by Indians. When Burgoyne demanded that his Indian allies surrender the culprits, the Indians refused and most left the British army.

Burgoyne now spent a month collecting supplies. He sent a foraging party of 600 men into Vermont but they were surrounded and attacked at Bennington (15–16 August) by a much larger force of New Hampshire militia, and all 600 were killed or captured. A relief party of similar strength suffered the same fate. These were serious losses – one-seventh of Burgoyne's army.

More bad news reached Burgoyne's army. A diversionary force of 1600 British and Iroquois under Colonel St Leger had been moving down the St Lawrence and then along the Mohawk, intending to join Burgoyne. However, St Leger's column, while besieging Fort Stanwix, was checked at Oriskany (6 August) by local militia. The

Indians, unhappy at the siege and made uneasy by reports of the approach of more American troops, left St Leger's camp. He thus had no option but to lift the siege and retreat to Canada.

The end of the campaign

Burgoyne was now isolated. The wisest course would have been to retreat to Ticonderoga. However, rather than admit defeat, Burgoyne determined to drive to Albany. The Americans were ready for him. On 19 August General Horatio Gates had replaced Schuyler as commander of the Northern Department. Gates had the confidence of the New England militia, as Schuyler did not. Aided by some able subordinates, not least Benedict Arnold, Gates prepared strong defensive positions north of Albany. The American successes in August encouraged New England militiamen to join Gates. By early September he had 7000 men. In mid-September, Burgoyne, with a similar sized army, pushed south.

On 19 September the two forces clashed at Freeman's Farm. Failing to defeat the rebels and sustaining significant casualties (556 men), Burgoyne found himself in a perilous position – 320 km (200 miles) from Canada, short of supplies and facing a well entrenched army, growing daily in size. Only a swift retreat could save the expedition. But on 21 September Burgoyne received a letter from General Clinton who promised to push northwards from New York. This gave Burgoyne renewed hope. He still gambled on breaking through the American lines to Albany, only 32 km (20 miles) away.

Given that there was no significant American force threatening New York, Clinton might have launched his move towards Albany earlier. In the event he did not leave New York until 3 October with 3000 men. Capturing a clutch of forts in the Highlands, he got close to Albany – but from Burgoyne's view not close enough. Burgoyne hoped that Clinton's campaign would force Gates to deplete his army in order to strengthen his rear. Gates did no such thing. Instead, he held firm on Bemis Heights. On 7 October Burgoyne attacked the American defences. Thanks largely to the heroism of Arnold (who had been relieved of his command just before the battle), Burgoyne's attack failed. He lost another 400 men – the Americans only 150.

On 8 October Burgoyne retreated to Saratoga, hoping that Clinton's army might still come to his rescue. It was a forlorn hope. By mid-October Gates had more than twice as many troops as Burgoyne who was effectively surrounded. On 14 October Burgoyne began negotiating with Gates who, worried by Clinton's advance, was keen to settle. Thus, Burgoyne (apparently) got good terms. Burgoyne's 5895 troops were to lay down their arms, march to Boston and to embark on British ships on condition they did not again serve in America. The surrender came into effect on 17 October. For the first time the rebels had defeated the British in a major campaign. (Congress found a series of excuses to reject Gates' terms. Thus Burgoyne's troops remained prisoners of war until 1783.)

British surrendered at Saratoga: October 1777 **Key date**

Who was to blame?
The American heroes were Arnold and the regulars of the Continental Army. Gates' role and that of the militia were exaggerated at the time and since. But who was to blame on the British side?

- Howe can be blamed for doing little to help Burgoyne.
- Burgoyne can be blamed for under-estimating the strength of the opposition.
- Germain can be criticised for failing to reconcile the plans of the two generals. With hindsight, he should have ordered Howe to co-operate with Burgoyne. But this was no easy matter. Germain, 4800 km (3000 miles) away in London, could not formulate too rigid a plan. He was dependent on the generals in America acting sensibly in the light of the circumstances.

The results of Saratoga
- On 21 October news of Burgoyne's surrender reached Howe. He at once wrote to Germain offering his resignation.
- Concerned about the situation in Pennsylvania, Howe ordered Clinton to send reinforcements. Clinton was thus forced to abandon the Highlands, a crucial area. Clinton believed the loss of Burgoyne's army might have been accepted as a necessary sacrifice had the British retained the Highlands.
- Burgoyne's surrender was a great morale booster for the Americans.
- The British government responded to the defeat by attempting to negotiate peace. In December, two days after the news of Saratoga reached London, North dispatched a secret agent to Paris to contact the American commissioners – Benjamin Franklin and Silas Deane – with a view to exploring the possibilities for ending the war.
- In February 1778 Parliament passed North's Conciliatory Propositions. Britain agreed to repeal the Coercive Acts, renounced the right to tax Americans and accepted that Americans could maintain their own army.
- A Peace Commission, headed by the Earl of Carlisle, was appointed to try to negotiate an end to the war. The commissioners could accept as part of the peace settlement the withdrawal of all British forces from America and were permitted to grant the Americans representation in the House of Commons. However, Britain's denial of American independence wrecked any hope of successful negotiations.
- Saratoga had important international consequences (see below).

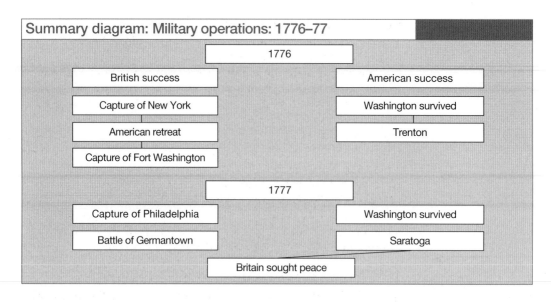

Summary diagram: Military operations: 1776–77

1776

British success
Capture of New York
American retreat
Capture of Fort Washington

American success
Washington survived
Trenton

1777

Capture of Philadelphia
Battle of Germantown

Washington survived
Saratoga

Britain sought peace

3 | The Extension of the War

Key question
What was the effect
of French intervention
in the War of
Independence?

In 1778 the war from Britain's point of view was to become a world war rather than simply a rebellion. This had important consequences for America.

The French alliance

From the start of the war, the Americans had realised the importance of France's help, even if her Catholicism and absolutist system of government made her less than a natural ally. The French King Louis XVI had no love of rebellion, democracy or republicanism. He feared the American experiment could provide a dangerous model elsewhere. Nevertheless, the French government realised that the war offered a wonderful opportunity to avenge the humiliating outcome of the Seven Years' War. If Britain lost her richest colonial possessions she would be weaker economically and in world power terms. Almost from the start of the war France secretly supplied the Americans with arms and gunpowder via fictitious companies trading in the West Indies. The French government had also encouraged some young army officers to go to America and place their service at America's disposal. (They included the Marquis de Lafayette, who became one of Washington's favourite officers.) However, Louis XVI had withheld formal recognition of American independence while the outcome of the war was in doubt. The French treasury was so depleted that some ministers believed that France should steer clear of another war at all costs.

In an effort to persuade France to join the war, Congress sent Benjamin Franklin as leader of a diplomatic mission to Paris. He arrived in December 1776, joining Silas Deane who was already in France purchasing war supplies. Franklin was to prove an inspired choice. His apparent simplicity and straightforwardness quickly attracted the admiration of Parisians.

American alliance
with France: 1778

Key date

Saratoga ended French fears of an American collapse and, by prompting North to make fresh concessions, allowed Franklin to play on French fears of a possible Anglo–American reconciliation. It is possible that France might have entered the war in 1778 even without Saratoga: the French government had decided to enter the war when naval preparations were ready. However, Saratoga helped overcome Louis XVI's doubts and made French intervention certain.

On 6 February 1778 France and America signed two treaties, one a commercial agreement, the other a defensive alliance to take effect when France eventually went to war with Britain – as she did in June 1778. By the terms of the defensive alliance, France and the USA guaranteed each other's New World possessions, promised to wage war until American independence was 'formally or tacitly assured' and undertook not to make peace separately.

Spanish and Dutch intervention

Key date

Spain joined the war: 1779

In April 1779 Spain entered the war against Britain. She did so as an ally of France, not of the USA. As a great imperial power, Spain had good reason to be wary about encouraging colonial rebellion. She joined the war not to help the Americans but to regain possessions lost to Britain – the Floridas, Minorca, Gibraltar and Jamaica. Spain agreed to stay in the war until American independence was secured. In return, France agreed to stay in the war until Spain recovered Gibraltar and to assist her recover Minorca.

In 1780 Britain, concerned that Holland was aiding France and Spain, declared war on her. The Dutch had few offensive ambitions. Their main aim was to hold on to their far-flung trading posts and colonies which were now threatened by Britain.

The League of Armed Neutrality

In 1780 Russia, Sweden and Denmark formed the League of Armed Neutrality. Its aim was the protection of neutral rights, given the British blockade of America. Prussia, Portugal and Austria joined in 1781 and Naples in 1783. The league adhered to the notion that neutral ships could freely trade at ports of nations at war. Although it accomplished little and posed no great threat to Britain, it bolstered the USA's international position while further isolating Britain.

Missed diplomatic opportunities

In the 1770s Britain missed several opportunities which might have averted the threat she faced after 1778:

- In the early 1770s France proposed an alliance with Britain against Russia. Had the alliance materialised, France might not have come to America's aid.
- Britain failed to ally with Russia. An Anglo–Russian alliance might have forced France to think twice about an American pact.
- Britain might have kept Spain out of the war by returning Gibraltar.

The results of French (and Spanish) intervention

After 1778 America became something of a sideshow for Britain. Her main concern was now France. The French population (25 million) was double that of Britain and Ireland. The French army was over 150,000 strong and since 1763 France had tried to construct a fleet capable of challenging British naval supremacy. As well as the threat of French invasion, Britain faced challenges across the globe.

French intervention produced a national war effort in Britain that the war against America had not roused. By 1782 Britain had 150,000 troops serving across the world. In 1778 the Royal Navy had 66 ships of the line available for service. By 1780 it had 95. By 1783, Britain had over 107,000 sailors and 617 ships of all types.

Britain could no longer devote the military resources to North America that she had done between 1775 and 1777. In 1778, sixty-five per cent of the British army was in North America. By 1780, only twenty-nine per cent of British troops were serving there (fifty-five per cent were guarding Britain against invasion). In 1778, forty-one per cent of British ships were in American waters: only thirteen per cent were there in mid-1780.

British forces had now to defend the West Indies, Gibraltar, Minorca and British possessions in Africa and India. Fortunately for Britain her European opponents were not as strong as they seemed:

- The precarious state of French finances meant that the French war effort was more limited than that of Britain.
- Spain's financial problems worsened because her access to the gold and silver of her American colonies was disrupted by the war. During the war, the number of Spanish ships actually declined. Spanish naval officers were strongly criticised by their French allies for their poor training and low standards of seamanship.
- Holland was no longer the great power it had been in the seventeenth century. In 1780 the Dutch had only thirteen ships of the line, the most modern of which had been built in 1753.

British finances were far better able to sustain a protracted struggle than were those of her enemies. Thus, she was able to fight France, Spain and Holland around the world and continue the war in America.

While the Americans benefited from additional assistance in arms, material and money, her new allies were more concerned with striking at Britain than they were with aiding America. Although a French naval squadron arrived in American waters in 1778, it soon departed for the West Indies, bent on capturing British sugar islands. France sent fewer than 10,000 troops to America and these men did little until 1781.

John Paul Jones

American privateers, with French assistance, were able to win some naval success. Scots-born John Paul Jones became a hero in both America and France. After attacking Whitehaven in 1778 (but doing little damage), he sailed to France where he was given command of a larger ship, the *Bonhomme Richard,* and four smaller ships. On 23 September 1779 he fought a naval battle off Flamborough Head, within sight of the Yorkshire coast, taking on the British frigate *Serapis*. Asked early in the battle if he wanted to surrender, the outgunned Jones said, 'I have not yet begun to fight.' He eventually triumphed, his crew capturing the *Serapis* as his own ship sank. Jones' exploits, however, were of small military significance.

Fighting in Europe

Once France joined the war, Britain had no option but to use precious resources for home defence. On 27 July 1778 the British and French fleets fought a major but inconclusive sea battle at Ushant, off the French coast. The Royal Navy was hard put to contain the French fleet. Spain's entry into the war added further to the strain. In July 1779 a combined French and Spanish fleet of 66 ships of the line headed north while 30,000 French troops massed ready for an attack on the Isle of Wight. The Royal Navy, with only 45 ships, avoided offering battle. This strategy worked. The French did not dare transport their troops until the British fleet had been defeated. The French and Spanish ships, their crews decimated by smallpox, scurvy and typhus, were finally dispersed by a gale and returned to their home ports. In 1781 another French–Spanish armada blocked the western entrances to the English Channel. Again sickness prevented the French and Spanish ships from making the most of their position.

Elsewhere, the British bases of Gibraltar and Minorca were besieged from 1779.

The British garrison in Minorca was forced to surrender in February 1782 after a heroic defence. Gibraltar, which faced several Spanish assaults from land and sea, managed to hold out, thanks largely to the Royal Navy's efforts to bring in reinforcements and supplies.

Africa

The war along the West African coast was essentially about improving access to supplies of slaves. French efforts to recover Senegal were unsuccessful. In 1779 British forces captured the French fort at Goree. In 1782 Britain captured several Dutch forts, including Accra, on the Gold Coast.

India

In India the British East India Company had its own army – mainly native soldiers – over 60,000 strong. The company forces were already engaged in war with a confederacy of Indian princes in 1778 – a war which dragged on until 1782. Even so the company took advantage of the Anglo–French war to occupy most of the French posts. Pondicherry, the most powerful, was captured after a 77-day siege. The capture of Mahe, the last French port, in March 1779 led to a major war with Haidar Ali of Mysore. In September 1780 a British force suffered a major defeat and Madras seemed likely to fall to the Mysorians. However, the arrival of reinforcements led by Sir Eyre Coote resulted in a series of British victories in 1781. Having captured all the Dutch trading posts in India, British forces took Trincomalee in Ceylon in 1782.

The West Indies

Between 1778 and 1783 a large part of British military and naval strength was committed to operations in the Caribbean. Many contemporaries believed West Indian colonies were more vital to Britain's prosperity than the American colonies. The islands purchased significant quantities of British manufactures, many of which were smuggled into Spain's colonies, and sent home vast volumes of sugar. The security of the islands was thus a primary objective of British policy. France was also aware of the value of her own West Indian possessions. Consequently, both countries were anxious to seize each other's islands.

In September 1778 French forces captured Dominica. A few months later Britain took St Lucia. In the summer of 1779 French Admiral d'Estaing seized first St Vincent and then Grenada. Once Spain joined the war, Jamaica, the jewel in the British West Indian Crown, was vulnerable to attack.

In February 1781 Britain seized the Dutch island of St Eustatius. In June 1781 the French failed to recapture St Lucia but did take Tobago. The French were even more successful over the winter of 1781–82, taking St Eustatius, St Kitts and Montserrat. France and Spain now began preparations to attack Jamaica. But the arrival of further ships from Britain meant that the combined fleets of Rodney and Hood now outnumbered French Admiral de Grasse's vessels. De Grasse left Martinique on 8 April 1782 aiming to attack Jamaica. On 12 April the two fleets met near the Isles des Saintes. The French lost five ships, de Grasse was captured and the projected attack on Jamaica was abandoned. Rodney and Hood had recovered command of the sea.

West Florida

By 1781 Spanish forces had cleared the Mississippi Valley of British troops.

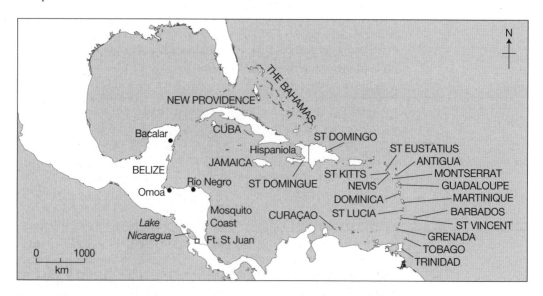

Figure 3.3: Areas in the Caribbean and Central America involved in the war.

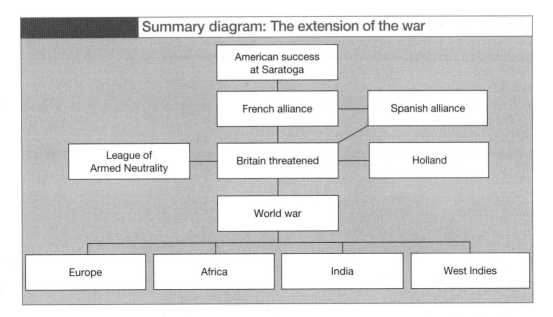

Summary diagram: The extension of the war

4 | The War in North America: 1778–81

Key question
Why was there no decisive battle in the Middle Colonies in the period 1778–81?

After 1778 Britain was able to devote less of her military resources to America. However, the Americans had their own problems. Thus, neither side was able to win a decisive victory until 1781.

Washington's problems in 1777–78

Although Saratoga boosted American morale, the winter of 1777–78 was one of trial and tribulation for the patriots. Gates' victorious army disintegrated as his militiamen returned home. Meanwhile, what remained of Washington's army endured great privations in their Valley Forge encampment. The place lacked almost everything an army needs for survival – food, fuel and shelter. Over 3000 men died and many more deserted.

Even Washington's own position seemed in jeopardy. There is no evidence of an organised conspiracy against him – though he and his aides believed otherwise – but both in and out of Congress there was an undercurrent of criticism. Some feared that military dictatorship might result from what John Adams called 'the superstitious veneration that is sometimes paid to George Washington'. Others questioned his military abilities and contrasted his sorry record with that of Gates. Matters came to a head in November 1777 with the publication of a letter written to Gates by General Conway expressing the hope that Gates would replace 'the weak general'. Gates, if not the organiser of a plot against Washington as the latter believed, was certainly ready to intrigue against him. Washington survived. So did his army – just. Its numbers fell to a few thousand. But so long as the army endured, Washington prevented the British from controlling the Middle Colonies.

General Sir Henry Clinton, commander-in-chief in North America from 1778 to 1782. How effective was he?

By the spring of 1778 Washington's fortunes had begun to mend. The Continental Army had been increased and re-equipped. Von Steuben, a German soldier of fortune whose fortunes were low in 1778, ensured that the American soldiers were better trained. By 1778, Washington was surrounded by a number of foreign military 'experts', few of whom had any great expertise. The young Marquis of Lafayette was one of Washington's favourites. He made up in zeal what he lacked in military skill. More importantly, Washington had a small corps of battle-hardened American junior-grade officers, and NCOs and men who had been blooded in combat and toughened by strenuous toil.

Clinton's problems in 1778–79

In February 1778 Germain wrote to Howe accepting his resignation, offered in October 1777. Howe's replacement was General Henry Clinton. In March Germain told Clinton that the main British military effort was now to be directed against France by means of 'an immediate attack upon the French possessions in the West Indies'. Clinton was ordered to send 5000 troops for an expedition against St Lucia and another 3000 to reinforce the Floridas. He was also instructed to evacuate Philadelphia and concentrate his forces in New York.

Clinton set off for New York in mid-June 1778 with 10,000 soldiers and a twelve-mile-long baggage train. He moved slowly, taking five days to cover 48 km (30 miles). At Monmouth Court House on 28 June an American attack on the British rearguard failed. Washington blamed the failure on his second-in-command, General Charles Lee. Lee insisted on a court martial to vindicate his conduct. Washington, who disliked Lee, gladly complied. The court martial found Lee guilty of disobeying orders and he was suspended from command for one year.

Meanwhile Clinton's army reached New York without further hindrance. He arrived in New York not a moment too soon. On 11 July a French fleet under Admiral d'Estaing arrived off Sandy Hook. D'Estaing had sixteen ships of the line and also brought 4000

French troops. In July and August American and French forces besieged Newport. Although massively outnumbered, the 3000 British troops held out. D'Estaing then sailed to the West Indies.

British forces raided the New England coast in the autumn of 1778. Clinton also tried to bring Washington to battle by sending troops into New Jersey. But Washington would not be drawn. Clinton continued his efforts to force Washington to fight a major battle in 1779 – without success. Clinton, who feared that the French navy might attack New York, was cautious – probably over-cautious. Accordingly, the main British army in America did very little for much of the period 1778–81. Frustrated and depressed, Clinton twice offered his resignation: both times his requests were turned down. Disgruntled, he remained in command, claiming shortage of troops and neglect by the government. In July 1779 General Cornwallis arrived in New York to become second in command to Clinton. The two men did not get on.

The military task facing Britain in America was now formidable. However, Britain's position was by no means hopeless. She still held a number of coastal enclaves, had opportunities in the South (see below), retained Canada and Florida, was able to launch offensives into the interior and might yet defeat the main American army. It was still possible that the continued British presence and war-weariness on the part of the patriots would lead to an upsurge of loyalist support and to conciliation of a substantial part of America.

American problems: 1779–81

In 1779, Washington faced difficulties which prevented him from taking the offensive. His greatest problem was lack of troops. The French alliance persuaded some soldiers that the fighting could be left to others. Many deserted or refused to re-enlist. In reality, the French provided little direct help to the Americans in North America. Although a French army of 5000 troops under the Comte de Rochambeau landed at Newport in July 1780, it remained inactive for a year.

In 1780 Benedict Arnold, one of America's war heroes, resentful of real and imagined slights at the hands of Congress, plotted to turn over the fortress of West Point to Britain for £20,000. The plot miscarried when Clinton's emissary, Major Andre, was captured with incriminating evidence that revealed the plot. Andre was hanged as a spy but Arnold escaped to fight, with some success, for Britain.

In January 1781 the Pennsylvania Line regiment mutinied. The mutiny was the result of long-smouldering discontent with conditions of service. Food and clothing were inadequate and pay (months in arrears) lost value as the American currency depreciated. The mutineers, who met with representatives of Congress, refused to return to duty until they were promised redress of their grievances. The promise was given. The success of the Pennsylvania Line encouraged the New Jersey Line to mutiny. Washington stepped in to nip this second rising in the bud, executing some of the ringleaders. In February Massachusetts and New Jersey troops clashed in a serious riot at Princeton.

For much of 1781 the Continental Army was in no position to threaten Clinton or influence the outcome of the war elsewhere. It remained badly supplied and paid. This was largely due to the financial problems of Congress and the individual states. By 1781 most Americans, civilians and soldiers alike, were war-weary, particularly as there seemed no end in sight.

The war in the West

The War of Independence saw a racial conflict between whites and Indians. Most of the 100,000 or so Indians who lived south of the Great Lakes and east of the Mississippi River chose to fight alongside the British. Various tribes saw the war as an opportunity to drive the Americans back. The British hoped that the Indian threat might prevent the Western settlements from lending support to the rebels in the East: it might even force the rebels to divert precious troops and supplies to the West.

Key question
Why were the Americans successful in the West?

The South-west

American campaigns in the South-west soon brought the Cherokees to terms. In May 1777 the Indians ceded considerable territory. Thereafter the South-west frontier was relatively peaceful. The Chickamaugas and Chickasaws occasionally attacked Tennessee settlements but the frontiersmen were strong enough to defend themselves.

Kentucky and Illinois

In 1777 Indian attacks left only three forts under American control in (what became) Kentucky. Alarmed by reports that the British commander at Detroit, Colonel Hamilton, encouraged the Indians by offering to buy patriot scalps, Virginia sent out George Clark with 175 militia to seize British forts in the North-west, a region which since 1774 had been technically part of Québec. By the summer of 1778, Clark controlled the old French settlements of Kaskaskia and Cahokia and proclaimed the region part of Virginia (see Figure 3.4). In December 1778, Hamilton, with fewer than 100 men, struck back, occupying Vincennes. After an epic 320-km (200-mile) march, Clark captured Vincennes (and Hamilton himself) in February 1779.

In 1780, Britain mounted an ambitious campaign aimed at breaking Clark's hold on the Illinois country and Kentucky and also interrupting Spanish control of the Mississippi. One force of about 1000 men, mainly Indians, commanded by Captain Hesse, marched through Wisconsin and down the Mississippi. At the same time Colonel Bird, with a similar-sized force, marched south through Ohio country and Kentucky. Failing to capture the Spanish base at St Louis, Hesse was forced to retreat. Meanwhile Bird's Indian forces attacked settlements along the Licking River, slaughtering scores of Americans. Bird, realising he was losing control of the Indians, headed back to Detroit. In August 1780 Clark crossed the Ohio with 1000 men and defeated Shawnee Indians at the Battle of Piqua.

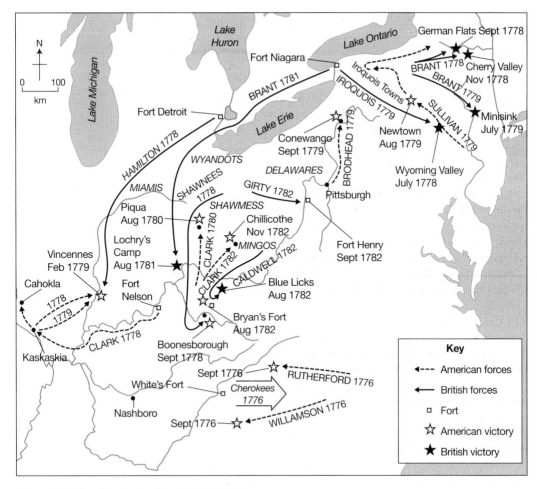

Figure 3.4: The War in the West, 1776–1779.

New York and Pennsylvania

Savage Iroquois raids on the western settlements of New York and Pennsylvania in 1778 persuaded Washington to send General Sullivan, with 2500 Continentals and several thousand New York militiamen to 'chastise' the Iroquois. On 29 August 1779 Sullivan routed a mixed force of Indians and loyalists at Newtown. The Indians retreated towards Niagara, leaving the Americans to wreak havoc on Indian settlements. Sullivan, however, was unable to take Niagara. In October 1781 1200 Indians and British troops raided American settlements in the Mohawk Valley. American forces defeated them at the Battle of Jonson (25 October) – the last major engagement of the war on the New York frontier.

The Indian impact

State governments kept up a constant pressure for assistance against Indian attack. However, the Indians were a mixed blessing as far as Britain was concerned.

- They were unreliable.
- They were divided.
- Savage Indian attacks antagonised neutrals and loyalists.

The Southern phase

In 1778 Britain decided to mount a campaign in the South where there were reputed to be large numbers of loyalists. The hope was to take control of Georgia and the Carolinas and then to advance northwards, reclaiming the colonies one by one.

Key question
How successful were the British in the Southern colonies?

Georgia

In late 1778 Clinton sent a 3000-strong expedition under Lieutenant-Colonel Archibald Campbell to Georgia, a thinly populated colony. In December Campbell captured Savannah, losing only three dead and taking over 500 American prisoners. Augusta fell in January 1779 and the rest of Georgia soon followed. Unlike many British officers, Campbell recognised the importance of winning the loyalty of Americans. He thus prohibited his troops from ill-treating the Georgians who responded by flocking to join a newly organised loyalist militia. In March 1779, the British defeated patriot forces at Briar Creek. The Americans lost 400 casualties and all but 450 of the survivors went home rather than rejoining General Lincoln's army in South Carolina.

Nevertheless, the British position in Georgia remained precarious. The 4000 white males of military age seem to have

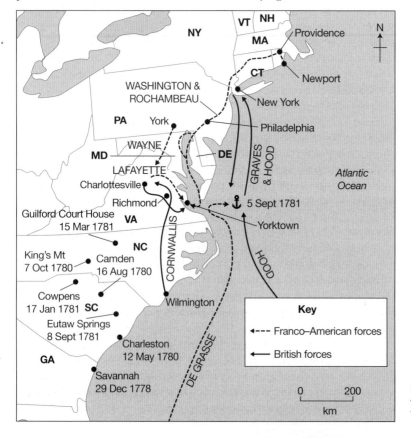

Figure 3.5: The war in the South and Yorktown.

been divided equally between loyalists and patriots. General Lincoln's forces still outnumbered those of the British. In September 1779, Admiral d'Estaing returned from the West Indies and anchored off the coast of Georgia. While the hurricane season lasted, he was prepared to co-operate with the Americans. Thus, a combined Franco–American force besieged Savannah. After a bloody battle which cost the attackers over 1500 casualties, the siege collapsed in mid-October. D'Estaing sailed away and Lincoln returned to Charleston.

South Carolina

On 26 December 1779 Clinton sailed from New York with 7600 men. His objective was Charleston, the largest town in the Southern colonies. After encountering a terrible storm, the dispersed British ships were forced to put in at Savannah for repair. Not until February 1780 did the siege of Charleston begin. Given its poor fortifications, Lincoln would have been best abandoning the city. However, he was under considerable political pressure to defend it. After a long siege Lincoln surrendered on 12 May. The British took 5000 American prisoners, 343 artillery pieces, 6000 muskets and 376 barrels of gunpowder. For the Americans this was the worst military disaster of the war.

The British were now able to move into the interior of South Carolina. On 29 May Colonel Banastre Tarleton and 300 dragoons defeated 350 Virginians at Waxhaw Creek. Tarleton's men butchered many of the Virginians even after they had tried to surrender. Tarleton's message was clear: 'If warfare allows me I shall give no quarter.' The atrocity called for vengeance. 'Tarleton's quarter' – that is, take no prisoners – became a rallying cry of American troops in the South. The fighting in the Carolinas was thus far more savage than elsewhere in America.

For a time it seemed that South Carolina had been brought under British control. The state government fled. Many patriots, believing the war was lost, took an oath of allegiance to the Crown. Clinton, fearing a French–American attack on New York, returned north, leaving Cornwallis in command of 4000 men in the South. Just before departing, Clinton issued a proclamation which helped to undermine British authority in the South. He required that all adult males should openly support the British or be treated as rebels. Accordingly, quiet neutrality was impossible: neutrals were forced to choose sides. Many Carolinians, while ready to take an oath of allegiance to Britain, were not prepared to fight against their former compatriots.

Nevertheless, initially the coastal communities of South Carolina gave Cornwallis no trouble. Most lowlanders took oaths of loyalty and joined loyalist militias. At the end of June Cornwallis reported that rebel resistance in South Carolina and Georgia had ended. However, while Britain controlled the coastal areas, the interior of the Carolinas was another matter. The people of this area, soured in the aftermath of the Regulator movement, had not been enthusiastic about revolution in 1775–76. But nor was the

General Charles Cornwallis. To what extent was Cornwallis responsible for British failure at Yorktown?

backcountry united for the king: it was divided against both itself and the Tidewater. Ethnic rivalries, especially Scots-Irish versus German, pre-dated the War of Independence. When the Germans expressed their loyalty to Britain, the Scots-Irish gravitated towards the patriots. An anticipated British attack on North Carolina stirred a ferocious war between loyalists and patriots during the summer of 1780. Loyalist forces were beaten at Ramsour's Mill (20 June), Williamson's Plantation (12 July), Flat Rock (20 July) and Thicketty Fort (30 July).

In August Horatio Gates, now the commander of Continental forces in the South, led an army of over 3000 men into South Carolina, hoping to defeat Cornwallis. On 16 August Gates was beaten at Camden by a 2000-strong British force. His army sustained 1800 casualties while British losses were just over 300. It was, as Cornwallis reported, 'a most complete victory', totally destroying Gates' military reputation and opening the way for a British invasion of North Carolina. On 18 August Tarleton's dragoons defeated patriot militia at Fishing Creek, inflicting over 500 casualties on the Americans. British casualties were 22.

North Carolina

Cornwallis began his invasion of North Carolina in early September. Although Gates' army at Hillsboro was in no condition to fight, patriot militia harassed British foraging parties. To make matters worse, as soon as Cornwallis advanced into North Carolina, South Carolina rose behind him. On 7 October a 1000-strong loyalist force was wiped out by patriots at King's Mountain. Cornwallis, abandoning his invasion of North Carolina, retreated south.

Over the winter of 1780–81 patriot and loyalist militias turned the backcountry regions of Georgia and the Carolinas into a wasteland of slaughter and plunder in which both sides routinely committed atrocities, torturing prisoners and hanging enemies without trial. Protecting loyalist areas proved a major problem for Britain. Cornwallis, short of men, was dependent on loyalists to make up numbers for his field army. The loyalists themselves, however, were greatly dependent on British military support.

General Nathanael Greene

In late 1780 General Nathanael Greene, a Rhode Island Quaker who had proved one of Washington's most loyal lieutenants, took command of the Continental Army in the South. Rather than risk his troops in major battles, Greene decided to divide his forces and rely on hit and run attacks, supported by patriot militia, hoping this would sap British strength. Thus he sent 700 men under Daniel Morgan to probe British defences in the South Carolina backcountry. Another group was sent to co-operate with militia in attacks on the British positions along the coast. The rest of the army stayed with Greene. While Greene has often been praised for his military skill, he lost every battle he fought in the South, despite enjoying significant numerical advantage and some able subordinates, like Daniel Morgan.

On 17 January 1781 Tarleton's hated British Legion was defeated at Cowpens by Morgan. Undeterred, Cornwallis determined to drive Greene out of North Carolina. On 15 March Greene and Cornwallis' forces came to blows at Guilford Court House. Outnumbered by more than two to one, Cornwallis won a costly victory – losing over 500 men – twenty-five per cent of his force. Cornwallis' army needed time to recuperate. Meanwhile, Greene decided to march into South Carolina. On 25 April Lord Rawdon, left in command in South Carolina, defeated Greene at Hobkirk's Hill. However, he was unable to follow up his victory and patriot forces continued capturing scattered British outposts. By mid-1781 only Charleston, Savannah and the remote Fort Ninety-Six remained in British hands in South Carolina and Georgia.

Virginia

In April Cornwallis, rather than return to South Carolina to deal with the threat from Greene, headed north towards Virginia. His force, less than 1500 strong, reached Petersburg on 20 May. Until 1780 Virginia had largely escaped the ravages of war. However, over the winter of 1780–81 Benedict Arnold had led a series of raids into the state, inflicting major physical damage. In March General Phillips had arrived in Virginia with 2000 more men. Cornwallis' junction with the British forces already in Virginia gave him command of an army of more than 7000 men.

The British presence in Virginia disrupted the state's ability to wage war and also led to several counties proclaiming support for Britain. However, most Virginians were committed to driving out the British. Having failed to destroy an American detachment led by Lafayette, Cornwallis moved towards the sea to maintain communications with Clinton in New York. In August he began to construct a base at Yorktown. If his army could be supplied by the Royal Navy it would be invincible and could cause mayhem. The success of this strategy depended on the Royal Navy retaining control of Chesapeake Bay. Clinton assured Cornwallis that he did not think there was any chance of the French 'having a naval superiority in these seas for any length of time, much less for so long a one as two or three months'. Unfortunately for the British a French fleet commanded by Admiral de Grasse, which had left Brest with twenty ships of the line in March, now appeared in American waters. Clinton, more fearful of an attack on New York than one on Cornwallis, failed to consider the prospect of the latter sufficiently seriously.

Yorktown

In May 1781 Washington learned that de Grasse's fleet was on its way. Washington had initially hoped to use the French army of Rochambeau and the fleets of Admiral Comte de Barras at Newport and de Grasse's larger force to attack New York. But Rochambeau persuaded him that Cornwallis was a better target.

In a rapidly executed and perfectly timed operation, for which Washington deserves much credit, the combined French–American army, 16,000 strong, reached Virginia in early September, confronting Cornwallis with a force twice the size of his own and trapping him on the Yorktown peninsula. The repulse of a British fleet on 5 September gave the French vital control of Chesapeake Bay. For a fortnight, Cornwallis was amazingly passive. In fairness, he expected that Clinton would send another fleet to either reinforce him or transport his army away. Delay in dispatching a relief expedition from New York sealed Cornwallis' fate. By October, his army at Yorktown, in a weakly fortified position and short of supplies, was trapped. On 19 October 1781, after a three-week siege, Cornwallis and his army of 7200 soldiers and 804 seamen surrendered. The British troops marched out of their positions to the tune of 'The World Turned Upside Down'.

On the morning of Cornwallis' surrender, Clinton sailed from New York with a relief force of 7000 men, conveyed by Admiral Graves' reinforced fleet. The British force arrived off Chesapeake Bay on 24 October, five days too late. Learning of Cornwallis' surrender, Clinton and Graves returned to New York.

The news of Cornwallis' surrender came as a total shock to most Britons. When North heard the news, he said, 'Oh God, it is all over.'

The results of Yorktown

In military terms, Cornwallis' surrender need not have been decisive. Britain still controlled New York, Charleston and Savannah and still had over 30,000 troops in America. The immediate aftermath of Yorktown did not see the collapse of the British position in America. American and French forces failed to co-operate in an attack on Charleston as Washington hoped. Instead, in November de Grasse sailed for the West Indies. Without French naval support the Americans could achieve very little. There was still widespread loyalism in the South and guerrilla activity by both sides continued throughout 1782. However, Yorktown was unquestionably a crucial victory. After Cornwallis' surrender the British government discontinued offensive operations in America and it was clear that the British public was sceptical about continuing the war.

Key date

British surrendered at Yorktown: 1781

Summary diagram: The war in North America: 1778–81

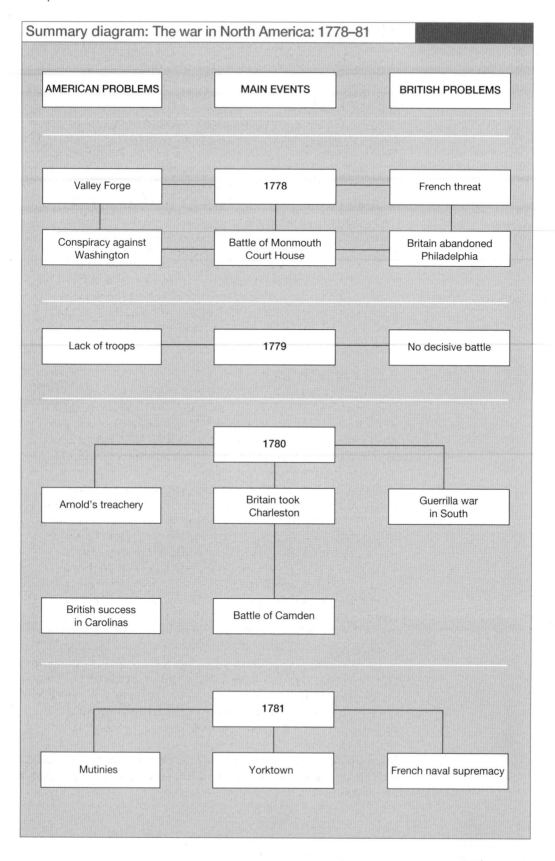

AMERICAN PROBLEMS	MAIN EVENTS	BRITISH PROBLEMS
Valley Forge	1778	French threat
Conspiracy against Washington	Battle of Monmouth Court House	Britain abandoned Philadelphia
Lack of troops	1779	No decisive battle
	1780	
Arnold's treachery	Britain took Charleston	Guerrilla war in South
British success in Carolinas	Battle of Camden	
	1781	
Mutinies	Yorktown	French naval supremacy

Key question

How successful were the Americans at peacemaking?

5 | Peacemaking

After Yorktown British opinion was ready to concede America independence.

The end of North

Although North had won a solid victory in the September 1780 general election, after Yorktown he faced increasing pressure from MPs who wanted to end the war. On 7 February 1782 North's majority fell to only 22 on a motion of censure. Germain resigned as colonial secretary on 10 February. On 27 February the Commons, to George III's chagrin, resolved to end military measures against the Americans. On 20 March North finally resigned. He was replaced by the Marquis of Rockingham. The Earl of Shelburne, who became colonial secretary, favoured peace. In April the new ministry ordered the evacuation of New York, Charleston and Savannah. (Savannah was evacuated in July 1782 but, because of the administrative and logistical problems involved, Charleston and New York were not evacuated until December 1782 and November 1783 respectively.) On Rockingham's death in July 1782, Shelburne became prime minister.

Key date

Resignation of Lord North: 1782

Peace negotiations

American representatives entered into informal talks with British officials in Paris in April 1782, months before the formal peace negotiations began in September. By now France was also keen on peace. The British Navy again ruled the waves, French finances were in a hopeless mess and the French government was concerned by the growing Russian threat in eastern Europe.

Shelburne, hoping to separate France and the USA, was prepared to be generous to the Americans. While John Jay and John Adams, the leaders of the American peace delegation, were suspicious of British motives, they also distrusted the French, suspecting – with good reason – that French Foreign Minister Vergennes was ready to support the Spanish claim to the trans-Allegheny region on which the US had set its heart. Without consulting either Franklin or the French, Jay and Adams opened separate discussions with Britain. After protracted negotiations, the American commissioners signed a preliminary peace treaty with Britain on 30 November 1782.

But for their almost paranoid suspicions of Franklin, Shelburne and Vergennes, Jay and Adams might have achieved an even better treaty: one which would have given the USA even more territory. Vergennes reproved their commissioners for going behind his back but accepted the outcome without undue protest. The terms of the treaty were accepted provisionally on 20 January 1783. Britain proclaimed an end of hostilities on 4 February. The Treaty of Paris was signed by Britain, the USA, France, Spain and Holland on 3 September 1783.

The Treaty of Paris

By the terms of the Treaty:

Peace of Paris: 1783

Key date

- Britain recognised American independence and agreed that the boundaries of the USA should extend west to the Mississippi River, north to the St Lawrence River and the Great Lakes and south to the 31st parallel, the northern boundary of Florida.
- The Americans were granted the 'liberty' to fish the Newfoundland Banks and to dry and cure fish in Nova Scotia and Labrador.
- The USA agreed that British merchants should meet with 'no lawful impediment' in seeking to recover their pre-war American debts and that Congress should 'earnestly recommend' to the states the restoration of confiscated loyalist property.
- Britain ceded Florida and Minorca to Spain.
- Britain regained the Bahamas.
- France regained St Lucia, Goree and Pondicherry and retained Tobago.
- Britain returned Trincomalee to Holland but retained Negapatam in India and won the right to navigate in the Dutch East Indies.

For the Americans the settlement was a major triumph. Especially surprising was Britain's willingness to concede the Mississippi River boundary. In 1783 the British still controlled most of the trans-Appalachian West. But Shelburne considered this and other sacrifices to be worthwhile. He hoped that a generous peace might lay the foundation for an Anglo–American commercial alliance and eventually even some form of political reunion. No one doubted that the loss of the American colonies was a disaster for Britain. Nevertheless, she had retained Canada, saved most of her West Indian possessions and strengthened her hold in India.

Summary diagram: Peacemaking

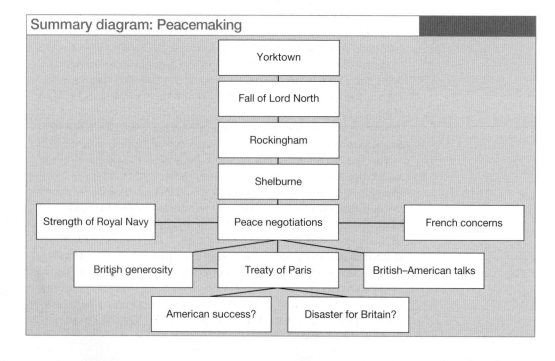

6 | The Key Debate

Did the British lose, or the Americans win, the War of Independence?

British failure

Britain was never going to find it easy to fight a war in America. However, the British did themselves no favours. In particular, British leaders made some important miscalculations early in the war. These included the assumption that the rebellion was localised and the overestimation of loyalist support. Better British diplomacy in the 1770s might have ensured that France and Spain thought twice about entering the war.

Much criticism has been directed both at individual commanders and the general calibre of British generalship. Howe was far too cautious. 'He is as valiant as my sword,' said a Hessian officer, 'but no more of a general than my arse.' He can be blamed for missing several opportunities to destroy Washington's army in 1776–77. Clinton was equally slow and timid. Alongside criticisms of cautious generalship, there are charges of over-confidence. Burgoyne was foolish to push on towards Albany in 1777. Cornwallis' invasion of Virginia in 1781 may not have been wise. British officers – military and naval – did not co-operate particularly well. British admirals, as well as British generals, can be criticised for unimaginative leadership. Admiral Rodney must bear much of the blame for Yorktown because of his failure to send sufficient ships from the Caribbean.

It may be that the government at home failed to direct and energise its generals. North was not a particularly impressive war leader. However, he did retain the support of Parliament for most of the war and did appoint some able men – not least Germain and Lord Sandwich – to key positions. Germain and Sandwich had no option but to leave much to the discretion of the generals and admirals. The main mistakes were made in America, not in London.

Arguably the employment of 30,000 Hessians was unwise. As well as alienating Americans, some historians claim they were not totally committed to the British cause. During the war some 5000 Hessians deserted. However, Britain would have found it hard to have waged war without the Hessians who provided over a third of British strength in America by 1778. Most of those who deserted did so after 1781 when the war was already lost.

Having failed to nip the rebellion in the bud in 1775–76 the British were unsuccessful in gaining local support. Indeed, they frequently offended neutral opinion or let down the loyalists. While both armies often behaved badly towards civilians, the British were notably worse. More importantly, British generals found it impossible to provide adequate protection for their supporters. The British had a bad habit of moving into an area, rallying loyalist support and then leaving their supporters in the lurch. If they ever had a chance of holding a population loyal to the king they squandered it by neglecting the Southern colonies from 1776 until 1779.

American success

American success was not just the result of British failure: it owed something to the Americans themselves. Most Americans were committed to the 'glorious cause'. Some 200,000 men fought at some time or another in Continental or militia armies. American deaths in battle amounted to nearly 8000 but some 25,000 also died in service as a result of disease and wounds. (This was 0.9 per cent of the population, compared with 0.28 per cent for the Second World War.) While the British army captured important towns and won most pitched battles, this success did not subdue the population. Whenever the British army moved out of an area, the people invariably reverted to the patriot cause.

George Washington's contribution to American victory was important. He had a difficult job. For most of the war the Continental Army was short of everything – men as well as supplies. During the course of the war at least one-third of the army deserted. But Washington kept it in being and improved its quality. The army was his creation. For many Americans his army *was* America. He could not risk losing it. His strategy was thus inevitably defensive, even though there was little glory to be won in a policy of retreat. He did not like the defensive war he had to fight but realised the necessity of fighting it. He had – and has – his critics. He was certainly no military genius and never defeated the main British army in the open. He tended to make plans beyond the capacities of his army and also chose some bad locations to give battle. Insecure, vain and ambitious, he sometimes permitted personal jealousies and emotional weaknesses to intrude on his tactical, strategic and personnel considerations.

But Washington's strengths outweigh his failures. Dealing with a host of state officials and Congress required enormous skill and tact. His attack on Trenton in 1776 showed efficiency and daring and the march to Yorktown in 1781 was a superb achievement. His career was the triumph not of intellect, but of character and courage. He displayed integrity and dedication, as well as a remarkable capacity for survival. Perhaps his greatest achievement was to soldier on and keep his army in being through a long succession of dark days. In the end to survive was to triumph.

There were a (limited) number of other reasonably talented American officers. Benedict Arnold was probably the best (before he deserted to the British).

The Continental Army became a reasonable fighting force. Its troops showed a steadiness under fire and demonstrated a brave endurance. Short of pay and supplies, the men withstood sufferings and privations, particularly at Valley Forge over the winter of 1777–78. While Washington held them in contempt, the militia units served a useful purpose. The ability of the militia to control most of the country not actually occupied by the British gave the Americans a huge advantage.

American success, Yorktown apart, owed more to American military achievement than to France. D'Estaing gave no effective help to Washington in 1778 and apart from an unsuccessful appearance off Savannah in 1779, no French fleet operated in American waters until 1781. France put only 9000 troops into America – of whom 3000 landed from Grasse's ships in 1781.

American diplomats – Franklin, Jay and Adams – turned European rivalries to America's advantage and produced a series of diplomatic victories, starting with the French alliance of 1778 and ending with the Treaty of Paris in 1783. The skill of Philadelphia merchant Robert Morris in seeking out arms and gunpowder from Europe was important in the early years of the war. No congressman played a more important role than John Adams in ensuring that, as he later remarked, the 'thirteen clocks were made to strike together'.

It is possible to claim that the outcome of the war was determined neither by British mistakes nor American prowess. The entry of France and Spain swung the struggle decisively in America's favour. The reallocation of British military and naval resources, caused by the broadening of the conflict, had important implications for the American war. France and Spain joined the war because they had old scores to settle with Britain, not because of brilliant American diplomacy.

Conclusion

Ultimately, the war was lost by the British rather than won by the Americans, and it was lost to the American landscape as much as to the Americans. All the British generals had to wage war in a difficult country with poor communications. Even if they had destroyed the Continental Army and occupied all thirteen colonial capitals, the British army would still have had to control a widely scattered and hostile population. Nevertheless, British defeat was not inevitable. If North had sent more troops to America earlier in the war, or if Howe had been less cautious, British forces might have won a decisive victory which could have been fatal to the patriot cause.

The British army, often against the odds, won virtually every major battle in the war. But it was unable to deliver a knock-out blow. Once France joined the war, it became less likely that Britain would conquer all the areas in rebellion. However, that did not mean that the success the Americans achieved in 1783 was inevitable. Cornwallis' surrender at Yorktown, which tipped the scales in favour of a peace settlement, was something of a fluke. It occurred after the sole significant French victory over the Royal Navy since 1690. If Yorktown had not occurred, it is hard to predict what would have happened. By 1782 Britain was better able to wage war than her European enemies. Before Yorktown a compromise peace between Britain and America was a real possibility. After Yorktown Britain had had enough of the American war. The Americans had won the war by not abandoning the struggle.

Some key books in the debate:
Jeremy Black, *War for America: The Fight for Independence 1775–1783*, Sutton, 1991.
Stephen Conway, *The War of American Independence*, Edward Arnold, 1995.
John E. Ferling, *Almost a Miracle: The American Victory in the War of Independence*, OUP, 2007.
Samuel B. Griffiths, *The War for American Independence: From 1760 to the Surrender at Yorktown in 1781*, University of Illinois, 2002.
Piers Mackesy, *The War for America, 1775–1783*, Harvard University Press, 1964.
Brendan Simms, *Three Victories and a Defeat: The Rise and Fall of the First British Empire, 1714–1783*, Allen Lane, 2007.

Study Guide: AS Questions

In the style of AQA

(a) Explain why the British were unsuccessful at the Battle of Saratoga in 1777. (12 marks)

(b) 'It was French and Spanish intervention that ensured American success in the War of Independence between 1778 and 1783.' Explain why you agree or disagree with this view. (24 marks)

Exam tips

(a) This question requires you to think of a range of reasons for British failure. You will need to consider Burgoyne's own inadequacies and the repeated failures of his campaign, but avoid falling into the trap of simply describing events. Instead, pick out issues such as speed, support, problems with supporting forces, e.g. Clinton, and even 'bad luck'. You should also comment on the role of others such as Howe and Germain, and don't forget American strengths, e.g. the parts played by Arnold and Gates and the effect on Americans of Burgoyne's Indian allies.

(b) The focus of this question is the reason for American success in the War of Independence. You will need to assess the importance of French and Spanish intervention, but you should balance this against other factors. Intervention, of course, meant that Britain had to face threats across the globe. It reduced Britain's ability to concentrate military resources on America and provided the colonists with arms, material and money. Britain also had to prepare for home defence.

On the other hand, the war with France was not solely aimed at helping the Americans and they put few troops into America, while the Spaniards merely wanted to regain lost possessions from Britain, rather than help colonists gain independence. British military miscalculations, the failures of individual generals, the lack of government direction, the British use of the Hessians and the behaviour of British supporters are all of relevance to the American success. A balanced answer should also take into account the Americans' own strengths – their commitment and military advantages combined with the contribution of George Washington. You will have to judge whether the contribution of France and Spain was the final element which swung the war in America's favour, but whatever your view, do ensure you argue throughout your answer and end with a well supported conclusion.

In the style of Edexcel

How accurate is it to say that the Americans won the War of Independence because their soldiers were better led? (30 marks)

Exam tips

The cross references are intended to take you straight to the material that will help you to answer the question.

Essentially the question is asking you to explain why the Americans won the war. You will need to organise your answer to make sure that you do concentrate a substantial part of it on whether the British military leadership was less effective than American military leadership, but you must also consider the range of other factors which led to the British defeat. Be careful not to get involved in a detailed narrative of the course of the war. Identify instead the key factors which explain the outcome of the war, and then refer to key situations and events only to support the points you wish to make. Note that the British should really have won the military conflict (pages 90–91), so its failure to do so needs explanation.

Since you will only have about 35 minutes to write your answer after you have planned what factors and events you will deal with, five clear points should be enough.

For example, you could consider:

- crucial misjudgements by British military leaders: Philadelphia, Saratoga and Yorktown (pages 98–107, 121–23)
- Washington's role (page 102) – but note the limitations of this (page 128) as well as its significance
- the Americans' advantage contrasted with the difficulties for the British of distance and terrain (pages 92–93, 128)
- misjudgements by the British authorities (pages 92–93, 127)
- the effects of foreign intervention; diverting British energies and strengthening American campaigns (pages 110–112, 128).

You must reach an overall conclusion. How important were the misjudgements of the British military leaders?

4

The Results of the War of Independence

POINTS TO CONSIDER

The American War of Independence is also called the American Revolution. Like any long war, it had significant consequences, not least the creation of the USA. But did those consequences amount to a revolution? This chapter will examine the results of the war, not least the notion of an American Revolution, by focusing on the following themes:

• Political developments within the states
• The national government
• The social impact of the war on America
• The economic impact of the war on America
• The impact of the war on Britain, France and Spain

Key dates

1776	Virginian Declaration of Rights
1777	Formation of Vermont
1777	Vermont abolished slavery
1780	Pennsylvania abolished slavery
1781	Articles of Confederation ratified

1 | Political Developments within the States

Key question
How much of a political revolution occurred in the thirteen states that made up the USA?

Arguably, the American rebels had not intended revolution. 'I say again,' said John Adams, 'that resistance to innovation and to unlimited claims of Parliament, and not any new form of government, was the object of the revolution.' Whatever the intent, Adams clearly thought that revolution was the result. In political terms, revolution usually means rapid, fundamental change as one set of power relationships and institutions collapses and another takes its place. Did this occur in the American colonies?

Republicanism

The political controversy between Britain and the colonies produced a political philosophy at the centre of which was a belief in the rights of man. Human liberty, in this conception, was derived from natural rights, not the British Constitution. At the heart of the new philosophy was republicanism. Tom Paine's *Common Sense* gave the terms republican and republicanism wide currency in America. He defined the word republic as 'the public good or the good of the whole'. In Paine's view, rule by nobility, oligarchy or faction was no more compatible with republicanism than rule by a king. The idea of republicanism was not yet interchangeable with the idea of democracy but it did imply a form of government which represented the whole people. Republicanism, essentially, was government by the consent of the governed.

In many ways America was well suited to republicanism. By 1763 the colonial legislatures had substantial power and most white men could vote. Colonial politics became even more democratic in the 1760s and 1770s. As the gentry passed resolutions against British tyranny in the colonial and provincial assemblies, men of lesser rank took to the streets to intimidate stamp distributors and royal officials. The Sons of Liberty (see Chapter 2, pages 45–46) contained many artisans, tradesmen and small merchants and helped to raise the political consciousness of Americans generally. The committees of correspondence, county meetings and committees of safety which spread across the colonies in 1774–75 brought many new men into politics.

Once allegiance to the Crown was repudiated republicanism became the only acceptable system of political values, providing philosophical underpinning and offering legitimacy for government and authority. Application of republican principles rested on the central proposition of popular sovereignty. In the words of the Virginia Declaration of Rights: 'All power is vested in, and consequently derived from, the people … magistrates are their trustees and servants, and at all times amenable to them.'

After 1775 Americans grappled with the implications of republicanism. What form should a republican government take? What rights should a republican government guarantee? Who should have the right to vote and hold office?

The transition from colonies to states

The political transition from colony to statehood was gradual. As British authority collapsed in 1774–75, most colonial assemblies reconstituted themselves as provincial conventions. To establish a legal foundation for these makeshift governments seemed an urgent necessity to American leaders who were deeply concerned for the rule of law and who feared the spread of civil disorder.

Congress dithered in 1775 when asked whether it would recommend colonies (soon to be states) drawing up new constitutions. Some states changed their constitutions before Congress decided. However, on 10 May 1776, Congress adopted a resolution by John Adams calling on all states that did not have a permanent constitution based on popular sovereignty to adopt one. Congress discussed the possibility of drafting a uniform model constitution, but Adams' view that each state should be entitled to draft its own constitution prevailed.

Between 1776 and 1780 all the states but two adopted new constitutions. (The exceptions were Rhode Island and Connecticut which merely revised their colonial charters, deleting all reference to royal authority.) The new constitutions embodied the principles of republicanism. That these principles were contested is reflected in the different constitutional arrangements adopted by the various states. Each state constitution reflected the balance of political power at the time of its writing, as well as an honest attempt by men of good faith to find the best way forward. Given the imperatives of the war, Americans wanted effective government. But they were also concerned about the dangers of excessive authority, as demonstrated by the British government which they had convinced themselves was conspiring to destroy their liberty.

Elitists v democrats

After 1775–76 the struggle about home rule was transformed into one about who should rule at home. Americans had to decide what type of government the new states should have and who should be allowed to vote and hold office. These issues were debated in newspapers, pamphlets, legislative chambers, committee rooms, pubs and homes. Broadly speaking, Americans divided into two camps – elitists and democrats.

The elitists were often men who had led the old colonial assemblies. They felt that while governments should maintain liberty, they must also preserve order. They feared that too much democracy might generate unstable governments which would result in anarchy. They thus sought to design republics in which the people would exercise their sovereignty by choosing the best men to govern and then standing aside to let them do so. They sought to create governments along the lines of the former colonial system, whereby:

- the franchise would be limited to property holders
- there would be (high) property qualifications for office holding
- the right to vote would be exercised relatively infrequently
- there would be a two-housed (bicameral) legislature, one representing the people and the other the elite
- governors would have wide powers.

The democrats were often men from humble backgrounds who had been politicised by their involvement in the resistance to Britain. Believing that ordinary Americans were capable of self-government, they sought to democratise the new governments. They thus tended to favour:

- a broad franchise (although no one advocated extending the **suffrage** to slaves or women)

Key term

Suffrage
The right to vote.

- no – or low – property qualifications for holding office
- frequent elections
- one-housed (unicameral) legislatures: they felt there was no need for an aristocratic second chamber
- a weak **executive**.

The state constitutions

Key question
What were the main features of the new constitutions?

Most of the new state constitutions were drawn up and put into effect by state legislatures without specific authorisation from the electorate. A few were the work of specially elected conventions. Massachusetts did most to ensure that its constitution had the explicit consent of the governed (see below). While varying in detail, the constitutions resembled each other in many respects and were broadly patterned on the colonial model:

- All the constitutions agreed that **sovereignty** ultimately resided with the people.
- All were concerned about the **separation of powers**. Virginia was the first state to spell out explicitly the proposition that 'the legislative, executive and judiciary departments shall be separate and distinct'.
- The usual provision was for a legislature consisting of two houses. (The only exceptions were Pennsylvania and Georgia.) The lower house was seen as directly representing the people. The upper house (or Senate) was seen as representing 'gentlemen'.
- All the original thirteen states required property ownership or payment of taxes to vote. Vermont (not admitted until 1791) was the only state to have universal manhood suffrage. However, property qualifications for voting were generally low. In most states over two-thirds of white men over the age of 21 had the right to vote. In some states, higher property qualifications were needed to vote for members of the Senate.
- Qualifications for office holding remained much the same as under the colonial governments.
- Every state (except Pennsylvania) had a single executive head – the governor – who was usually chosen by the legislature. The deep suspicion of executive authority (one of the legacies of the colonial past) resulted in governors being denied, initially at least, many of the powers enjoyed by their royal predecessors. Eleven states, including Vermont, set one-year terms for governors and most governors were little more than figureheads. Only in Massachusetts and New York were the governors given the power to veto legislation.

Government limitations

Although most constitutions affirmed the principle of the separation of powers, authority was in practice largely concentrated in the legislatures – particularly the lower houses. But the power of the legislatures was limited, first by the (usual) requirement to hold annual elections and second by the inclusion in most constitutions

Key terms

Executive
The power or authority in government that carries the law into effect: a person (or persons) who administer(s) the government.

Sovereignty
Ultimate power.

Separation of powers
A system of government in which the power is shared between the legislative, the executive and the judiciary, ensuring the government is not too strong.

Key date

Virginian Declaration of Rights: 1776

of declarations (or bills) of rights. The Virginia Declaration of Rights, written mainly by George Mason in 1776, provided the model. It enumerated those fundamental English liberties which Americans had come to regard as their own: freedom of expression, worship and assembly, the subordination of military to civil power, the right to jury trial, protection against cruel and unusual punishments and guarantees against self-incrimination, against arrest without knowing one's accuser and against search warrants. The written constitutions thus set out not only the powers of the governments but also their limits.

It is worth considering the way that two states – Pennsylvania and Massachusetts – drew up their constitutions.

The Pennsylvania constitution

By 1775 those who formed the social and political elite of Pennsylvania were divided. Some, like Joseph Galloway, became loyalists. The moderates, whose leaders included John Dickinson, Robert Morris and James Wilson, devoted much of their attention to continental rather than state matters. Accordingly, Pennsylvania's divided elite was swept aside by radicals. In June 1776 the radicals called for a special convention to draft a new state constitution. Traditional property requirements for voting were waived, benefiting the previously under-represented frontier areas.

The Pennsylvania constitutional convention, consisting of 96 delegates (including Benjamin Franklin), sat from July until September 1776. Those who drafted the constitution, and later defended it, tended to be Scots-Irish Presbyterians, men of moderate economic status, and residents of the northern and western parts of the state. The resulting document was the most radical experiment in republican government to emerge from the Revolution:

- Legislative powers were vested in a single assembly.
- The assembly was to be elected annually by all taxpayers over the age of 21.
- All voters were entitled to stand for office.
- Instead of a governor there was to be an elected twelve-member executive council.

Implementation of such a democratic constitution brought about drastic changes. After 1776, the men entering power came from a lower stratum of society than their predecessors. Not surprisingly, this provoked opposition. In 1779, conservatives founded a Republican Society with the object of repealing the Constitution. For the next decade Pennsylvanian politics were dominated by the struggle between Constitutionalists and Republicans.

The Massachusetts constitution

In June 1775 the Massachusetts provincial assembly adopted the colony's 1691 charter with minor modifications as a temporary frame of government. The first effort to draft a more permanent constitution was rejected by the Massachusetts voters in 1778, mainly because it lacked a bill of rights and had been drafted by the assembly and not by a specially elected convention. In 1779 the assembly called for elections to a special constitutional convention to which delegates would be sent from every town. This convention, with 300 delegates, met in September 1779. The resulting document, largely the work of John Adams, closely resembled the previous colonial system:

- There was to be a bicameral legislature.
- The legislators were to be elected by males over 21 who earned £3 per year in freehold property or had £60 in total property.
- Senators were required to have £600 total property and representatives £200.
- The governor, elected to a four-year term, had extensive powers, including the right to veto legislation.

In March 1770 the constitution was sent to the towns for ratification. In June the convention declared that it had been approved. Paradoxically, the far from democratic constitution was arrived at by – apparently – very democratic means. In reality, the towns rejected the document: the convention, desperate to establish a permanent government, juggled the figures so it could declare ratification. Despite the final 'fixing', the Massachusetts process helped to establish the principle that the 'sovereign' people should have a role both in drafting and in ratifying constitutions.

Elite v new men

In most states the new arrangements were hardly models of democracy. The new constitutions reflected the eighteenth-century belief that political rights should be confined to property holders. A man without property, it was held, was not sufficiently independent to be entrusted with political power. Property qualifications restricted the electorate in virtually every state and, for office holding, were sometimes so high as to exclude all but the really wealthy. In some states, for example South Carolina, Maryland and Virginia, the elites retained their power. In Virginia, a core of about 40 major families continued to provide the state's leaders.

Nevertheless, the suffrage, already extensive in America pre-1775, was widened further as nearly all states reduced property qualifications for voting. Thus, most state governments became more responsive to popular opinion. The departure of many loyalist office holders created vacancies for new men – often of modest means. This trend was accentuated by the temporary absence of many patriot leaders in Congress, the army and the diplomatic service. The enlargement of the legislatures and the better representation in them of frontier districts also led to a change of personnel.

According to historian Jackson Turner Main, the state legislatures after 1775 were significantly different from those before it. Pre-1775 the voters overwhelmingly selected their

Key question
To what extent were the states democratic?

representatives from among the rich. By 1783 the proportion of the wealthy in the legislatures had dropped from forty-six to twenty-two per cent. Members of the old elite families had declined by more than half. Pre-1775 small farmers and artisans had accounted for only about a fifth of the members of the colonial assemblies: afterwards they constituted a majority in some Northern legislatures and a sizeable minority in the South. While the wealthy and well educated continued to dominate American politics, ordinary folk had a far greater voice in affairs.

Cosmopolitans v localists

The assumption had been that the primary division in American politics would be between the rich and the many. In the event this division proved to be only one of several. Jackson Turner Main claimed that the main division was that between agrarian–localist interests on the one side and commercial–cosmopolitan interests on the other.

In the North the cosmopolitans came from commercial areas and in the South they comprised large property owners. Most lived along navigable rivers, had connections in towns and with large-scale commerce, were wealthy and, above all, had wide interests and experience and a broader outlook than their fellow citizens. They welcomed activist government (provided they could direct it) and supported conservative monetary policies.

In contrast the localists were predominantly rural, owned small properties, lived in remoter interior areas and had narrower intellectual, economic and social horizons. They were suspicious of government and opposed banking, business and urban interests.

Nevertheless, party organisation was slow to form. While cliques and factions existed in most states, there was no real party system in place by the mid-1780s. There were no carefully worked out platforms and, Pennsylvania apart, very little orchestrated campaigning.

Politics in the states

For most of the period from 1775 until 1787 the individual states remained the main stage for political activity. While Congress directed the war, it possessed little further authority. Each state controlled its own finances, trade and economic policy and dealt with a host of political and social issues. Critics of the new constitutions complained that they were dangerously democratic and not conducive to good government. However, according to historian Colin Bonwick, the states' record of effective administration was 'far better than contemporary, and later critics have allowed'.

Many problems facing the states flowed directly from the processes of becoming independent. Some states had difficulty asserting their authority throughout their territory and several faced threats of secession. Two New York counties – Gloucester and Cumberland – formed themselves into a separate state of Vermont in 1777. While the state did not receive official recognition until 1791, Vermont's existence from 1777 was a reality that even New York could not ignore.

The war created other problems. The operations of both armies often made civil administration difficult and sometimes impossible. The occupation by the British of New York City (1776–83), Philadelphia (1777–78) and Charleston (1780–82) made things difficult for New York state, Pennsylvania and South Carolina respectively. Financial problems were particularly severe. The states had no option but to increase taxation. In every case the revenue raised was insufficient. The states were thus forced to finance the war by issuing paper currency. This led, inevitably, to inflation. By the 1780s state finances were a major problem.

States also had to deal with the problem of loyalism. Every state required men to take oaths of allegiance to the state. In some states, those who refused to take the oath could not practise trade or their professions. In many places they had to pay extra taxes. All states had laws for confiscation of loyalist property. In some states loyalists were banished or imprisoned.

Liberal trends

Americans prided themselves that their republican governments were more humane than British governments. Some efforts were made to help the insane and poor but the efforts were not much further advanced than those in Britain. The criminal codes, always less harsh than Britain's, were made even more liberal in most states.

Pre-1775 most colonies possessed established churches. After 1775, states debated whether religious establishment was inconsistent with individual liberties. New York, New Jersey, Delaware, Maryland, North Carolina, Georgia, South Carolina, Pennsylvania and Virginia prohibited established churches. In

Table 4.1: Disestablishment of the churches

Colonies	Churches	Year disestablished
Massachusetts		1833
Connecticut	Congregational	1818
New Hampshire		1819
New York	Anglican (in NY City and three neighboring counties)	1777
Maryland		1777
Virginia		1786
North Carolina	Anglican	1776
South Carolina		1778
Georgia		1777
Rhode Island		
New Jersey	None	
Delaware		
Pennsylvania		

Note the persistence of the Congregational establishment in New England.

Virginia, James Madison and Thomas Jefferson worked to ensure that religion would become entirely a private matter. In 1786 Jefferson's Act for Establishing Religious Freedom was finally approved by the state legislature. It prohibited all forms of state intervention in religious affairs. No church was to enjoy privileges denied to others and no man was to suffer any formal disadvantages because of his religion. Nevertheless, the triumph of religious freedom did not occur everywhere. All the New England states except Rhode Island continued to require taxpayers to support 'public Protestant worship' though non-Congregationalists could insist that their taxes went to their own denominations.

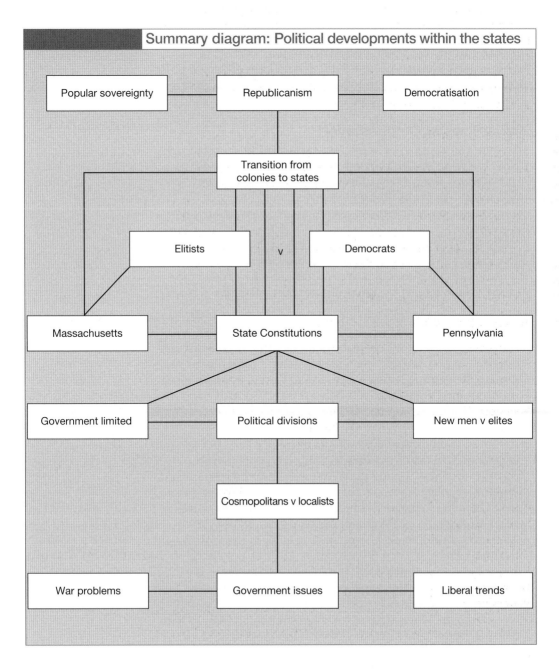

Summary diagram: Political developments within the states

2 | The National Government

Key question
How strong was the national government?

The task of framing new state constitutions was accomplished much more smoothly than that of creating a central government for the states as a whole. Although some form of national government was essential, the emergence of a vigorous national union was far from inevitable. While opposition to British policy after 1763 stimulated continental unity and the outbreak of fighting made collaboration imperative, any sense of American nationality was, at most, embryonic. Most Americans thought of themselves as Virginians or New Yorkers first and Americans second. The colonies had rebelled against Britain in order to control their own internal affairs. Moreover, the struggle with Britain had bred a distrust of central authority. Since a strong national government would necessarily diminish the states' authority, many Americans resisted it as being a repudiation of the Revolution itself. In the midst of a war to check tyranny, Americans had no wish to create a new one.

The Articles of Confederation

Congress, which began in 1774 as an extra-legal protest body, was poorly fitted to exercise national authority. It consisted of delegates from states eager to load it with responsibility but reluctant to cede it effective power. It functioned more as a conference of the states' representatives than as an autonomous government.

In June 1776 Congress appointed a committee of thirteen (with one man from each state) to draw up a constitution. A month later the committee produced a draft constitution – the Articles of Confederation. Largely the work of John Dickinson, the Articles provided for a central government with limited powers:

- Congress, which would act as the government of the USA, was composed of one body in which each state, whatever its size of population, had one vote. State delegations consisted of two to seven persons. Congressmen were elected annually and limited to three terms in six years.
- There was no provision for a national executive or a national judiciary.
- Congress could declare war, raise an army and navy, borrow and issue money, conclude treaties and alliances, apportion the common expenses among the states, settle interstate boundary disputes, regulate Indian affairs, make requisitions on the states for money and men (in case of war), set standards for weights and measures and establish and regulate post offices.
- Important measures, such as treaties, needed the approval of at least nine states.
- The Articles themselves could not be amended without the consent of all thirteen states.
- All powers not specifically granted to the Confederation were reserved to the states. Crucially, Congress had no power to levy taxes, regulate trade or enforce financial requisitions.

The Confederation, in Dickinson's view, was little more than a 'firm league of friendship'. However, such was the hostility towards centralised authority, even of so limited a kind, that the Articles did not obtain congressional approval until November 1777. They would come into force only when ratified by all the states.

After Congress submitted the Articles to the states, its members acted on the assumption that they would be ratified and behaved as if the new constitution was in force. In fact, ratification was not a simple matter. As a result of disputes over Western land claims, the unanimous consent of the states, necessary for the constitution to become effective, was not obtained until Maryland ratified on 1 March 1781. Maryland did not sign up until Virginia agreed to surrender to Congress its territorial claims north and west of the Ohio River.

<table>
<tr><td>**Key date**</td><td>Articles of Confederation ratified: 1781</td></tr>
</table>

National government problems

Throughout the war, the USA had only a rudimentary central government. To make matters worse, Congress was in session only intermittently and had no fixed abode. Its members often found better things to do than attend its sessions. (It only just managed to get a **quorum** to ratify the Treaty of Paris in 1783.) Turnover was high, partly because many prominent members were appointed or elected to other posts.

<table>
<tr><td>**Key term**</td><td>**Quorum**
A minimum number of officers or members necessary for transaction of business.</td></tr>
</table>

Nevertheless, Congress conducted national affairs for six years, implementing as well as formulating policy. Gradually it devised a system of administration, operating through committees of its own members established to deal with particular subjects. The Secret Committee of September 1775, for example, arranged for imports of munitions and other military supplies. Other committees, founded in 1776, dealt with military, naval and financial matters. Major decisions, however, remained the responsibility of Congress itself.

Military matters were a crucial concern. At first Congress implemented policy through state committees and assemblies which were called upon to raise troops, requisition supplies and put the country on a war footing. But from 1777 it created small executive boards, consisting in the main of professional appointees, to run the war. Congress exercised close supervision over military affairs in part to enforce the principle of civil supremacy over military commanders – a task made easier by Washington's acceptance of the principle.

Financing the war imposed an acute burden on Congress, which lacked much of the power customarily possessed by governments. Unlike the states, it enjoyed no authority to impose taxes. There were no banks, no existing national currency and no bullion reserves. Congress was thus obliged to rely on issuing paper money which caused huge inflation. Congress tried to solve its financial problems by leaning on the states. The states provided some money but, given their own financial problems, did not give enough. In 1780 Congress, virtually bankrupt, required the states to share in guaranteeing a new federal currency. They were also ordered to raise taxes to redeem the old currency. The states tried to comply but the plan failed. By 1781 the continental currency had expired.

In 1783 the Articles faced a problematic future. One of the defects of the Confederation was that it was established by the states and not by the people. There was no element of direct popular election. Moreover, the war had been a powerful unifier and peace diminished one of the most powerful imperatives to union.

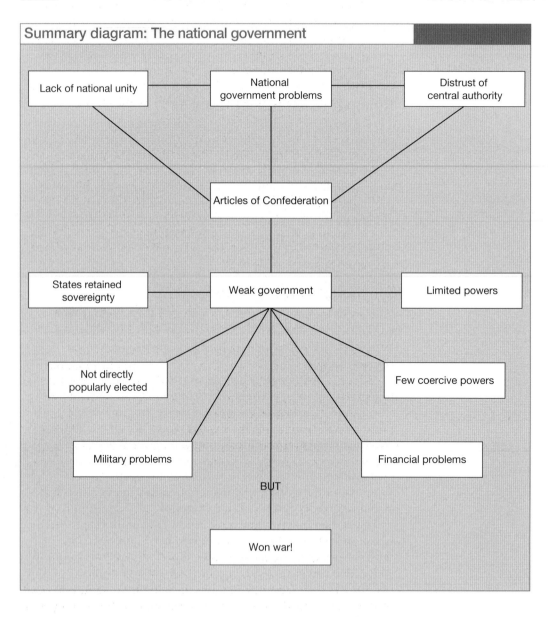

Summary diagram: The national government

Key question
Was there a social revolution in America?

3 | The Social Impact of the War on America

No one doubts that the lives of most Americans were deeply affected by the war. However, historians disagree about the extent to which the structure of society was affected by the conflict.

The effect of loyalist emigration

By 1783, 80,000 to 100,000 loyalists had left their homes and gone into exile. Most went to Britain, Canada and Nova Scotia (where they were given substantial land grants), or the West Indies. It was once thought that the sudden disappearance of the loyalists had levelling effects, providing new men with land and opportunities.

However, it is now accepted that loyalists came from all social classes: they were not simply the elite. The American Revolution was not, in Wright's phrase, one of 'Nobs versus Mobs'. Thus American society was not decapitated by their departure. In so far as there was now more room at the top, it was quickly occupied, not by the poor but by the already well-off.

During the war, state governments confiscated land and other property worth millions of pounds from loyalists. While confiscation led to some restructuring of ownership, the extent varied from area to area and overall was limited. The imperatives of war finance made it essential for the state governments to sell to the highest bidder. Thus, confiscated land was usually sold as a unit and at prices which ordinary men could not afford. Great patriot landowning families, who could obtain credit, were able to expand their estates substantially.

A more egalitarian society?

Some historians are convinced that the War of Independence profoundly changed society, resulting in more equality:

- Republican ideology had social effects. While Americans continued to accept the principles of social stratification, they were not prepared to acknowledge those not based on individual merit. Hereditary privilege in all its forms, from monarchy down, was taboo. Two states forbade the creation of titles of nobility. Many state constitutions prohibited hereditary office holding.
- New men, of lower social status, now sat in state legislatures. These men challenged the social and political supremacy of the old elite. They believed that they were entitled to share in the direction of a nation they were helping to create and demanded that their interests be considered even if they conflicted with those of the rich. The outcome was a significant realignment of relations between the elites and their social inferiors, with the latter showing less deference towards their 'betters'.
- Many ordinary Americans became officers in both the Continental Army and militia units as a result of merit, not social status. This helped erode social barriers and furthered a sense of equality.

- Some of the outward marks of social deference disappeared. Republican simplicity decreed less ceremony in the law courts. Judges no longer wore wigs and scarlet robes in the English fashion.
- The acquisition of territory west of the Appalachians created opportunities for landless Americans to acquire their own farms.
- Some states abolished slavery (see below).
- Women gained more equality (see below).
- Indentured servants almost disappeared as a result of the war. Many gained freedom through their military service while immigration traffic in contract labour ceased during the war.

But other scholars claim that the Revolution did not profoundly disturb the social fabric:

- Few American leaders sought to create a new social order. Virtually all of them accepted that class distinctions were natural and inevitable. They made no attempt to redistribute wealth or to promote social equality. Many did not feel that indentured servitude or slavery was at variance with the new nation's libertarian ideals.
- Social classes did not change in significant ways. Except for its loyalist component, the old colonial aristocracy survived the war intact. In 1787, over eighty per cent of the 100 wealthiest Virginians had inherited their wealth. Most of the prime developed land that was sold during the war was purchased by existing land owners. Thus the rich became richer, widening the economic gap between themselves and the rest of society.
- In most states, the general pattern of land holding remained essentially unchanged with tenancy as pervasive as it had been before the war.
- Indentured service had been declining before the war. Never the most reliable kind of labour, indentured servants simply had to flee west to escape the obligations of servitude.
- The war had a limited effect on slavery (see below).
- The war had a limited impact on the status of women (see below).
- America had been, and remained, a nation of self-sufficient farmers.

The impact of the war on slavery

Prior to 1775, most white colonists had taken slavery for granted as part of the natural order of society. Many American leaders (for example, George Washington and Thomas Jefferson) relied on slave labour to provide them with the status, time and wealth to make themselves effective leaders. However, the Revolution represented a fundamental challenge to the institution of slavery. At the heart of the Revolution was the belief in human liberty. It was difficult to reconcile the Declaration of Independence's assertion that 'all men are created equal' with the fact that one in six Americans were slaves because of their skin colour and ancestry.

Key question
What effect did the war have on slavery?

Slaves at work in the late eighteenth century. What seems to be the nature of the work?

Black action

Some blacks saw the War of Independence as an opportunity to secure their freedom. In pursuing that objective, black males were willing to side with the patriots or the British, depending upon which side offered them the best chance for success. For most, Britain seemed to offer the best hope. One of Washington's first acts as commander of the Continental Army was to ban all blacks from service – a move endorsed by the Continental Congress in November 1775. That same month Lord Dunmore promised freedom to any Virginian slave who fled a rebel owner to serve the British. The result was that many blacks became loyalists.

Table 4.2: The 1790 Census (showing the number of slaves)*

States	Free White	All other free persons	Slaves	Total
Vermont	85,268	255	16	85,539
New Hampshire	141,097	630	158	141,885
Maine	96,002	538	none	96,540
Massachussets	373,324	5,463	none	378,787
Rhode Island	64,470	3,407	948	68,825
Connecticut	232,674	2,808	2,764	238,246
New York	314,142	4,654	21,324	340,120
New Jersey	169,954	2,762	11,423	184,139
Pennsylvania	424,099	6,537	3,737	434,373
Delaware	46,310	3,899	8,887	59,096
Maryland	208,649	8,043	103,036	319,728
Virginia	442,117	12,866	292,627	747,610
Kentucky	61,133	114	12,430	73,677
North Carolina	288,204	4,975	100,572	393,751
South Carolina	140,178	1,801	107,094	249,073
Georgia	5,886	398	29,264	82,548
Total	**3,140,205**	**59,150**	**694,280**	**3,893,635**

*Data excerpted from the US Census Bureau (1978), *First Census of the United States*, (Baltimore).

However, some slaves did fight for American independence. By tradition Americans, especially New Englanders, allowed slaves to serve in the militia in times of crisis. Thus, despite the Continental Army ban, blacks continued to serve in Northern militias. By 1777 Washington and Congress bowed to chronic manpower shortages and accepted blacks in the ranks of the Continental Army. Enlisted slaves expected to receive their freedom in exchange for their service.

Before undertaking the Southern campaign in 1779 General Clinton issued a proclamation in which he declared that any slaves captured in service to the rebels would be sold, but that those who deserted the rebels and served Britain would receive 'full security to follow within these lines, any occupation which [they] shall think proper'. Although not an explicit promise of freedom, Southern slaves interpreted it as such. Thousands – perhaps one in six of the South's slaves – fled to the British lines. In the main the runaways were welcomed by the British who employed them as labourers and servants. The British were almost as reluctant to arm the slaves as the patriots.

At the end of the war, Britain transported some 20,000 black loyalists out of America:

- Most were resettled in the West Indies as slaves.
- Others, who had taken up arms, were absorbed into the British army, fighting for Britain in the Caribbean during the French Revolutionary Wars.
- Some 3000 were given their freedom and given land in Nova Scotia.

The North

Even before the war, some white Americans, particularly Quakers, had begun to denounce slavery and the slave trade. In 1771 the Massachusetts assembly banned the slave trade with Africa. Rhode Island and Connecticut followed suit in 1774. As the Revolutionary crisis heightened awareness of ideological principles, so the anti-slavery movement gathered strength in every state from Pennsylvania northwards. The task of abolishing slavery in the North was relatively simple since there were relatively few slaves. Blacks comprised only three per cent of New England's population and six per cent of that of the Middle Colonies.

Vermont banned slavery in its 1777 constitution. In 1780 Pennsylvania adopted a law requiring gradual emancipation of slaves when they became adults. In 1784 Connecticut and Rhode Island passed similar measures. Between 1781 and 1783 Massachusetts' courts ended slavery in the state by a series of decisions in response to suits brought by slaves who sought their freedom based on the state's 1780 constitution which declared all men free. New Hampshire courts followed Massachusetts' example.

However, in New York and New Jersey, the only two Northern states with sizeable slave populations, opposition was sufficiently

Key dates

Vermont abolished slavery: 1777

Pennsylvania abolished slavery: 1780

strong to delay the passage of gradual emancipation laws until 1799 and 1804 respectively, and even then the process of emancipation took decades to work itself out. (Slavery was not officially abolished in New York until 1827 and in New Jersey until 1846.)

The South

Racial attitudes and assumptions were deep in the Southern states where eighty-five per cent of slaves lived. Most Southern whites were determined to maintain slavery which they saw as an instrument for increasing production, enabling them to enjoy the rewards of greater wealth. Anti-slavery agitation had little impact in most Southern states.

Nevertheless, a few Southern slave holders acknowledged that slavery was a moral evil and supported freeing slaves. The most significant change to the slave system in the South after 1783 was the liberalisation of the **manumission laws**. Some planters, motivated by revolutionary ideology, took advantage of these laws to free their slaves. (Others simply used the legislation to free their children who had been born to slave women.) After 1783 there was a dramatic increase in the number of free blacks in the upper South. In 1780 they totalled less than 5000. By 1810 there were more than 180,000. Manumission was most common in Maryland and Virginia. In 1810 twenty per cent of Maryland's blacks were free. Between 1782 and 1810 the number of free blacks in Virginia rose from 2000 to 30,000. However, in the lower South, where the slave population was greatest, far fewer slaves were freed. Less than 300 slaves were manumitted in South Carolina between 1770 and 1790.

In addition to liberalising manumission, several Southern states also prohibited participation in the trans-Atlantic slave trade which was disrupted by the war. Virginia prohibited the trade in 1778 and Maryland in 1783. However, these actions were motivated more by local conditions than a concern over the inhumanity of the trade or revolutionary concern for liberty. By closing the African slave trade in the upper South, planters hoped to maintain the value of their slaves, the population of which was growing naturally.

After 1783 pent-up demand led to increased prices for slaves. Slavery expanded westwards on a massive scale once cotton became a profitable crop in the 1790s. From 1790 to 1807, more slaves were imported into North America than during any other similar period in colonial times.

George Washington and slavery

Washington, who owned some 250 slaves, was troubled by slavery. Revolutionary ideology was partly responsible for his thinking. So was his discovery that blacks could match the courage exhibited by white soldiers in the Continental Army. Washington also realised that slavery was an inefficient system of labour, especially for a wheat farmer such as himself. However, he found it

---

Key term

Manumission laws
Laws which allowed owners to free their slaves.

impossible to cut his ties to slavery. The preservation of the
Union, not the end of slavery, was his guiding principle and thus
he did not speak out against it. Only in his will did he free his
slaves, hoping his example would be followed by other planters.
Few copied him.

Free blacks

Most white Northerners held similar racist attitudes to those of
white Southerners. Consequently, free blacks, both in the North
and South, suffered from discrimination and segregation.
Economically they had the most menial jobs. But the free black
community, by its very presence, was a challenge to the slave
system. In the face of white intolerance, ex-slaves worked hard to
construct their own independent cultural life, forming their own
churches and voluntary organisations.

Conclusion

The war did something to weaken slavery. Most of the slaves who
had fought against Britain were given their freedom at the end of
their army service. All the Northern states realised that slavery
seemed incompatible with revolutionary ideology and acted to
provide for the gradual emancipation of slaves. After 1783 slavery
no longer went unchallenged or unquestioned.

But arguably the Revolutionary generation was remarkable for
its failure to take more action against slavery:

- The overwhelming majority of Southern slaves were not affected
  by the abolition of slavery in the North.
- Abolition in parts of the North was so gradual as to allow slave
  holders to sell their slaves in the South if they so chose.
- The framers of the Constitution in 1787 were unwilling to take
  any meaningful action against slavery for fear of destroying the
  Union (see Chapter 5).

The impact of the war on the status of women

The duration of the conflict meant that women of all races,
regions and classes endured great hardship. Some women were
made homeless. Some were raped. Many lost loved ones. However,
for some women, the war presented opportunities to exercise
greater control over their lives. As many as 20,000 women served
with the military forces in an ancillary capacity – as cooks,
laundresses and prostitutes. Moreover, women replaced absent
husbands as temporary heads of households. Many historians insist
that the war greatly affected women's lives:

- Mary Beth Norton claims that the Revolution brought a dramatic
  shift as women moved from submission to a world over which
  they had some control. Women, she claims, were no longer
  content to be 'good wives' and ignorant of the larger world.
  Instead they read newspapers, discussed politics with their
  menfolk and ensured that their daughters had the best
  education possible.

Key question
Did the status of
women change as a
result of the war?

- Other historians think a notion of 'republican motherhood' emerged during the revolutionary era. The first task of 'republican mothers' was to train their sons for active citizenship. But if they were to succeed in moulding republican citizens, they needed to imbibe a fair amount of republicanism themselves. This justified women's participation in public life.
- Historian Harry Ward claims that ordinary American families became less patriarchal. Just as the colonies had repudiated royal paternalism, Americans came to believe that the family should be founded on mutual trust and respect, without a domineering head.

However, these claims are not substantiated by much evidence. It is easier to claim that the Revolution produced no significant changes or benefits for American women. Women were still expected to confine themselves to the traditional domestic sphere – homemaking, childrearing, feeding and clothing their families. Women were not allowed to vote or hold public office. Nowhere was there any significant improvement in the legal status of women. The property of a married woman remained under the control of her husband. In legal, economic and political terms, American women remained in a subordinate position within a patriarchal social order.

The impact of the war on Indians

The war had disastrous consequences for Native Americans. According to historian Edward Countryman the transformation of power relations between whites and Indians in the trans-Appalachian west was among the most radical changes wrought by the war. After Britain's defeat, most Indian tribes had little option but to sue for peace. Thus the US concluded treaties at Fort Stanwix, New York and Hopewell, South Carolina in 1784 in which it won concessions of land from the Iroquois, Choctaws, Chickasaws and Cherokees. The new republic had little sympathy with Indians. As well as losing huge amounts of land, the Indians were largely excluded from the rights and privileges of citizenship.

Some tribes in the North-west continued their resistance. The Delawares, Shawnees, Miamis, Chippewas, Ottawas and Potawatomis formed an alliance – the Western Confederacy – to resist American encroachments. Covertly armed by the British, the Western Confederacy would prove a serious obstacle to American settlement. Not until 1794–95 were the Indians of the North-west finally defeated.

Summary diagram: The social impact of the war on America

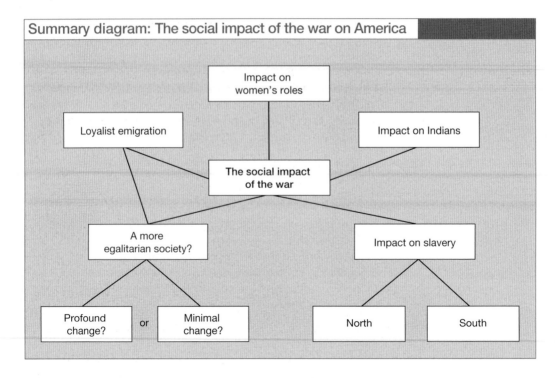

4 | The Economic Impact of the War on America

The economic effects of the war were generally – but not totally – negative.

Key question
What were the main economic effects of the war?

The negative effects

- Boston, New York City, Charleston and Philadelphia were all occupied at one time or another and their populations fell considerably.
- Those areas that experienced significant military operations suffered. Property was destroyed or stolen. American troops could be as destructive as the British.
- Large numbers of American merchant ships were seized by the Royal Navy.
- American trade was seriously affected by the British blockade.
- The fact that America was no longer part of the British mercantilist system had a devastating effect on some merchants and some businesses. Pre-1775 forty per cent of all colonial exports and virtually all colonial imports had gone through Britain or British colonies.
- The loss of the subsidy provided by Britain for indigo cultivation resulted in indigo growing almost ceasing.
- Production of tobacco was reduced to a third of the pre-war levels.
- The New England fishing industry was temporarily destroyed.

- Hyper-inflation, the result of a shortage of goods and the printing of vast quantities of paper money, was damaging to day-to-day economic activity.
- The requisitioning of large numbers of wagons and carts by the competing armies had a disruptive effect on internal transport.
- The production and price of American products were affected by the flight of large numbers of slaves who sought British protection.

The beneficial effects

- Freed from the constraints of the Navigation Acts, Americans could export directly to European markets.
- Privateering was a risky but potentially very profitable operation for some towns and some individuals. American privateers captured British vessels worth about £18 million.
- The sharp reduction in imports of manufactured goods from Britain had a stimulating effect on American manufacturing. The main beneficiaries were the iron, textile, paper, pottery and shoe-making industries.
- Military demands boosted domestic production of uniforms, munitions and guns.
- The Continental, French and British armies required vast amounts of food. Farmers outside the immediate war zones did especially well.
- British-held areas, especially New York, boomed during the war.
- Some traders, for example, Robert Morris, who negotiated for government military supplies, made huge profits.

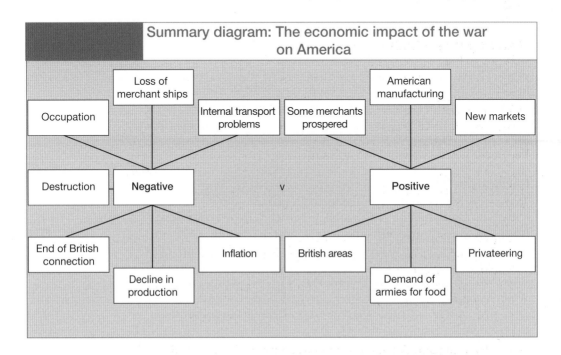

Summary diagram: The economic impact of the war on America

5 | The Impact of the War on Britain, France and Spain

Key question
What effect did the war have on Britain?

Historian Stephen Conway believes that the war's impact on Britain was 'both wide-ranging and profound'. In Conway's view, the events of 1775–83 'provided a lengthy preview of the tests and strains to come' in the French Revolutionary and Napoleonic Wars between 1793 and 1815. But did the war have any immediate impact on Britain?

The impact of the war on Britain
The financial and economic impact
Historians disagree about the impact of the war on British finances and on the British economy. On the negative front, the cost of the war was enormous. By 1783 the National Debt stood at a towering £232 million. To meet the interest charge alone required £9.5 million. This necessitated increased taxation which had a detrimental impact on economic activity. The war also led to the disruption of overseas trade. Between 1775 and 1778 British imports fell by twenty-six per cent and exports by eighteen per cent. Those who traded with the thirteen colonies were particularly badly hit. Once France, Spain and Holland entered the war, many European markets were also closed. In the ensuing recession both the stock market and land values plunged to alarmingly low levels. The capture of over 3000 British merchant vessels by American privateers led to trade contraction, as did the navy's demand for merchant shipping to transport troops and supplies.

However, there was a positive side. Some industries benefited from the war – especially textiles and naval building. Recruitment to the army and navy took men out of employment. Thus wages remained reasonably high. If some markets were lost, British exports to other areas increased. British privateers also made good profits. Some 120 privateers were operating out of Liverpool alone in 1779. Britain quickly recovered economically from the war. The restoration of trade contact with America helped. By 1785 Britain's trade with her ex-colonies had attained its pre-war level. Trade with Europe also quickly revived. The value of British exports to Europe doubled between 1783 and 1792.

Relations with Ireland
The war provided useful leverage for Irish patriots hoping to reduce British dominion. The parallels between the constitutional situations of the Americans and the Irish appeared close. Although Ireland had her own parliament, it was elected only by Protestant voters and only Anglicans were supposed to sit in it. It was also subject to the control of the English Privy Council and the Westminster Parliament. Moreover, the Irish had economic grievances, not least British restrictions on Ireland's overseas trade. Determined to change matters, the Irish adopted a non-importation agreement directed against British goods. This and the emergence of large bodies of armed 'volunteers' persuaded

North to press ahead with the redress of Irish grievances, in an effort to stop Ireland going the same way as America:

- In 1780 Ireland was granted freedom to trade with the British colonies and restrictions on the export of woollen goods were removed.
- In 1780 Protestant non-Anglicans were allowed to take public office.
- In 1782 the British Parliament repealed the Irish Declaratory Act and formally recognised the legislative independence of Ireland.

In the circumstances, keeping Ireland loyal could be seen as something of a triumph for the British government.

The political impact

In Britain the war led to pressure for constitutional reform. There was increasing opposition to the war, not least from landowners who disliked the way the war was being run and the steep rise in taxation. There were demands to end what was perceived to be undue influence exercised by the executive on the legislature through its control of MPs who were financially dependent upon the government. Many feared that Parliament had become a rubber stamp for the decisions of the ministers.

In 1779–80 petitions from nearly 40 groups (or associations) arrived at Westminster. The common demand of the so-called Association movement was 'economic reform' – a reduction in the influence of the king's ministers by the cutting of the number of places in government pay and the prevention of certain office holders from sitting in the Commons. Many associations also pressed for parliamentary reform – the creation of 100 new county

William Pitt the Younger, son of William Pitt (the Elder).

seats, the abolition of **rotten boroughs** and the extension of the franchise. The radical fringe of the Association movement went even further. The Westminster committee demanded universal manhood suffrage, the secret ballot and equal electoral districts. The strength of the Association movement was impressive. At its height in 1779–80 it achieved an extraordinary degree of national consensus, so much so that the Commons passed a resolution which declared that the 'influence of the Crown has increased, is increasing and ought to be diminished'.

However, the Association movement soon declined. The influence of the Gordon Riots of June 1780 had a major impact. The Gordon rioters held London at their mercy for nearly a week and engaged in an orgy of murder and destruction. The cause of the riots was religious prejudice, their aim to repeal the liberal measure of relief for Roman Catholics passed in 1778. (North's ministry had supported relief because it was thought the measure would encourage further Catholic enlistment in the armed forces.) The leader of the anti-papists, Lord Gordon, called his movement the Protestant Association. Frightened men of property – wrongly – made a connection between the rioters and the political activities of the Association movement. Moreover, the riots convinced many moderates that the time was not ripe for introducing political reforms.

Nevertheless, reform seemed very much on the agenda in the early 1780s. Before 1782 would-be reformers in Parliament congregated loosely round the two main Whig groups, led by Rockingham and Shelburne. The most promising talent in the Rockingham group was Charles James Fox. William Pitt (the Earl of Chatham's son) was the starring light in the Shelburne group. In the complex politics which followed North's resignation in 1782, the initiative was taken by Fox. In order to control the Commons, Fox made a cynical alliance with his old enemy North. The 1783 Fox–North ministry was strongly opposed by George III, who hated Fox, and Pitt, who detested North. In late 1783 the king instructed the Lords to defeat Fox's proposed East India Bill and asked Pitt to form a ministry. In the spring of 1784 a general election was called.

The result was decisive. Pitt triumphed. George III was delighted. At last he had a prime minister in whom he had confidence and who had a comfortable majority in the Commons. After 1783 Pitt showed little interest in extending the franchise. The return of prosperity also removed the stimulus to political reform.

Britain's imperial status

The loss of the thirteen colonies did not spell the end of the British Empire. Britain had managed to cling on to Canada and thus continued to control much of North America. Elsewhere the rest of the Empire remained essentially intact in 1783. Indeed, it had continued to grow in India. Britain's diplomatic status and influence quickly recovered after 1783, both in Europe and overseas.

Rotten borough
A place that sent members to Parliament though it had few or no inhabitants.

Key term

The impact of the war on France and Spain

France appeared to be a major beneficiary of the American war:

- Her main enemy Britain had been defeated.
- She had gained territory in the West Indies.

However, France was driven to near bankruptcy by her role in the American war and her financial crisis set in train the events that led to the French Revolution in 1789.

The winning of independence by Britain's colonies was a dangerous example to Spain's American colonies. It would take many years for the South Americans to follow suit – but follow they ultimately did and by the early 1820s Spain had lost all her South American colonies.

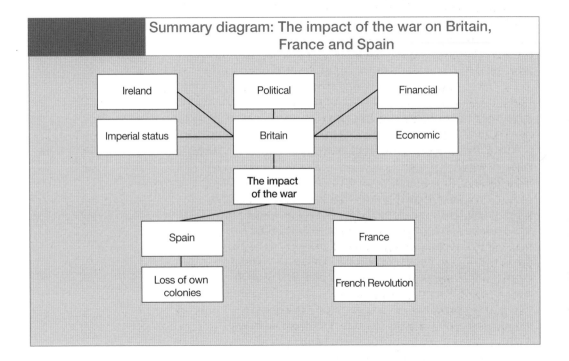

Summary diagram: The impact of the war on Britain, France and Spain

6 | The Key Debate

How revolutionary was the American Revolution?

During the congressional debate over independence, John Adams wrote, 'We are in the very midst of a Revolution, the most complete, unexpected and remarkable of any in the history of nations.' But historians continue to debate just how revolutionary the American Revolution was. In fact, there is little agreement about what the Revolution actually was:

- Was it simply the decision of the thirteen colonies to declare independence?
- Did it arise from the strains of war?

- Did it lie in the replacement of monarchy by a republican government?
- Did it take place in Americans' mentality and ideology or in the real world of social and political relationships?
- Was it an enormous transformation that bound together many separate changes?

Historians do not even agree about how long the Revolution lasted. Did it start in 1763, 1765 or 1775? When did it end? In 1781 with Britain's surrender at Yorktown? In 1783 with the Treaty of Paris? In 1787 with the drawing up of the Constitution? In 1788–89 with the inauguration of the Constitution? One recent historian has suggested that the Revolution continued down to 1815!

Arguably, the American Revolution hardly deserves its name. The events which led to the creation of the USA can be seen as merely the culmination of political, economic and social trends at work in the thirteen colonies long before independence. Certainly the American Revolution had none of the cataclysmic quality associated with what happened in France in 1789 or in Russia in 1917. There was little social upheaval or class conflict, no radical reorganisation of government or the economy, no challenge to existing religious beliefs, no descent into anarchy or dictatorship, no reign of terror. The Americans in 1775 were struggling for political independence, not for social revolution. American republicanism was not synonymous with egalitarianism and the USA did not immediately become a democratic society.

The new states looked very similar to the old colonies in government terms. Rich supporters of independence retained much of their power. Many white men were still excluded from participation in politics. Women and blacks scarcely benefited from the Revolution politically or socially. The conservative elite who created the Revolution remained in control of what they created. Thus, it is possible to conclude that the American Revolution was simply a successful war of independence which ended British rule but otherwise left things pretty much as they had been.

But a case can be made for there being a 'real' revolution. Colin Bonwick insists that 'there can be no doubt that the United States which entered the nineteenth century was very different in many, if not all, respects from the colonial America from which it emerged'.

John Adams observed that the real revolution was over before a shot was fired, for its essence lay in the changes of heart and mind that turned Britons who lived overseas into Americans who lived in their own country. By 1776 Americans, who had initially resisted British impositions by citing their rights as 'Englishmen', were speaking of the natural rights of men everywhere and were emphatically denying they were Englishmen.

The Revolution also – eventually – produced a federal union out of thirteen distinct colonial communities. The new nation was based on a body of ideas which differed from – indeed consciously repudiated – those of the Old World. Those ideas not only affected contemporary beliefs and attitudes but influenced succeeding generations of Americans. Many Americans, for example, were struck by the inconsistency of claiming freedom for themselves while keeping others in bondage.

Participation in the pre-war protest movement against Britain led to an increase in political consciousness among Americans who were previously marginalised within the political process. The experience of war led ordinary Americans to demand and win a greater voice in the new governments which were formed during and after the conflict. Those governments derived their authority from the people. Although total democracy was not established, the Revolution had a profoundly democratising effect. The previously dominant elites were obliged to admit their social inferiors to a share of political power.

Ordinary people thus came more to centre stage. Americans, in historian Edward Countryman's view, began to say that a private was as good as a colonel, a baker as good as a merchant, a ploughman as good as a landlord. Some even began to think and say the same about blacks and women. Certainly, the ideals and history of the Revolution gave the quest for equality of blacks, women and poor whites a legitimacy it had not previously enjoyed.

Nor were the results of the Revolution confined to America. As the first war for national independence in modern times to result in the rupture of an imperial connection, it was to serve as an inspiration to other colonial peoples. 'It is impossible indeed,' thought Esmund Wright, 'to find limits to the consequences for the world that have followed from the events that took place on the narrow Atlantic seaboard in the years from 1763 to 1783.'

Some key books in the debate:

Colin Bonwick, *The American Revolution*, Macmillan, 1991.
Edward Countryman, *The American Revolution*, Hill and Wang, 1985.
Francis D. Cogliano, *Revolutionary America 1763–1815*, Routledge, 2000.
Robert Middlekauff, *The Glorious Cause: The American Revolution, 1763–1789*, OUP, 1982.
Harry M. Ward, *The War for Independence and the Transformation of American Society*, Routledge, 1999.

Study Guide: AS Question

In the style of Edexcel

How accurate is it to describe the changes in American society in the years 1776–89 as a social revolution? (30 marks)

Exam tips

The cross-references are intended to take you straight to the material that will help you to answer the question.

At the heart of the Revolution was the belief in human liberty (page 134), but did it go on to create a more free and equal society? This question asks you to weigh up the significance of the social changes in America and to decide whether they were great enough to be called a revolution.

To consider whether a more equal society was created you could explore the following questions:

- Was there greater social mobility? For example, how great were the changes in land holding, wealth and hereditary privilege (pages 145–146)?
- Did the position of women improve (pages 150–151)?
- What was the impact on the position of the Native Americans (page 151)?
- How far did the position of slaves improve?

This last area will give you most to explore. You can examine the impact of manumission laws (page 149), the prohibition of the slave trade in some areas (page 149) and the prohibition of slavery in some states (page 148). Note the limitations to these however (page 150).

You will need to do more than describe changes; you will need to show clearly what criteria you are using to measure whether these amounted to a 'revolution'. How significant were the differences? How widespread? If much of American society was not greatly changed in practice, you could conclude that significant change for sections of society or in just some areas of America cannot be called a revolution.

5 The American Constitution

Key dates

1781	The Articles of Confederation became fully operational
1786	The Annapolis meeting
1786–87	Shays' Rebellion
1787	The North-west Ordinance
1787 May–September	Meeting of the Constitutional Convention
1788	Constitution ratified
1789	George Washington inaugurated as first president

1 | The Political Situation: 1781–87

Key question
How well did the Confederation deal with the problems of the 1780s?

The USA was governed by the terms of the Articles of Confederation from 1781 until 1789. Numerous problems faced the new regime.

Weak national government

Key date
The Articles of Confederation became fully operational: 1781

During the eight years the Confederation was in operation, the USA had only the semblance of a national government and at times not even that. Charles Thomson, secretary of Congress, complained that 'a government without a visible head must appear a strange phenomenon to European politicians and will I fear lead them to form no very favourable opinion of our stability, wisdom or Union'. Congress, in which each of the thirteen states had one vote, had some of the qualities of a national government, but it was in session only intermittently and had no fixed abode. Withdrawing from Philadelphia in 1783 to escape angry soldiers demanding back pay, it drifted successively to Princeton, Annapolis and Trenton before settling in New York in 1785. Attendance at sessions was thin.

Once the Articles came into full effect in 1781, three executive departments were set up – foreign affairs, finance and war. The three departments functioned with varying degrees of success. Their main problem was that the Confederation government had no coercive power over states or individuals within the states. Moreover, once independence was achieved, the states attached less importance to unity and became absorbed in their own affairs. They exercised rights they had specifically relinquished and responded belatedly or not at all to Congressional requisitions. Most ambitious politicians preferred to serve within their states rather than in Congress. Most decisions affecting the lives of Americans were made at state level, not by Congress.

The West

The Treaty of Paris (see page 126) gave America control over virtually the whole region south of the Great Lakes and east of the Mississippi. The Revolutionary period witnessed an unprecedented flood of pioneers into the trans-Appalachian region. By 1790 the population of Kentucky had risen to 73,677 and Tennessee's reached 35,691. A coherent policy on Western land distribution and territorial government was essential. American politicians, fearing that the new Western territories might declare independence from the USA, realised the need for systems that would bind the Western communities to the old seaboard states. As early as 1779 Congress had resolved that the West would eventually be organised into new states, to be admitted to the Union as equals. This was confirmed by the 1784 Ordinance.

Key question
How successful were the Confederation's Western policies?

The 1785 Land Ordinance

The 1785 Land Ordinance outlined a surveying system for the sale of North-west land. Government surveyors would first divide land into six-square-mile townships. Each township was then divided into sections of one square mile (640 acres). Four sections in every township were to be set aside as bounty land for ex-soldiers and one for the maintenance of schools. The rest of the land was to be sold at auction in 640-acre lots at not less than one dollar an acre. This provided a relatively quick and certain means of setting out lines, reducing the potential for disputes among land purchasers.

The 1787 North-west Ordinance

The North-west Ordinance prescribed a set of procedures for organising and admitting to statehood new territories. It provided that during the initial phase of settlement a territory would not be

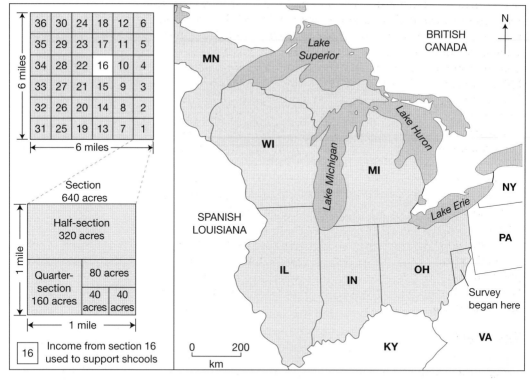

Figure 5.1: Surveying the North-west: 1785–87. Sections of a township under the Land Ordinance of 1785.

Key date

The North-west Ordinance: 1787

self-governing but would have a governor and judges appointed by Congress. When the territory had 5000 adult male inhabitants, it could elect a legislature with limited powers. It could also elect non-voting representatives to Congress. Finally, when its population reached 60,000, it could form a constitutional convention and apply to Congress for admission as a state on equal terms with existing states.

Key question

How successful were American policies with Britain and Spain?

Foreign policy

Although it had won independence from Britain, in 1783 the USA could not be considered among the foremost world nations in terms of its strength. Its population, production, wealth and military and naval power were far inferior to those of its rivals. In 1784 the federal army was less than a hundred strong. Yet the new nation shared the North American continent with Britain to the north and Spain to the south and west.

Relations with Britain

Despite promising in the Treaty of Paris to evacuate American soil 'with all convenient speed', Britain still clung to a number of frontier posts south of the Great Lakes in order to safeguard the fur trade and maintain contact with the Indians of the North-west. As a pretext for continuing to occupy the frontier posts Britain cited the American failure to observe those clauses of the peace treaty concerning the repayment of pre-war debts and the restoration of loyalist property. Although Congress had urged the states to place no obstacle in the way of British merchants recovering pre-war debts, the states had ignored the advice. They had likewise turned a deaf ear when Congress 'earnestly recommended' the return of confiscated loyalist property. A government so obviously weak at home could scarcely command respect abroad. Thus when John Adams was sent to London in 1785 with instructions to demand the evacuation of the frontier posts and seek a commercial treaty, he was rebuffed. Britain claimed there was little point negotiating with the federal government since Congress was unable to compel the states to implement its treaties.

Relations with Spain

Problems posed by relations with Spain were even more complex and dangerous to American unity. Spain, like Britain, opposed American westward expansion. Strengthening her ties with south-west Indians, Spain schemed to create an Indian buffer state to protect her own possessions. Spanish control of the Mississippi River – the strategic key to the entire area south of the Great Lakes – was a huge advantage. In 1784 Spain seized Natchez on the eastern bank of the Mississippi and closed the river to American navigation, thus depriving Western settlers of a vital outlet for their goods. Some American leaders feared that settlers in Tennessee and Kentucky might transfer their allegiance to Spain.

In 1786 Foreign Secretary John Jay initiated a treaty with Spain whereby in return for limited access to Spanish markets, the USA agreed to give up for 25 years the right to use the Mississippi. However, with five Southern states opposed, the treaty could not be

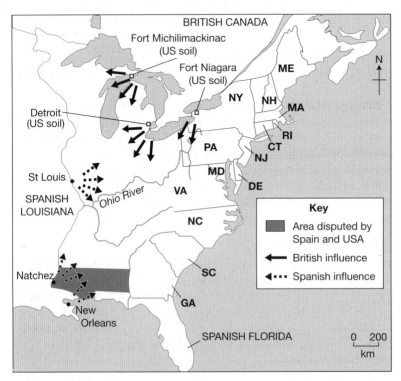

Figure 5.2: Disputed territorial claims: Spain, Britain and the USA.

ratified by the required nine. Westerners were furious at Jay's willingness to sacrifice their interests to those of Eastern merchants. Some talked of setting up an independent Western republic, under Spanish protection.

The failure to achieve a commercial treaty with Britain, the presence of the British in the North-west and the disputes with Spain all demonstrated the weakness of the Confederation in foreign affairs.

Economic problems

Key question
How serious was the economic situation?

The American economy suffered considerably from the destruction of war and the separation from Britain (see pages 152–53). Economic difficulties were compounded by imports of large quantities of British goods after 1783. Between 1784 and 1786 the USA imported from Britain goods worth over £7.5 million, selling less than one-third of that in return. American debt and the flow of **specie** outside the country to meet the trade deficit helped to depress trade and to slow economic recovery. To many at the time, the economic situation looked bleak: prices were depressed, private and public indebtedness heavy and trade regulation chaotic.

Key term

Specie
Gold or coined money.

The fact that control over commercial matters was retained by individual states weakened the USA's bargaining position. When Massachusetts tried to prevent the dumping of British goods in America, New Hampshire eagerly absorbed them. After 1784 there were increasing demands that the Articles should be amended to allow Congress to regulate both international and American trade. The proposal aroused considerable intersectional rivalry since each area had different interests. The mercantile and industrial interests of New England and the Middle states wanted a protective tariff against British competition. In contrast, Southern states, as exporters of agricultural products, preferred free trade.

However, all was not doom and gloom on the economic front:

- The US population grew considerably from 2.75 million in 1780 to 4 million in 1790.
- The prospect of western expansion was a great bonus.
- There were new markets available in Europe and the Far East. Prices obtained for American commodities remained high with tobacco and wheat doing especially well.
- Many of the British trading restrictions could be evaded, especially by Americans trading in the West Indies.
- Barriers to interstate trade were dismantled during the 1780s.

Financial problems

Key question
Why were financial problems a particular source of concern?

The Confederation inherited serious financial problems, including a nearly worthless currency (see page 153) and huge debts. In 1783 the national debt stood at a massive $41 million: the foreign debt – to Holland, France and Spain – comprised nearly $8 million and domestic debt the remaining $33 million. The debt was one problem. Paying the interest on the debt – about $2.4 million per year – was another.

The fact that the government was unable to pay its soldiers was particularly serious. Over the winter of 1782–83 army officers met at Newburgh, New York, and pressed hard for back pay and half-pay pensions. The possibility of a coup was defused only by George Washington's use of his considerable authority. In June 1783 dissatisfied soldiers surrounded the Pennsylvania State House, forcing a humiliated Congress to abandon Philadelphia.

Robert Morris

Bankruptcy was averted only through the dexterity and wealth of Robert Morris, appointed superintendent of finance in 1781. A Philadelphia merchant who had made huge profits during the war, Morris used some of his own money to meet expenses. Keen to develop a systematic financial policy, Morris believed it was essential to create a strong national government with powers to:

- set up a national bank
- secure control of the public debt (instead of parcelling it out to the individual states)
- levy import duties.

Robert Morris, the superintendent of finance. How successful was Morris?

The Bank of America

Morris succeeded in having his privately financed Bank of North America chartered by Congress (1781). Morris hoped the bank would become a national bank (like the Bank of England), servicing the outstanding loan obligations of the government and affording it credit. His hopes soon collapsed. The bank's notes fell below specie value which hindered their acceptance. Nor did it receive as much capital as expected. The government severed connection with the bank in 1784.

The public debt

Morris wanted the national government to secure control of the public debt so that it would then have to be given taxing power to raise money. His hopes were to be disappointed. The states preferred to assume responsibility for servicing directly that part of the debt held by their own citizens instead of responding to Congressional requisitions for the same purpose. Thus by 1786 the states had incorporated a large part of the national debt into their state debts. This was a blow to the status of Congress and meant that it had little justification for seeking enlarged financial powers.

Import duties

Morris supported efforts to amend the Articles so as to give Congress authority to levy a five per cent duty on all imports. The necessary unanimity, however, proved unattainable.

The situation by 1787

A disappointed Morris resigned in 1784. The financial situation remained serious. By 1786 Congress had levied over $15 million in requisitions from states but only $2.5 million had been paid. The states which failed to meet their obligations could not be compelled to do so. The only major source of independent income for the national government was from the sale of western lands, but this developed slowly, yielding only $760,000 before 1788. Congress was able to meet its normal expenses: the cost of government administration was minimal – $128,332 in 1787. But there was an immense debt still owed overseas and Congress did not have enough revenue to pay the interest, let alone the principal.

Creditors versus debtors

The various states faced similar financial problems. In an effort to reduce their war debts, the states imposed heavy taxes. Those in debt were particularly hard hit by the financial situation. By 1783 the paper continental currency had ceased to circulate and some states had stopped issuing paper currency. Lacking the specie necessary to pay their taxes and meet their debts, debtors demanded an increase in paper money. Most creditors opposed this, contending that paper money would simply lead to inflation and economic instability.

By the late 1780s it seemed the debtors were winning. In 1787 seven states were issuing paper money. Rhode Island went to the greatest lengths, not only making paper money legal tender but even compelling creditors to accept it. The value of Rhode Island paper money depreciated sharply and creditors fled the state to avoid having to accept it. For conservatives Rhode Island was a horrifying symbol – an attack on private property. The experiment in republican government seemed to have given way to anarchy.

Disturbances

In September 1786, the governor of New Hampshire called out 2000 militiamen to disperse several hundred farmers threatening the legislative assembly after it reneged on a promise to issue paper money. There were similar disturbances by angry farmers in Vermont, Pennsylvania, New York and Virginia.

Shays' Rebellion

The most serious trouble arose in Massachusetts. The Massachusetts state legislature, controlled by men from the commercially oriented eastern counties, rejected the demand for paper money and insisted that taxes be paid in scarce specie. Many farmers, unable to pay the heavy taxes, lost their land: some were imprisoned. By the summer of 1786 western Massachusetts was seething with discontent. When the state legislature adjourned without heeding the farmers' demands for paper money, riotous mobs roamed from place to place, preventing the courts from hearing debt cases.

By the autumn the malcontents had found a leader in Daniel Shays, a bankrupt farmer who had been a captain in the war. In January 1787 Shays led an armed band of several hundred men toward the federal arsenal at Springfield. The rebels were easily dispersed by 1000 militiamen and by February the insurgency had been put down. Nevertheless, Shays' rebellion alarmed conservatives throughout the country. Again it seemed that anarchy loomed. In conjunction with the paper money issue in Rhode Island, Shays' Rebellion gave a crucial impetus to the movement to strengthen the power of the national government.

Shays' Rebellion: 1786–87

Key date

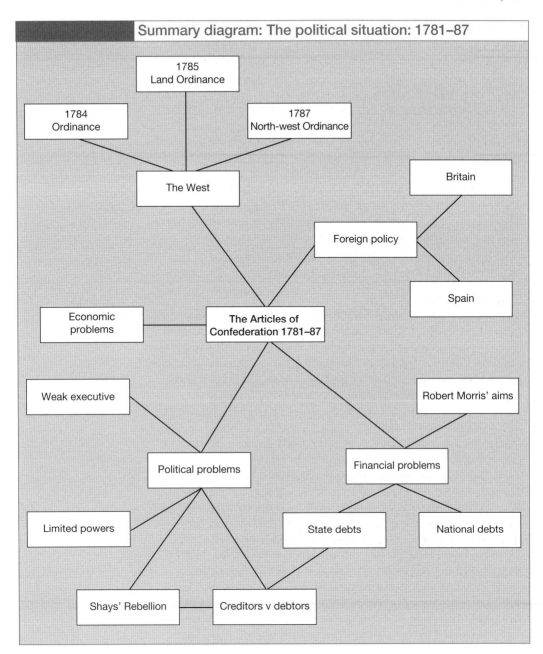

Summary diagram: The political situation: 1781–87

Key question
Why did many
Americans wish to
strengthen the
national government?

2 | The Demand for Stronger National Government

By the mid-1780s many Americans were dissatisfied with the Articles of Confederation and demanded stronger national government:

- Many were appalled by the powerlessness of the national government in foreign affairs and commercial matters.
- Creditors wanted a national government that would put a stop to what they saw as the irresponsible legislation of states that issued paper money.

- Those who wanted constitutional reform feared that the weakness of the Articles threatened impending disintegration and chaos.

American nationalism

Most Americans were primarily loyal to their states. Nevertheless, there were distinct signs of growing national consciousness. The struggle for independence had increased the sense of being American. The war, besides mixing men from different states in the Continental Army and Congress, had produced a crop of national heroes (for example, George Washington) and national shrines (for example, Bunker Hill). National symbols appeared in profusion:

- Congress adopted the Stars and Stripes as the national flag in 1777.
- The bald eagle took its place on the Great Seal of the USA in 1782. (Benjamin Franklin, thinking the eagle a bird of bad moral character, would have preferred the turkey as America's emblem!)

Nationalism inspired the political leaders who led the movement for constitutional reform. Men like Alexander Hamilton, Robert Morris, George Washington and James Madison were mortified at Congress' weakness. They wanted a unified republic that would command the respect of the world – a truly national society in which local and state attachments were subordinate to American loyalties.

Conservative nationalism

Most of the nationalist leaders were men of substance. Some were horrified by the type of new men who now occupied so many seats in the state legislatures and even more horrified by what they considered to be the low standards of the consequent legislation. Nevertheless, the nationalists were far from crude reactionaries – as some historians have suggested. They supported much of the revolution's central ideology, not least popular sovereignty. But they lacked faith in the ability of the common people to exercise careful judgement and abhorred what they saw as democratic excesses in state and local government. Fearing that the weakness of the Confederation endangered the republican experiment, they favoured the creation of a strong national government whose power was vested in the hands of the wealthy and well educated. Such a government, they believed, would curb democratic excess at home while promoting American interests abroad.

Support for the Articles of Confederation

The view that the USA was falling apart was not shared by all Americans. Many believed that the Confederation was working reasonably well:

- The Americans had gained independence under the Articles.
- The state governments were more responsive to people's demands than ever before.
- Some feared that a stronger central government would replicate the British government.

- Most Americans equated a high degree of local self-government with the preservation and enjoyment of personal liberty.
- Most people continued to identify with their state governments.
- Most state governments muddled along competently enough by eighteenth-century standards.

While many Americans accepted the need for some reform of the Articles in order to strengthen the national government, most thought the individual states should retain considerable powers.

Interstate disharmony

Although state boundary disputes, jurisdictional rivalry and western issues were mostly resolved by 1787, sectional animosity remained a problem particularly in relation to the levying of tariff duties. From 1782 to 1785 all the states except New Jersey placed duties on imports, affecting both interstate as well as foreign commerce, for the purpose of raising revenue. By 1786 the New England states, New York and Pennsylvania had increased import duties to make them protective. States put their own interests first: some imposed higher tariffs than others against foreign – especially British – goods.

Virginia and Maryland agreement

The immediate origins of the Constitutional Convention lay in a dispute between Virginia and Maryland over navigation on the Potomac River. Such interstate disagreements were not uncommon during the 1780s and the national government was largely powerless to act as an arbitrator in them. In 1784 James Madison proposed that commissioners from the two states meet to negotiate a solution. Meeting at Washington's Mount Vernon estate in March 1785, the delegates quickly reached agreement on the navigational issues. They then went beyond their brief and suggested that their states should co-operate on financial and customs policy, and recommended that an appeal should be made to Pennsylvania to join in future deliberations on matters of common interest. Madison, who had served in Congress and witnessed its ineffectiveness at first hand, saw an opportunity for interstate co-operation for constitutional reform. In the wake of the Mount Vernon meeting, he proposed a resolution to the Virginia assembly for a national convention to discuss commercial regulations.

The Annapolis meeting

Key date

The Annapolis meeting: 1786

Madison's resolution had effect. In September 1786, twelve men, representing five states (New York, New Jersey, Pennsylvania, Delaware and Virginia) met in Annapolis to discuss commercial problems. In practical terms, a meeting of such an unrepresentative body could not propose reforms, commercial or otherwise, to the nation with any credibility. But the Annapolis meeting brought together men from different states who agreed on the need for constitutional change. Most, like Madison, realised that it was impractical to hope for amendments to the Articles by Congressional action. The Articles could be amended only with the unanimous agreement of all thirteen states – an unlikely event.

The meeting thus proposed that a convention of all the states should be held in Philadelphia in 1787 'to devise such further provisions as shall appear to them necessary to render the constitution of the federal government adequate to the exigencies of the Union'.

Congress was not at first enthusiastic, but after the shock of Shays' Rebellion it called upon the states in February 1787 to send delegates to a convention in Philadelphia in May 'for the sole and express purpose of revising the Articles of Confederation'.

Profile: James Madison 1751–1836

1751	– Born in Virginia into the planter class
1775	– Chairman of his county's revolutionary committee
1776	– Helped draft Virginia's state constitution
1780	– Became the youngest member of the Confederation Congress
1787	– Played a crucial role in drafting the Constitution
1787–88	– Contributed to the *Federalist Papers* (see page 185)
1789	– Drafted the Bill of Rights
1801–09	– Served as Secretary of State
1809–17	– President of the USA

Madison was a man of deep conviction. His firm attachment to Virginia did not prevent him from loving the Union. A supporter of political liberty, he feared tyranny by the majority. Nevertheless, he believed liberty could survive in a republic only if the people were faithfully represented.

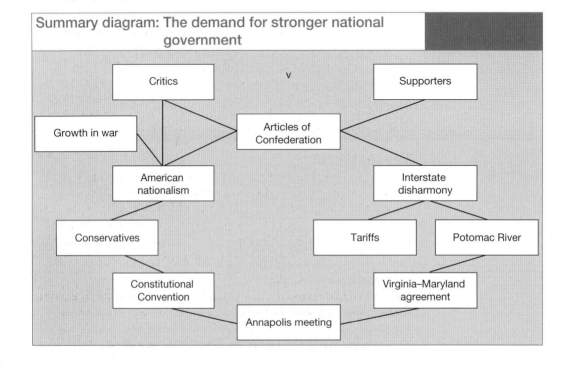

Summary diagram: The demand for stronger national government

Key question
What were the aims of the Founding Fathers?

Key date

Meeting of the Constitutional Convention: May–September 1787

Key question
Why was Madison's role so crucial?

3 | The Constitutional Convention

Thomas Jefferson described the Constitutional Convention which met in Philadelphia in May 1787 as 'an assembly of demi-gods'. Many historians have agreed. The Convention delegates (the Founding Fathers) have been seen as intervening at a crucial moment to save the American Revolution. Their masterpiece – the Constitution – is seen as re-launching the republic and laying the foundation of all that followed. However, there are historians who view the Convention as a meeting of self-interested elitists who sought to undermine the Revolution's democratic principles. For some, the Constitution represents a counter-revolutionary subversion of liberty.

The influence of James Madison

The Constitutional Convention was scheduled to begin its deliberations on 17 May 1787. But when the appointed day arrived, the delegations of only two states – Pennsylvania (the hosts) and Virginia – were present. Poor weather and poorer roads delayed the arrival of the other delegates. The Virginian delegation contained two key men: George Washington and James Madison. Washington was the most famous and respected American. His presence would lend credibility to the Convention and its work. Washington, who believed that the Confederation was 'shadow without substance', was convinced of the need for a stronger union.

Madison, although not as well known as Washington, was to have the greatest impact at the Convention. Intellectually gifted, he was determined to strengthen the national government and came to Philadelphia with a clear idea of what he thought needed to be done. In April 1787 he wrote a lengthy memorandum, 'The Vices of the Political System of the United States', in which he outlined the present defects and the remedies – the creation of a powerful national republic with a centralised government. He circulated the memorandum among the prospective delegates. Moreover, while waiting for the delegates from the other states, Madison won the support of Virginia's other representatives – including Washington – for his plan for a stronger federal union. By the time the other delegates arrived, Madison was ready to dominate the opening stages of the Convention.

The delegates

By 25 May, 29 delegates from seven states had arrived and the Convention, meeting in the Philadelphia State House, began its work. Over the next few weeks a further 26 delegates straggled in. Every state was represented except Rhode Island, which declined to participate. The 55 delegates (74 had actually been appointed to attend) brought a broad range of experience in public service:

- All had held public office.
- Forty-two had served in Continental or Confederation Congresses.
- Three were present and four were former governors of their states.
- Twenty had helped to draft their states' constitutions.

The delegates thus had practical experience of the strengths and limitations of republican government as it had been experimented with at state and national levels.

The Convention was a remarkably talented group – even if it lacked the abilities of Thomas Jefferson and John Adams who were then serving as envoys to France and Britain respectively. With an average age of 42 the delegates were relatively youthful: 30 had fought in the War of Independence; 34 had legal training; 26 were college graduates; nineteen were slave owners. The fact that there were no blacks, native Americans, women or 'poor' was hardly surprising. By law and custom, these groups were outside the recognised polity in eighteenth-century America. Small farmers, artisans and Westerners, who had won an increased voice in American politics since the 1760s, could not afford the time to attend.

The principles of the Founding Fathers

There was no great ideological rift between the delegates. Virtually all agreed on the necessity to strengthen the central government. But few wished to centralise power to the extent of abolishing state sovereignty altogether. There was general agreement on the need for balanced government. No one branch of government – executive, legislative or judiciary – should be allowed to monopolise power. Likewise a balance must be struck between property and numbers. Most delegates distrusted democracy, believing the government should be in the hands of men with experience and standing. John Jay summed this up when he said 'the people who own the country ought to govern it'. Nevertheless, most accepted that the people must have a voice in government.

Despite a large measure of agreement on principles, there was no unanimity on details.

- While the delegates accepted the need to extend the power of the federal government, they disagreed as to how powerful it should be.
- They disagreed about whether the legislature should consist of one house or two.
- Representation was the most contentious issue. Should all the states be equally represented in the federal legislature, irrespective of size, as was the case under the Articles? Or should representation be based on population, an arrangement which would give Virginia, with 747,000 people (of whom 300,000 were slaves), twelve times as many representatives as Delaware, which had only 60,000?

The key men

Apart from James Madison (who spoke 161 times), other key delegates were the Pennsylvanians James Wilson (who spoke 168 times) and Governeur Morris (who spoke 163 times). Wilson, who had been born in Scotland, was a successful lawyer. Gouverneur Morris, with a crippled arm and only one leg, was far more vocal than his namesake Robert Morris (ex-Superintendent of Finance), another of the Pennsylvania delegates. The presence of George Washington and Benjamin Franklin was crucial. Although rarely speaking, the mere fact that they were present gave the Convention prestige. Washington was unanimously chosen to preside over proceedings.

Economic motivation

Key question
Were the Founding Fathers motivated by economic self-interest?

In the early twentieth century, historian Charles Beard depicted the Founding Fathers as reactionaries whose aim was to destroy popular rule. According to Beard, they had considerable investments in **certificates of public credit**. They thus stood to gain economically if a strong central government was established. (The market value of the public credit certificates was then likely to rise.) Beard argued that the debate over the Constitution centred on rivalry between the holders of personal property (money, public securities, manufacturing, trade and shipping) and real property (land). By the mid-twentieth century Beard's thesis had been generally accepted.

Key term

Certificates of public credit
Printed statements recognising that the holders were owed money by the government.

However, in the 1950s, historians Robert Brown and Forrest McDonald showed that Beard's research was sloppy. In reality the Founding Fathers' capital was largely invested in land and real estate, not public securities. Perversely, some of the largest holders of certificates of public credit voted against the proposed Constitution.

No one doubts that the Founding Fathers represented the richest groups in the USA or that they were determined to construct a system that would ensure their wealth was protected. However, economic interest alone did not determine the framing of the Constitution. The Founding Fathers were men of ideas and principles. Most believed that the survival of liberty was at stake. From their understanding of classical literature, they were convinced that excessive democracy was as dangerous as the monarchical tyranny from which Americans had just freed themselves.

The process of debate

At the start of proceedings, the delegates made several crucial decisions:

- They resolved to keep their deliberations secret, thus insulating the Convention from outside pressures and encouraging frank discussion.
- They agreed that the voting should be by state rather than by delegate.

The Virginia Plan

The Convention's first step was to consider a draft constitution, introduced on 29 May. Largely the work of Madison, the Virginia Plan provided for a national legislature of two houses, in each of which representation was to be proportionate to the population. The first house of the legislature would be directly elected by the voters in the states. The members of the second house would be elected from among those of the first. The legislature was to have wide powers: it was to elect both the executive and the judiciary. The states would be reduced to little more than administrative units since the central government was to have the power to veto acts of state legislatures and to interfere directly – using military force if necessary – in cases where the states were incompetent 'or in which the harmony of the United States may be interrupted'.

Given that the Virginia Plan was the first proposal put before the Convention, it set the agenda. For the rest of the summer the delegates would debate and amend it. Although there would be significant changes, the Virginia Plan would remain at the centre of the Convention's deliberations.

The New Jersey Plan

The Virginia Plan put the smaller states immediately on the defensive. In the national legislature, the representatives of the smaller states would easily be outvoted by the representatives of the larger states. (The combined populations of Virginia, Pennsylvania and Massachusetts included almost half the country's population.) Though congenial to the larger states, the Virginia Plan was bitterly opposed by the smaller ones, as well as by delegates who objected to the amount of power which would be concentrated in Congress.

In an effort to preserve the interests of the smaller states, William Patterson of New Jersey presented an alternative scheme (on 15 June) providing for a single legislative chamber, in which each state would have one vote. The New Jersey Plan envisaged merely the amendment of the Articles. Though Congress was to be given enlarged powers, including authority to tax and to regulate commerce, state sovereignty would be largely preserved. Although the Convention rejected the New Jersey Plan on 19 June (by seven states to three), the issue of representation in the national legislature went unresolved. For the next fortnight the issue was debated with increasing acrimony. A Grand Committee, with one delegate from each state, was finally appointed (2 July) to work out a compromise.

The Great Compromise

The Grand Committee's report is referred to as the Great Compromise. In essence, it bowed to the demands of the small states. All the states, whatever their population, would have equal representation in the upper house (the Senate). However, the lower house (the House of Representatives) would have proportional representation: thus larger states would have more representatives. Representation and direct taxation would be distributed according to the results of regular censuses. The Great Compromise was accepted (by five votes to four) on 16 July, after a fierce debate.

North v South

The issue of slavery representation divided Northern and Southern delegates. The Southern states wanted slaves to be included in the population total when allotting Congressional seats, but left out in determining liability for direct taxation. The Northern states, by contrast, wanted slaves excluded from representation, since they were neither citizens nor voters, but included for tax purposes since they were a form of property. The Convention eventually accepted the formula whereby a slave was counted as three-fifths of a person for the purposes of both representation and direct taxation.

Other issues
- On 26 July the Convention accepted the argument for a single executive.
- Crucially, the Convention agreed to drop Madison's federal veto over state actions.
- No agreement could be reached on some matters, for example, the precise role of the proposed national judiciary. Hence the delegates took refuge in evasion. It recognised, as Madison put it, that ambiguity was the price of unanimity.

The Committee of Detail
On 26 July the Convention adjourned. A Committee of Detail was charged with producing a draft constitution. It had to make sense of the various recommendations and amendments to the Virginia Plan made over the previous two months. The committee, chaired by Rutledge of South Carolina and including Randolph of Virginia and Wilson of Pennsylvania, worked for ten days, fleshing out many of the features of the Constitution. Randolph and Wilson seem to have written most of the report which became the proposed Constitution.

Continued debate
Debate on the report of the Committee of Detail occupied five weeks from 6 August to 10 September. During this debate, slavery re-emerged as an issue. The proposed Constitution prohibited Congress from banning the slave trade. Some Northern delegates wanted to end the trade. Delegates from the Carolinas and Georgia, by contrast, insisted that their states would never accept the new Constitution if the right to import slaves was impaired. However, it was not simply a case of North versus South. Some Northern delegates, more concerned with securing a constitutional settlement than they were with slavery, argued against interfering with the trade. Moreover, some Southern delegates wanted to abolish the slave trade: this would increase the value of their – excess – slaves. In late August it was agreed that Congress would not have the authority to abolish the slave trade until 1808.

The Constitution agreed
On 8 September a Committee of Style was appointed to tidy the draft Constitution into its final form. Most of the work was done by Governeur Morris. On 17 September 39 of the remaining 42 delegates approved the Constitution. To side-step the probable opposition from the state legislatures, the Convention recommended that the proposed Constitution should be submitted for ratification to popularly elected conventions in each state.

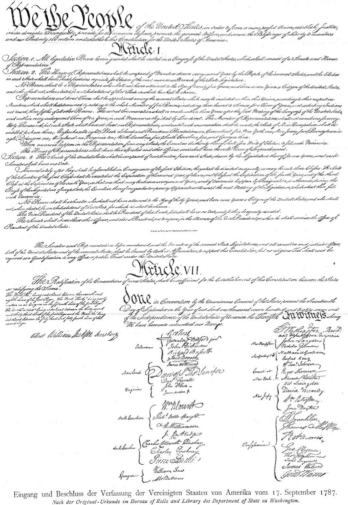

Eingang und Beschluss der Verfassung der Vereinigten Staaten von Amerika vom 17. September 1787.
Nach der Original-Urkunde im Bureau of Rolls and Library des Department of State zu Washington.

Washington's copy of the final draft of the first page of the Constitution.

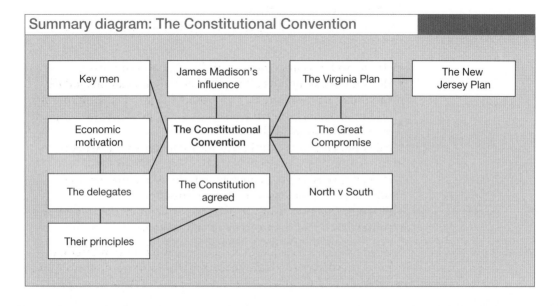

Summary diagram: The Constitutional Convention

- Key men
- James Madison's influence
- The Virginia Plan
- The New Jersey Plan
- Economic motivation
- The Constitutional Convention
- The Great Compromise
- The delegates
- The Constitution agreed
- North v South
- Their principles

Key question
To what extent was the Constitution a bundle of compromises?

4 | The Constitution

Separation of powers

The Constitution proposed a division of authority between executive, legislature and judiciary. The separation of powers (see Chapter 4, page 136) was intended to permit the other two branches of government to check the third should it exceed its authority. Each was to be independent of the other, so that members of the executive branch were denied membership of the legislature.

The powers of the federal and state governments

Like the government of the Confederation, the federal government was authorised to maintain an army and navy, coin and borrow money and make treaties with foreign powers. But it was given some additional powers, notably to levy taxes and to regulate commerce. Moreover, in the 'elastic clause' Congress was authorised to 'make all laws which shall be necessary and proper' for executing its powers. The Constitution and all laws and treaties made under it were declared to be the supreme law of the land, superior to any state law.

The states were specifically forbidden from waging war, engaging in diplomacy, coining money or laying duties on imports. Moreover, they were deprived of some powers they had hitherto exercised: in particular, they were not to issue money or make treaties. Nevertheless, the states retained considerable powers:

• The slavery issue was left to the states.
• Each state could determine its own suffrage in elections to the House of Representatives.
• The states could regulate their own intrastate or internal commerce.
• States continued to exercise jurisdiction in many important areas of civil, criminal and family law.

The Federal Executive

The federal government's executive authority would be exercised by a president:

• He was to be commander-in-chief of the army and navy.
• He could make important appointments, for example, judges and diplomats (with Senate approval). To avoid corruption, the president was prohibited from appointing members of Congress to executive posts.
• He could conclude treaties (in association with the Senate).
• His signature was required to make Acts of Congress law.
• He could veto acts of Congress (but the veto could be over-ridden by a two-thirds vote of both houses).
• He could be removed from office only on impeachment for and conviction of 'high crimes and misdemeanors'.

Presidents were to be elected for a four-year term by an Electoral College, to which each state was to send the same number of electors as it had senators and members of the House of Representatives.

The Federal Legislature

Congress was to comprise the House of Representatives and the Senate:

- The House of Representatives was elected directly by voters for a two-year term.
- The Senate comprised two senators from each state and was elected by state legislatures. They were to serve for six years, one-third elected every two years.
- Congress had the power to raise money and the power to make laws. It also had the power to declare war, to ratify treaties (two-thirds of the Senate had to agree), to impeach, and (with a two-thirds' majority) to over-ride the president's veto.

The Federal Judiciary

Although much was left vague, it was agreed that:

- an independent national judiciary should be established
- there should be a Supreme Court – appointed by the president with the approval of the Senate.

Amending the Constitution

Amendment of the Constitution required a two-thirds' majority in each house of Congress and a seventy-five per cent majority of the states.

Criticisms of the Constitution

A common view in 1787 – and one shared by some historians since – was that the Constitution represented a conservative backlash, curbing a growing democracy:

Key question
How successful was
the Constitution?

- The Electoral College would stand between the people and the president.
- The senators would owe their office to the state governments, not direct election.
- Six-year terms would give senators considerable immunity from popular pressure.
- The House of Representatives would represent constituencies as large as 30,000 people, half the population of the state of Delaware.
- The two-year term of its deputies was twice as long as the terms of most state assemblymen.

All these arrangements served to insulate the people's servants from the people.

Historians have attacked the Constitution for its defence of slavery (not changed until the thirteenth Amendment in 1865). They have also criticised some of the Constitution's ineffective provisions. The Electoral College has, on occasions, prevented the candidate with the most popular votes from becoming president. The need for a two-thirds' approval of the Senate for treaties has handicapped the formulation and execution of foreign policy. It is also possible to claim that the system of checks and balances ensured that nothing much would ever get done. Historian

Richard Hofstadter described the Constitution as 'a harmonious system of mutual frustration'.

For all the Convention's efforts to construct detailed systems, much of the Constitution was couched in general terms and many issues were left open. It was unclear, for example, whether the Constitution should be strictly construed or more loosely interpreted. More importantly, the boundaries between federal and state power were far from sharply defined. Nor was it clear whether states could leave the new 'club' they had joined. These questions would provide the staple of constitutional debate for decades to come and were not to be finally settled until the Civil War (1861–65) – a war which cost 620,000 lives.

In practice the Constitution did not operate as envisaged. The Founding Fathers' model was parliamentary, not presidential, yet presidents – eventually – came to dominate the American political scene. Although the Founding Fathers envisaged that both houses of Congress would be equal, within three generations the Senate, with its longer tenure, had become more powerful than the House. The latent power of the Supreme Court would also have surprised the Founding Fathers. Since the chief justiceship of John Marshall (1801–35) the Court has pronounced regularly on the validity of Acts of Congress. American political and social advance has thus often been determined more by the pronouncements of the judges than by Acts of Congress. The Constitution has 4000 words: the Supreme Court's interpretations of it number over 450 volumes.

Praise for the Constitution

It is doubtful whether the Constitution entirely satisfied anyone in 1787. 'I confess that there are several parts of the Constitution which I do not at present approve,' said Benjamin Franklin, 'but I am not sure I shall never approve them ... I consent, Sir, to the Constitution because I expect no better and because I am not sure that it is not the best.' Nineteenth-century British Prime Minister William Gladstone went further, describing the Constitution as 'the most wonderful work ever struck off at a given time by the brain and purpose of men'. Arguably the Founding Fathers' work was a masterpiece of ingenuity and enlightened statesmanship, informed by democratic ideals, which helped save the American Revolution.

The Constitution accepted that the sole fount of legitimate political authority was the people: its preamble opened with the phrase 'We the People of the United States'. All the officers of government were to be the agents of the people. The Founding Fathers remained true to the representative principle at almost every point.

The strong national government was still made as weak and as divided as could safely be managed. Fearing tyranny in any form, the Founding Fathers were hostile to the concentration of authority in any one man or institution. They deliberately created a system of checks and balances:

- the executive versus the legislative versus the judiciary
- the House of Representatives versus the Senate

- popular election versus indirect election
- the federal government versus state governments.

At the same time, the Constitution reconciled the interests of:

- large and small states
- slave and free states
- the federal government and state governments
- patrician leadership and popular sovereignty.

The fact that the Constitution was a sketch not a blueprint was a strength. Much was left for the future to clarify. The Constitution has thus been a living document, constantly reinterpreted and made responsive to new social and political needs. The Founding Fathers' good sense and political realism are evident from the fact that the Constitution has stood the test of time. With relatively few amendments (27 since 1787), a document devised 200 years ago for a small, rural republic is still the fundamental law for the world's greatest power. No other written constitution has lasted so long.

Summary diagram: The Constitution

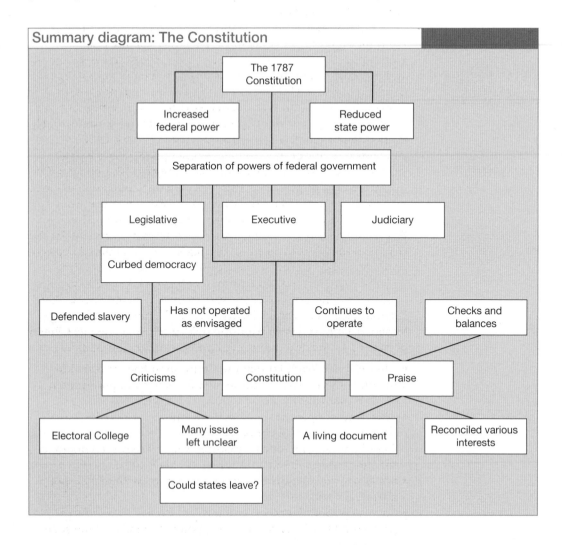

Key question
Why was the
Constitution ratified?

5 | The Ratification of the Constitution

When the Convention finished its work, it immediately transmitted a copy of the proposed Constitution to Congress. On 28 September, Congress unanimously voted to submit the document to the states for ratification according to the method outlined by the Convention. The new document would thus become operative when ratified by nine – not all thirteen – states. Moreover, the Constitution would be submitted to specially elected state conventions, not the state legislatures. Such a procedure would confer on the Constitution a status which the constitutions of all but one of the states (Massachusetts) lacked, namely that of being based directly on popular consent.

Key question
What were the
Federalists'
advantages?

Federalists v Anti-Federalists

The process of ratification provoked bitter debate in every state. The contest was marked by discourse of the very highest order concerning the meaning of republicanism. It was also marked by cynical political tactics.

The supporters of the Constitution won an important first point when they appropriated the word 'Federalist' to describe themselves. (Given that their intentions were for increased central and less state power, the word was probably a more apt title for their opponents.) The fact that the Federalist opponents were dubbed 'Anti-Federalists' immediately cast them in a negative role.

In the struggle over ratification the Federalists were most strongly supported by men of property and position: planters, merchants and lawyers. Many of their Anti-Federalist opponents were small farmers, especially from the more isolated regions. But opinion did not divide neatly along lines of class or economic interest. Some rich men were Anti-Federalist. Many poor men, like the labourers and artisans of the cities, were Federalist. Every major town had a Federalist majority. According to historian Jackson Turner Main, the crucial socio-economic factor in distinguishing Federalists from Anti-Federalists was their level of engagement in commercial trading.

Anti-Federalists were aware of the problems of the 1780s but believed that the proposed cure was far worse than the disease. Anti-Federalist leaders – Patrick Henry, Richard Henry Lee and George Mason of Virginia, James Winthrop of Massachusetts, George Clinton of New York – made a number of criticisms of the Constitution:

- They claimed (rightly) that the Convention had exceeded its mandate in proposing a whole new framework of government to replace the Articles.
- They feared a powerful national government would destroy the sovereignty of the individual states.
- They believed that state legislatures were more representative of the people than the new Congress was likely to be.
- Some saw the Constitution as an attempt to establish a despotic aristocracy.
- Many deplored the absence of a Bill of Rights – a list of legally protected liberties such as were appended to many of the state constitutions.

Anti-Federalists also raised a host of specific objections, all reflecting a suspicion of centralised power: the federal government's new taxing power was potentially oppressive, the president would have too much power, the members of the House of Representatives (initially fewer than 60) would be too few to represent adequately the varied interests of the country.

Federalists addressed the criticisms in hundreds of pamphlets and newspaper articles. Their greatest fear was that rejection of the Constitution would lead to collapse of the union, anarchy, interstate warfare and ultimately the loss of American independence.

Federalist advantages

It seems likely that at the outset a majority of American voters were opposed to the Constitution. Nevertheless, the Federalists had several advantages:

- They offered a specific set of solutions to the pressing problems that faced the nation. While most Anti-Federalists conceded that some political reform was necessary, they had no alternative to offer the public.
- Federalist support was strong in the towns. Local people thus often gave delegates to state ratifying conventions (which met in towns) the impression that most people favoured the Constitution.
- The support of the two most famous men in America – Washington and Franklin – added lustre to the Federalist cause.
- Anti-Federalist support, scattered across isolated small farms, was difficult to organise.
- The vast majority of newspapers were Federalist owned and inclined. Only five major newspapers – out of approximately a hundred – consistently opposed the Constitution.

Where their support was strong the Federalists moved rapidly to secure approval and where it was weak they delayed, allowing themselves time to campaign effectively. The crucial states were Pennsylvania, Massachusetts, Virginia and New York – the largest and most influential.

Delaware, New Jersey, Georgia, Pennsylvania and Connecticut

In some states ratification was easily achieved. Of the first five states to ratify, Delaware (7 December 1787), New Jersey (18 December, 1787) and Georgia (2 January 1788) did so unanimously. Pennsylvania (12 December 1787) approved by a comfortable majority (46–23) and Connecticut (9 January 1788) by an overwhelming one (128–40). Thus the Federalist cause built up an early momentum.

Massachusetts

In Massachusetts there was a long and spirited contest. The stance of revolutionary stalwarts Samuel Adams and John Hancock was vital. Both had Anti-Federalist leanings. When the Massachusetts convention met in January 1788 Federalist pressure was put on

Key question
How was the
Constitution ratified?

Constitution ratified:
1788

Key date

both men. Pro-Constitution demonstrations by Boston artisans persuaded Adams to support the Constitution. Hancock changed sides when Federalists suggested that he might be vice president if the Constitution were ratified. Eventually, moderate Anti-Federalists were won over by a Federalist pledge to consider appending a Bill of Rights to the Constitution. Thus on 9 February 1788, the Federalists triumphed by 187 votes to 168.

Maryland, South Carolina and New Hampshire

Maryland (63–11) voted in favour of the Constitution on 28 April 1778 and South Carolina (149–73) fell into line on 23 May. On 21 June New Hampshire (57–47) became the ninth state to ratify. Remote and non-commercial, the state had been initially strongly Anti-Federalist. When its people elected their convention, they instructed it not to ratify. When it met over the winter, it followed instructions. But rather than reject the Constitution, it adjourned until June without taking a final decision. That gave the Federalists an opportunity. Raising the issue in town meetings, they put pressure on delegates to change their minds. According to historian Forrest McDonald, the New Hampshire convention finally ratified on an afternoon when Federalists had got a number of their opponents drunk enough at lunch to miss the session. Technically the Constitution could now go into force. However, without Virginia and New York it could hardly succeed.

Virginia

In Virginia, the opposing forces were evenly balanced. Patrick Henry's eloquent attacks on the Constitution, ably seconded by Richard Henry Lee's *Letters from a Federal Farmer,* had a profound effect. However, Washington's support for the Constitution and Madison's reasoned advocacy, along with his promise to work for a Bill of Rights, was crucial. On 26 June 1788 the Virginia Convention ratified by 89 votes to 79. In essence in Virginia the division was between the commercial Tidewater counties (Federalist) and the less well developed regions (Anti-Federalist).

New York

When the New York convention met, Alexander Hamilton thought that four-sevenths of the people of the state were against the Constitution. He, Madison and Jay, using the joint pseudonym Publius, wrote a series of 85 articles for the New York press, urging the adoption of the Constitution. These essays, subsequently published as *The Federalist Papers,* came to be regarded as a classic of American political thought. However, they do not appear to have had a significant influence on contemporary opinion. More important in softening the intransigence of the New York Anti-Federalists was Virginia's decision to ratify and the fear, cultivated by Hamilton, that New York City would secede (leave) if the state rejected the Constitution. On 26 July 1788 New York's convention approved ratification by 30 votes to 27.

The C E N T I N E L.

States—like the gen'rous vine supported live,
The strength they gain is from th'embrace they giv
THE FEDERAL PILLARS.

UNITED THEY STAND—DIVIDED FALL.

New York's approval of the Constitution (26 July 1788) inspired this comment in the *Massachusetts Centinel*. There was high hope that North Carolina would ratify the Constitution but Rhode Island was more problematic.

Conclusion

Although North Carolina and Rhode Island still stood aloof, the new Constitution could now begin to function. As its last act the Congress of the Confederation ordered national elections for January 1789.

Only about a quarter of adult white males voted for the state ratifying conventions. The rest were either disfranchised or disinterested. Those most likely to stay away were farmers in isolated communities. Federalist success was the result of several factors –

Table 5.1: Ratification of the Constitution

	State	Date	Vote in Convention	Rank in population	1790 population
1	Delaware	7 Dec 1787	Unanimous	13	59,096
2	Pennsylvania	12 Dec 1787	46 to 23	3	433,611
3	New Jersey	18 Dec 1787	Unanimous	9	184,139
4	Georgia	2 Jan 1788	Unanimous	11	82,548
5	Connecticut	9 Jan 1788	128 to 40	8	237,655
6	Massachussets (incl. Maine)	7 Feb 1788	187 to 168	2	475,199
7	Maryland	28 Apr 1788	63 to 11	6	319,728
8	South Carolina	23 May 1788	149 to 73	7	249,073
9	New Hampshire	21 June 1788	57 to 47	10	141,899
10	Virginia	26 June 1788	89 to 79	1	747,610
11	New York	26 July 1788	30 to 27	5	340,241
12	North Carolina	21 Nov 1789	195 to 77	4	395,005
13	Rhode Island	29 May 1790	34 to 32	12	69,112

better organisation, big names, newspapers and Anti-Federalist divisions (see above). However, the Bill of Rights concession was crucial. Federalists could easily accept a concession that did not materially alter the Constitution.

The 1789 election

Key question
Why was the 1789 election so important?

The election of 1789 gave the Federalists control of the new government. There were large Federalist majorities in both the Senate and the House of Representatives. Electoral College representatives met and voted in February. As the most famous and popular man in the country, George Washington was chosen as president: no one stood against him. John Adams was elected vice president. Washington was inaugurated as the first president of the USA on 30 April 1789.

The new government entered office with several advantages, not least the fact that the worst of the post-war depression was over and the economy was expanding. There was also widespread public support for both the new government and the Constitution. Despite the passion that had characterised the ratification debates, the Anti-Federalists accepted the popular verdict and agreed to participate in the new political system in good faith.

The importance of Washington

Key date
George Washington inaugurated as first president: 1789

Washington proved to be an excellent first president. Scrupulously following his mandate as outlined in the Constitution, he realised his actions would set important precedents. Although he said and wrote little, he attached great importance to the need to create a vigorous and effective executive under his direction. He selected his cabinet on the basis of three criteria: merit, service and geography. He appointed Thomas Jefferson as secretary of state and Alexander Hamilton as secretary of the Treasury. Henry Knox, the secretary of war, continued in the office he had held under the Confederation. Edmund Randolph became attorney general. Washington insisted that members of his cabinet were his subordinates and his right to dismiss them was reluctantly conceded by Congress.

The Judiciary Act

The Constitution had created a federal judiciary but left the detail as to how it should be structured, what its precise responsibilities should be and what its relationship with the state courts should be for settlement at another time. The 1789 Judiciary Act addressed many of these issues. The Act established a Supreme Court with district courts in each state and circuit courts of appeal. By creating an entire apparatus, the Act ensured that federal laws and rights would be adjudicated uniformly throughout the nation and exclusively in national courts.

The Bill of Rights

On 24–25 September 1789 the House and Senate approved a number of proposed amendments to protect civil liberty and limit federal power and submitted them to the states for ratification.

Of these, the states approved ten, including those guaranteeing freedom of religion and of speech, the right to bear arms, protection from unlawful searches, the right to due process of law and the right to a speedy trial by jury. Other amendments prohibited quartering soldiers with civilians in times of peace, excessive fines and cruel and unusual punishments. The amendments took effect in December 1791 when Virginia became the last state to ratify them. The adoption of the ten amendments (known as the Bill of Rights) helped to convince North Carolina (1789) and Rhode Island (1790) to enter the new union.

Party politics

While all politicians were committed to making the new Constitution work, they disagreed vehemently as to its character. To men like Hamilton it was an expansive grant of power for national purposes and could be implemented only by constructing a federal government committed to activist policies. Hamilton advocated a broad 'implied powers' reading of the Constitution. But to Madison and Jefferson the Constitution was intended to protect and preserve the liberty of individual citizens and the autonomy of the states. While they wished for a strong union, they did not want an activist federal government. They thus supported a stricter interpretation of the Constitution that limited the actions of the government.

Disagreements about the nature of the federal government soon led to rivalries and the development of political parties (not envisaged by the Founding Fathers) as the elite – including the men surrounding Washington – fell out about financial and foreign policies. Ironically, the development of a party system – deplored by Washington – helped give life to the Constitution.

The USA in 1790

In social and economic terms, the America of 1790 was not far removed from that of 1760. Most Americans continued to work on the land. Only three per cent of the population lived in the six towns of more than 8000 people (Philadelphia, New York, Boston, Charleston, Baltimore and Salem). Philadelphia, with 40,000 people, was still the largest city. There was little by way of manufacturing industry. There were few good roads. It still took at least four days to travel from Boston to New York by land. The trans-Appalachian West was another world – isolated and remote.

But in other respects, America in 1790 was a very different place from what it had been when George III assumed the throne. The change from colonial status to statehood had been far from smooth. It had resulted in a long and costly war. The war and its outcome had helped transform the way Americans thought about themselves and how they dealt with one another. The American Revolution was essentially a political revolution. In declaring independence, the Americans raised a host of constitutional questions:

- What form should their new governments take?
- Who was entitled to participate in those governments?
- What should be the relationship between the states and the national government?
- What rights did citizens have?

At state and national level, Americans had experimented with a range of governmental structures in their search for answers to these questions. But American leaders never wavered in their commitment to republican government – that is, government where sovereignty was derived from the people.

Summary diagram: The ratification of the Constitution

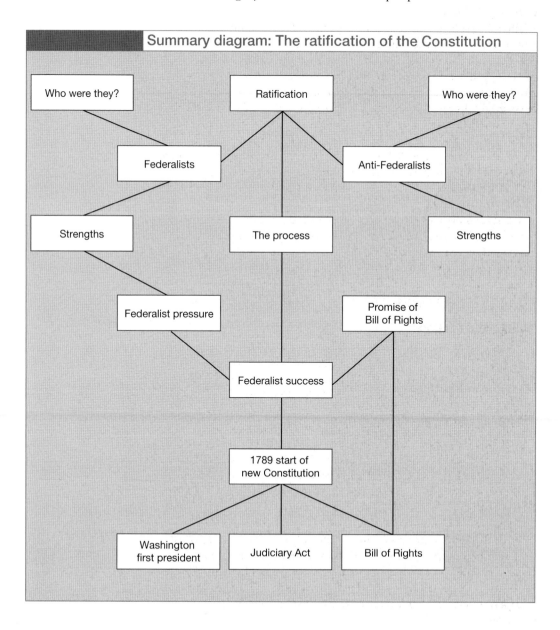

6 | The Key Debate

Did the Founding Fathers 'ride to the rescue of the American Revolution'?

In the late nineteenth century historian John Fiske called the years from 1781 to 1787 the 'Critical Period'. He depicted the Articles of Confederation as a weak government, unable to deal with a host of political, social and economic problems. Fiske claimed that the USA was close to disintegration until the Founding Fathers rode to the rescue, drafting a more effective Constitution. For much of the nineteenth century, the Constitution was seen as the fitting end of the Revolution. Most nineteenth-century historians, especially the influential George Bancroft, believed that the Revolution had been a struggle to secure American liberty: the Constitution was seen as liberty's greatest protection.

However, in the twentieth century historians like Charles Beard, Merrill Jensen and Jackson Turner Main had a different view. They saw the years from 1781 to 1787 as years of achievement, not failure. Rather than defenders of the Revolution, they claimed the Founding Fathers were upper-class conservatives, conspiring to protect their own economic interests. Thus by the mid-twentieth century, the Constitution was depicted as a reactionary document – the product not so much of democracy but of devious men who feared it.

It is now generally accepted that the 1780s was not a period of unrelieved gloom. Nor is it fair to blame all the troubles of the period on the weakness of the Articles of Confederation. In some respects the Confederation acquitted itself well, ensuring that the USA won independence and successfully regulating Western settlement. The Articles aimed to prevent the central government from infringing the rights of states. Arguably, there was nothing wrong in the USA remaining a loose collection of independent states.

Nevertheless, the authority of Congress steadily diminished after 1783. With peace, the states no longer felt the necessity of co-operating with each other or with Congress. Thus, the once-respected institution became increasingly weak and moribund. By 1785 American finances were in disarray and the USA was treated with contempt by Britain and Spain.

American nationalists wanted a stronger central government. The result – the Constitution – has survived the test of time. As have the Founding Fathers. Over the last 60 years historians have put the Founding Fathers back on their pedestal. Stanley Elkins and Eric McKitrick found them to be the 'Young Men of the Revolution', driven not by self-interest but by youthful energy and the frustrations they had known as congressmen, diplomats and army officers. John Roche saw them as modern politicians who understood the need for reform and who carefully calculated the best strategy for achieving it. Esmond Wright stressed that the Founding Fathers were patriots, 'men with principles as well as pocketbooks'. If they represented property they spoke for many constituents for most Americans were property owners. They sought to create a strong government not only, and perhaps not mainly, to curb democracy, but also to preserve the Union and the gains of the Revolution.

While the Critical Period may not have been as critical as its critics implied, the Articles of Confederation certainly deserves some criticism. The Founding Fathers may not have been 'demi-gods', but they did produce an extraordinary document which ensured that the 'great experiment' in republicanism would endure at a national as well as a state level. In that sense, they came to the rescue of the Revolution.

Some key books in the debate:

Thornton Anderson, *Creating the Constitution: The Convention of 1787 and the First Congress*, Pennsylvania State University, 1993.
Colin Bonwick, *The American Revolution*, Macmillan, 1991.
Jack N. Rakove, *Original Meanings: Politics and Ideas in the Making of the Constitution*, Knopf, 1996.
Harry M. Ward, *The American Revolution: Nationhood Achieved 1763–1788*, St Martin's Press, 1995.

Study Guide: AS Question

In the style of Edexcel

How well was the American Constitution designed to meet the problems faced by the USA after 1783? (30 marks)

Exam tips

The cross-references are intended to take you straight to the material that will help you to answer the question.

Success in this question depends first on a clear identification of the problems so that you can reach a judgement about how well the Constitution dealt with them.

You could identify three main problems:

- the powerlessness of the national government in foreign and commercial affairs (pages 163–65)
- the financial problems caused by irresponsible actions of individual states (pages 165–68)
- the differing state interests and the threat of chaos and disintegration of the Confederation in the face of this (pages 169–171).

You should then link the key terms of the Constitution directly to these, showing the way in which problems were addressed. At the heart of the problem was the issue of the power of individual states relative to central authority.

How did the Great Compromise (page 176) deal with that? What relationship was established between the powers of federal and state governments (page 179)? In what ways were the powers of states curtailed (page 179)? In what way did the new office of president (page 179) strengthen the position of the USA? How were conflicting ideas about slavery (page 176) dealt with?

To reach an overall judgement, decide whether most key problems had been addressed, or whether serious weaknesses or difficulties remained. The assessment on pages 180–82 will help you here. Was just the right amount of power left with individual states? Were the differing interests of states taken sufficiently into consideration? What is your decision?

Glossary

Arbitrary power   Power that is not bound by rules, allowing a monarch to do as he or she wishes.

Artisans   Skilled manual workers.

Autonomy   Independence or self-government.

Backcountry   The western areas furthest from the coast.

Boston town meeting   The town council of Boston.

Certificates of public credit   Printed statements recognising that the holders were owed money by the government.

Charter   A formal document, granting or confirming titles, rights or privileges.

Circular letter   A letter of which copies are sent to several persons.

Colony   Territory, usually overseas, occupied by settlers from a 'mother country' that continues to have power over the settlers.

Congregationalists   Members of a church that has a form of government in which each congregation is independent in the management of its affairs.

Continental Army   The main American army.

Corporate colonies   The corporate colonies Connecticut and Rhode Island possessed charters granted by the king which gave them extensive autonomy.

Deflationary   The situation resulting from a decreasing amount of money in circulation. People have insufficient money to buy goods or to invest.

Economic self-sufficiency   The situation when a country or a community produces all it needs for itself and is not dependent on others.

English/British   England and Scotland signed the Act of Union in 1707. Thus it is correct to term policy British (rather than English) after 1707.

Enlightenment   This is the name given to a school of European thought of the eighteenth century. Those influenced by the Enlightenment believed in reason and human progress.

Enumerated commodities   Listed items which were affected by the Trade and Navigation Acts.

Executive   The power or authority in government that carries the law into effect: a person (or persons) who administer(s) the government.

Feudal   Describing the system of social organisation prevalent in most of Europe in the Middle Ages, in which powerful land-owning lords granted degrees of privilege and protection to lesser subjects (holding a range of positions) within a rigid social hierarchy.

Franchise   The right to vote.

Freeholders   People who own, rather than rent, their land.

Frontiersmen   People who lived close to the borders of the colonies or in Indian territory.

General warrant   A warrant that allowed the government to make an arbitrary arrest for a political offence. A general warrant did not name an accused individual but merely specified the crime.

Glorious Revolution, The   In 1688 King James II fled from Britain. William III and Mary became joint monarchs. Parliament assumed greater control.

Guerrilla war   Warfare by which small units harass conventional forces.

Hessians   German auxiliaries who fought for Britain.

Industrial Revolution   The economic and social changes arising out of the change from industries carried on in the home with simple machines to industries in factories with power-driven machinery.

Jacobites   Supporters of James (Jacobus in Latin) Stuart, the eldest son of James II, who was driven from the throne in 1688. Strong in the Highlands of Scotland, the Jacobites led rebellions in 1715 and 1745.

Liberty Tree   An actual (but also symbolic) tree in Boston, representing freedom from tyranny.

Light infantry   Foot soldiers who travelled with the minimum of equipment and were thus able to move quickly.

Manumission laws   Laws which allowed owners to free their slaves.

Mayflower   The name of the ship on which the Pilgrim Fathers – a small group of English Puritans – sailed to America in 1620.

Mercantilism   The belief, widely held in Europe in the seventeenth and eighteenth centuries, that economic self-sufficiency is the key to national wealth and power.

Militia   A force, made up of all military-aged civilians, called out in times of emergency.

Minutemen   Men who were pledged to rush to America's defence at a minute's notice.

Oligarchy   Goverment by a small (usually wealthy) exclusive class.

Order-in-council   An order made by the sovereign with the advice of the Privy Council.

Patriots   Americans who supported independence. They are sometimes called rebels.

Patronage   The right of bestowing offices – offices usually given to supporters, family or friends.

Planters   Southern landowners who owned more than 20 slaves.

Porphyria   A physical condition affecting the nervous system, inflicting huge pain and symptoms which can sometimes be taken for insanity.

Presbyterians   Protestants with a system of church government by elders or presbyters, rather than bishops and archbishops.

Privateers   Privately owned vessels granted permission by a government to capture enemy ships.

Privy Council   The private council of the British king, advising on the administration of government.

Proprietary colonies   These were colonies in which the Crown had vested political authority in the hands of certain families: the Calvert family (in Maryland) and the Penn family (in Pennsylvania and Delaware).

Prorogued   Dismissed or postponed.

Quorum   A minimum number of officers or members necessary for transaction of business.

Redcoats   British troops who wore red uniforms.

Rotten borough   A place that sent members to Parliament though it had few or no inhabitants.

Separation of powers   A system of government in which the power is shared between the legislative, the executive and the judiciary, ensuring the government is not too strong.

Ships of the line   The great wooden battleships employed from the seventeenth to the mid-nineteenth centuries.

Sinecure   An office without much, if any, work: in other words, a cushy job.

Sovereignity   Ultimate power.

Specie   Gold or coined money.

Strategy   Long-term military planning.

Suffrage   The right to vote.

Tarred and feathered   Victims were stripped naked, covered with hot tar and then rolled in goose feathers.

Tidewater   The eastern areas nearest the coast.

Tories   Members of the Tory party – the great English political party in the late seventeenth and eighteenth centuries. The party usually opposed change.

Whigs   Members of the Whig party – one of the great English political parties in the late seventeenth and eighteenth centuries. The party usually upheld popular rights and opposed royal power.

Index